MANAGING *more* EFFECTIVELY

About the Author

Madhurendra K. Varma is the Managing Director of 'Aakankshaa', a human resource management consultancy firm, based in Ranchi, Bihar. After studying industrial and labour relations at Cornell University as a Fulbright Scholar, he joined industry and occupied senior positions in various corporations—including ESSO, Indian Oxygen Limited and Philips India—before starting his own firm. He also worked as the Executive Director of the All India Management Association.

During a rich and varied career, Madhurendra Varma has been a member of the Planning Commission's Working Group on Industrial Relations; a member of the Governing Council of the All India Management Association; and a member of the Central Board of Film Certification. Since starting his own firm in 1984, he has provided consultancy to a wide range of organizations including Visakhapatnam Steel Plant, SAIL (Bokaro and Bhilai steel plants), ISO/SWED Forest Consortium, Standard Batteries Ltd, Century Rayons, and Kirloskar Oil Engines Ltd.

While he has contributed over 30 articles to journals and edited volumes, this is his first full-length book.

MANAGING
more EFFECTIVELY

A professional approach to get the best out of people

Madhurendra K. Varma

Foreword by Prakash L. Tandon

Response Books
A division of Sage Publications
New Delhi / Thousand Oaks / London

First published in 1997 by

Response Books
A division of Sage Publications India Pvt Ltd
32 M–Block Market, Greater Kailash–I
New Delhi 110 048

Sage Publications Inc	**Sage Publications Ltd**
2455 Teller Road	6 Bonhill Street
Thousand Oaks, California 91320	London EC2A 4PU

Published by Tejeshwar Singh for Response Books, typeset by Print Line, New Delhi, and printed at Chaman Enterprises, Delhi.

Library of Congress Cataloging-in-Publication Data

Varma, Madhurendra K., 1924–
    Managing more effectively: a professional approach to get the
best out of people/Madhurendra K. Varma: foreword by Prakash L.
Tandon.
        p.   cm.
    Includes bibliographical references and index.
    1. Industrial management. I. Title.
HD31.V377   658—dc21 1997   97-11576

ISBN 0-8039-9373-0 (US-Hb) 81-7036-621-6 (India-Hb)
        0-8039-9374-9 (US-Pb) 81-7036-622-4 (India-Pb)

Sage Production Editors: Rakhshanda Jalil and Urmi Goswami

Contents

Foreword

For this very remarkable book, let me begin with its philosophy.

Management is both a science and an art: a science for the mathematical, technical and quantitative inputs; an art, because it has to deal with people—be they workers, customers or the public. But as management is an applied science combined with art, it has to go through the cycle of knowledge taught in a class-room, illustrations of its application through case-studies, and taken to the field for practice. The experience gained is examined at post-experience seminars, programmes and conferences; and then it is further examined and conceptualized and formed into a new theory. And thus the cycle of theory, practice, conceptualization and new theory goes on.

Management, in its practice, requires as inputs various disciplines such as marketing, finance and accounts, HRD and personnel management and psychology, science and technology. These disciplines are applied in an inter-disciplinary manner and not independently—with their mutual interactions.

Management's most important task is decision-making, is done in conjunction with different disciplines; The process of decision-making is not hierarchical and vertical but horizontal and consultative. The involvement of different disciplines at different levels creates decisions which are acceptable to all those affected by them. This hastens the process and enriches the quality of implementation. Each manager concerned contributes to the process by pooling his knowledge during the process of decision-making and of fulfilling further tasks created by implementation.

Management, therefore, has the unique quality that in its working as a team it can achieve something which can make 'the whole greater than the sum of its parts'.

Mr Varma has kneaded all this and much more into his book. *Managing More Effectively* is the title that Mr Varma has chosen, which is most appropriate. As Peter Drucker, the guru of management in America, said some years ago: to be a good manager is something, but to be an effective manager is much more. A good manager may do everything right and yet may not achieve much; the effective manager obtains results, though through good means.

In the 11 chapters, Mr Varma has touched upon different aspects of management, the attributes and qualities that make one a good and effective manager and a leader. In each chapter he has drawn upon his vast and diverse experience, spread across a range of multinational and national firms and industries, in teaching and in mangement administration. He, however, goes further: he has conceptualized his experience for the benefit of management practitioners, teachers and researchers.

It is a book to be strongly recommended to all interested in management, and others who would like to widen their knowledge and wisdom about human behaviour, its ideals and achievement in life. He follows the dictum of Gita, highlighted in the commentary by Dr Radhakrishnan, our great philosopher and leader: 'He (the manager), for the task set to him or by himself, looks not to the personal gain but to the satisfaction derived from the fulfilment thereof'.

Prakash L. Tandon

Formerly:
Chairman, Hindustan Lever Ltd;
Chairman, State Trading Corporation;
Chairman, Punjab National Bank; and
Director-General, National Council of
Applied Economic Research (NCAER)

Preface

Another book on 'effective management' when the book-shelves are already crammed with innumerable books on the subject? True, but then this book, is different. To begin with, it is neither a textbook nor a management refresher. It adopts an approach focusing on typical, practical issues, drawn from real-life workplaces. It offers practical suggestions to managers with a view to improving their effectiveness.

This book is the outcome of my four decades of work experience as a manager. I have drawn on the 'realizations' of management principles as I have observed them permeating various activities at the workplace. I was always keen on 'thinking through' whatever I did, was asked to do, or what others did. What has fascinated me and still does is the ripple effect that decisions, decision-making process, communication, delegation, leadership, interpersonal relationships, etc., make at the workplace. I have had an irresistible urge to seek meanings in terms of the 'what', 'why' and 'what became' of the managerial inputs. And this is what this book is essentially about.

The book covers the different aspects of managerial effectiveness—professionalism, motivation, leadership, delegation, communication, decision-making, time-management, management of tensions at work. Off hand, these topics may appear to be much-discussed. However, in this book, I have kept the modern-day concerns in central focus, while understanding managerial effectiveness.

The acceptance of management as a professional field, as medicine, law or accounting are regarded, is fairly new. Peter Drucker in his book, *The Practice of Management*, notes that management was mistakenly being seen largely as an expression of rank and power. Management, thus, became the function of managing of subordinates not businesses. In the past fifty years or so, certain broad management principles have been gaining significance. As a result, management is now accepted as a practice, in which people form a key and precious resource; and the key functions of businesses is that of marketing and innovation. That principles of management have gained ground is obvious from the growing realization that enterprises must identify, and keep srengthening, what they do best, what is now known as 'core competencies'; and that quality pays for itself.

Modern-day innovations such as total quality management, building on core competencies, filling the performance gaps, adaptability gaps and opportunity gaps are contemporary tributaries that have originated from the perpetually relevant topics of managerial effectiveness. It is these 'perpetually relevant' concepts that this book attempts to analyze in a new light, as what makes these concepts relevant contemporary concerns is how topical their treatment is, not their labels.

Divided into eleven chapters, the book acquaints the reader with the practicalities of the Indian management scenario before discussing the various facets of managerial effectivity. The book ends with the discussion of the significance of the competence and character of a good manager. Finally the acid test of an effective manager is if he has developed the reflex for doing the right thing at the right time.

I hope that the book will be of practical use to its readers.

Madhurendra K. Varma

ONE

Professionalism in Management: Myth or Reality?

CHAPTER OBJECTIVES

- Survey the current management scene—its concerns and their contemporaneity
- Provide a backdrop to the management scene in India in earlier—even ancient—days to assess the level of professionalism
- Discuss the meaning of professionalism in management and how professionalism can be achieved

---

Introduction

The practice of management can be dated to the beginning of history, while conscious thinking and enunciations about management are relatively new.

Even during pre-historic times, mankind observed certain basic principles of management in order to achieve desired results, although they were unaware of the principles behind their efforts. It is only during the last hundred years or so that rational thinking and enunciations on management have gathered momentum. To a great extent, this has liberated business and industry from the 'hit-or-miss' syndrome. The primary thrust of the researches on this subject has been to identify and suggest such elements and sequence of efforts that may produce desired results in a far more predictable manner.

A cave-dweller may have unwittingly brought into play the quint-essence of management practices, when he set out to achieve his objective of, say, killing an animal for food or driving away the prowling tiger. If he was doing this single-handedly, he determined his strategies, and evaluated the odds and risks vis-à-vis his own strength and cunning. He then proceeded with his actions. Among other things, his actions must have included lining up the required resources. With his intelligence and the implements and skills in his possession he must have tried to make the best use of those resources, including choosing the right timing for his actions. If he acted in collaboration with others, he must have instinctively selected them on the basis of their capabilities and commonality of interest (unless they were thrown together by some act of God). This inevitably resulted in the emergence of a 'leader' through a natural process of acceptance by all those involved in the activity. Then, together, they must have broken down the job into tasks, and distributed each task to the one most suited for it. During the implementation of these actions, further decisions must have been taken, either singly or in consultation with others, as to what more or new things have to be done in order to achieve the desired objective. All this must have entailed continuing communication, motivation, delegation, reviews *and* ultimately a reward for each of those involved through amicable sharing of the fruits of the achievement.

Mankind has progressed from its primitive days through the practice of management—never mind whether man knew or cared to know anything about the principles behind what and how he managed his affairs!

With progress toward civilization, each country devised its own 'system' of management in order to minimize the hit-or-miss element in obtaining desired results. This was more in the nature of ensuring orderly compliance of well-tried methods so that the needs of the government, industry and various sectors of society were fulfilled properly.

It would be interesting to recall here how meticulously the society and mercantile activities in our country were organized and administered as early as the fourth century BC during the reign of Chandragupta.[1] Within the framework of Kautilya's *Arthashastra*, the all-important armourers and shipbuilders were employed directly by the state for obvious reasons; and the rest worked either individually or, in most cases, as members of guilds. The guilds fixed rules of work, the quality of finished products, and their prices in order to safeguard both the artisan and the customer. Tax was levied on all manufactured articles, and the date of manufacture was stamped on them so that the customers could distinguish between fresh and stale goods! The behaviour of the guild members was controlled through guild courts.

Management in the sphere of administration was also well organized. The city of Pataliputra (present-day Patna) was administered by 30 officials, divided into six committees, each having five members. These committees, according to Megasthenes, the Greek emperor Seleucus's ambassador, were responsible for questions relating to:

♦ industrial arts;
♦ the welfare of foreigners;
♦ the registration of births and deaths;
♦ trade and commerce;
♦ supervision of the public sale of manufactured goods; and
♦ collection of sales tax (which at that time too was 10 per cent of the purchase price).

It would also be interesting to present here an imaginary, though true, picture of how, not so long ago, an individual with meagre means but with a lot of self-confidence and commonsense at his command, managed his enterprise. Depicted below are the efforts of a humble entrepreneur, a peanut vendor, as we knew him in our school days in the 1940s. He followed the following *eight* steps:

1. Before embarking upon his *enterprise*, this person despite his poverty and inadequate resources did indeed run through an unwritten *project report* in which he weighed various alternatives, keeping in view the opportunities and limitations he thought he could foresee.
2. He finally took a *policy decision* that roasted peanuts were the most appropriate and promising (though, perhaps, not the best) 'goods and services his *enterprise* was in a position to provide.
3. He selected specific cultivators at the outskirts of the city from whom he could procure raw, fresh groundnuts. Perhaps he cajoled them into supplying the groundnuts to him at a special price at specified intervals and with negotiated 'credit facilities'. Quite likely, he also lined up alternative suppliers. He thus followed the discipline of *purchasing and materials management*.
4. In selecting his *ghonsar* (clay-oven) and in fixing up the service charges for roasting the groundnuts, he selected his *third party technical collaborators,* and determined his *production schedules*.
5. He established the pattern of positioning himself near a high school during tiffin hours. He would then go over to the nearby railway station in the afternoon when three trains make their

scheduled stops, and then brave the evening cold in front of the cinema house on the main thoroughfare. He thus showed his multiple *selling sense* of:

♦ selecting his clientele;
♦ selecting his vantage selling points; and
♦ selecting his selling cycles.

In other words, he displayed—or learned and displayed—his *marketing and selling techniques.*

6. He developed his own colourful and rich sales slogans in spicy language and (atrocious) singing style, and he varied these to suit the localities he was positioned in. He was thus acting as his own *advertising agent.*

7. He also decided upon what portion of his sale-proceeds would be spent on the upkeep of his family and what would be ploughed back into running and expanding his business. He thus exercised the functions of *financial management.*

8. Above all—and because of all the above—he functioned as his own *Managing Director!*

Fascinating though it is, this is, of course, an over-simplified presentation based on an extended metaphor. The attempt here is simply to emphasize that management, as a function, permeates each and every level of human effort in the management of resources for producing goods and services leading to rewards for entrepreneurs. And there is nothing 'modern' about this function. What is new, and growing, is the attempt to study and codify management as a practice in order to:

♦ break down this function into its various components;
♦ study each component objectively;
♦ recognize the dynamics of these components when they interact;
♦ see what 'inputs' a manager can introduce to channelize the dynamics into productive forces, leading to achievement of desired and desirable goals; and
♦ above all, pursue the one major concern of the growing body of management studies and experiments which is to *unlock the mysteries of human motivations.*

Dedicated and painstaking researches have yielded for us a set of golden ground rules and principles. These have stood the test of time and trying situations, and have convincingly transformed management into both a science and an art. Thanks to these, we have come a long way. The earlier concept that management constituted managing subordinates stands replaced by the present-day realization that it consists of managing businesses *primarily through people*. These people need to be managed not merely as subordinates but as vibrant human beings whose high potential can be tapped in most cases by sensitive and imaginative leadership.

It is in this context that somewhere, some time, the realization dawned upon both the thinkers and practitioners of management that management must be professional. It must be free from ad hocism, whims and fancies; it must have a certain code of conduct, and ensure predictable results based on understandable cause-and-effect phenomena.

This search for professionalism, however, has almost always been beset by challenges and puzzles. Let us analyze them.

Challenges Confronting Modern Management

The Dilemma of Roles

It is important for business enterprises today to be clear about their role, that is, which activities they are involved in and in which they are *not*. Also, they need to know where they ought to draw the line between what role *they* perceive for themselves and what *others* would like them to play.

Here are some horns of the dilemma:

Profits A business enterprise exists and functions for creating and delivering value satisfactions at a profit. Of course, profit must not be confused with profiteering—the latter being an obsession with exploiting others through dishonest means. But profit (or surplus, if you like) must be generated to sustain continuous research and development, technological upgradation, diversification and expansion which, together, propel the enterprise toward growth.

Who Should Determine Their Role? The business world is dogged by an excess of unsolicited advice about their role. They face the dilemma of *(a)* where to draw the line on their role in the context of continuing public euphoria; and *(b)* who should draw this line. One would not mind if a hospital manages its affairs and revenues in such a manner that it remains self-dependent, provided, of course, it does not lose sight of the main purpose of its existence which is to provide quality medical services to its patients at affordable costs. By the same token, a business enterprise stands to be judged today by its *economic performance* coupled with the quality of goods and services offered by it. True, it can—and should—also be judged by the extent to which it fulfills its social obligations.

Achievements   A business enterprise must never lose sight of the fact that the real testimonial and goal of an effective management is *purposeful* achievements—not merely efficient functioning.

Quality, Quantity and Service   New and more complex demands are now being placed upon business enterprises. Till a few years ago, the criterion for determining the activities of an enterprise was quantitative, that is, specify the product; assess its demand; control the costs and get the best possible results. In other words, take care of the bottom line! However, occasional recessions and the government's recent liberalization policies have opened up our markets to multinational companies on the one hand and accentuated the ambitions of our indigenous industries to go global, on the other. The price our industries have to pay—one that they are quite willing to pay—is that they must concentrate on quality and service.

Response to Change through Innovations   A modern organization has to be very alert and anticipate desirable changes so that it proacts to them with sensitive innovativeness and not merely reacts either routinely or in panic. This must be manifested in how effectively it uses its resources with skill and experience, and in the results it achieves. The results, in turn, are evaluated not only in terms of the traditional bottom lines of annual reports; they are judged more in terms of how dedicated they are to further emphasize the qualitative aspects of *(a)* what their products, prices, delivery schedule and service are like; *(b)* how well the interests of consumers are served and protected; and *(c)* how much the community and other stakeholders are benefited in the ultimate analysis. *Modern enterprises must justify their usefulness to themselves, to their customers and to society.*

The Challenge of Managing Working People Today

This is a challenge which has always been there, and meeting it effectively is of paramount importance. Here are *four* ways of doing it:

1. A new assertiveness coupled with greater expectations and ambitions now prevails among the working people today. They expect a great deal not only in regard to remuneration and career growth, but also of the quality of life at their workplace. People want newer challenges to their skills and creative urges so that their talent and expertise are constantly on trial, and they can *see* and *show* clear evidence that their time and efforts do yield worthwhile results.

2. The education and upbringing of a large number of people these days have sharpened their sensitivity. On the one hand, they expect their superiors to exercise authority, while on the other, they are not willing to submit to authority without questioning its rationale. Their commitment to achieve and their performance are far better where they are allowed to participate in decisions on matters that concern them. Therefore, exercise of authority needs to be dispersed down the line imaginatively—not concentrated in a few hands at the top.

3. Top management no longer has the monopoly on conceiving efficiencies and imposing them down the line. Even where efficiencies conceived are otherwise sound, the fact that they are being handed down from the top does harbour a risk; it can vitiate the motivation needed for adoption or acceptance of such efficiencies. Top management must, therefore, promote the practice of:

   ♦ encouraging, or at least welcoming, initiatives from lower levels to evolve efficiencies appropriate to their levels—as answers to problems, challenges and opportunities as perceived by them; and

   ♦ implementing such efficiencies bottom upwards. In other words, a much greater practice—not merely pious talks—will have to be integrated in the very reflexes of the organization as conscious plans of actions, in order to *(a)* enrich the jobs with the help of suggestions from the bottom; and *(b)* secure the employees' participation in reorganizing their work, their work content and their quota of contributions toward total task performance.

4. Top management must enrich its language of communication, dialogue and negotiations. Above all, it must bring in transparent integrity in its actions and intentions if it expects its communication to be believed. It will have to recognize that, in managing its human resource, it is not enough to be 'rational'; it will have to be 'relational' as well.

A Case for Professionalism in Management

The Indian Streams

In our country, the 'river' of management—with its various characteristics, dynamics, strengths and weaknesses—can be said to have evolved out of three main tributaries. A certain managerial culture has been evolving that may, hopefully, emerge duly distilled through a maturing process, and one day result in greater professionalism in the Indian management scene.

In the Indian context, the following questions need to be addressed:

1. Have these three streams been a help or a hindrance in the flowering of professional management?
2. What do we really mean by professional management? And why do we need professional management?
3. What must be done now to promote professional management?

The Three Streams: Help or Hindrance?

Until recently, that is, till the 1980s, the concept and culture of the three streams of management had been flowing separately. Earlier efforts to draw upon the respective strengths of each and to synthesize them did not seem to meet with much success. In most cases, a trader organization continued to shun modern management principles and practices. It managed its affairs essentially on its trading reflexes—sometimes even whims—despite repeated setbacks that cried out as object lessons. Similarly, most of the family-owned organizations tended to be used by the proprietors either as an extended ego trip or as an out and out money-making machine.

It must, however, be said that the three streams have never remained water-tight. It was often found that influences of each of these streams could be found within the same organization in varying

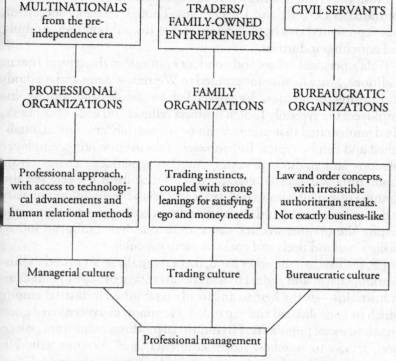

FIGURE 1.1 The Three Main Streams of Indian Management

degrees. There have been instances where a proprietor or a bureaucrat moved up from his traditional position and graduated to becoming a truly professional manager. Of course, he would have had to unlearn much of his earlier inherent traits. It can, therefore, be conceded that each of the three streams has something positive to contribute to professional management—*provided* one is made to interact with the other in the right proportion.

It is necessary here to mention some exceptional pioneers whom we can justly be proud of. They came from trading/family-owned organizations as well as from the multinationals operating in India during the pre-independence days.[2] These are the great entrepreneur-industrialists—leaders driven by vision and faith in themselves. They staked everything to achieve their commercial and industrial dreams and ambitions, and founded business dynasties which continue to dominate Indian industry in spite of considerable resistance from successive governments and competitors.

From the arena of family-owned organizations, I wish to cite two contrasts: G.D. Birla and J.R.D. Tata. Though enviably successful, they represented two opposite approaches toward building, running and enriching industries.

Birla's personal values and conduct epitomized the typical Indian traditions. Since he was not exposed to Western systems and methods of running industries, he succeeded in inculcating among his employees the typically Indian business reflexes and code of conduct. He demonstrated that industry can be successfully envisioned, established and run by typical Indian ways of decision-making, employee relations and traditional values. Another remarkable characteristic about Birla was that he graduated with ease from the reflexes and cunning of a small (almost pedestrian) trader to the discipline, tenacity and conviction of an industrialist and succeeding in carving a niche despite the unobtrusive resistance from the then European industrialists, unkind press and cocktail-party ridicule.

J.R.D. Tata, on the other hand, had a naturally westernized sophistication, charm and style. He had the advantage of starting out as an industrialist—as the heir to an already established industrial empire which he consolidated and expanded. He almost always enjoyed good press and social popularity. His industrial products range from power, steel, trucks to watches, soaps, cosmetics, and common salt. His industrial practices bore the unmistakable stamp of the special Tata touch—be they decision-making, employee relations or cultural issues.

From among the pre-independence multinationals, I cite just two names of truly professional managers: Prakash Tandon and Ajit Narain Haksar. They were the pioneers who made lasting contributions not only to their respective organizations but also to the management scene in India.

Prakash Tandon was the first Indian chairman of Hindustan Lever Limited. He was a former chairman of the State Trading Corporation and Punjab National Bank, and later Director-General of the National Council of Applied Economic Research. A visionary and risk-taking professional, he demonstrated that post-independence India had its share of professional business managers who could streamline and consolidate the country's corporate enterprises. He is widely considered to be among the world's best business professionals.

Ajit Narain Haksar was appointed the first Indian chairman of the Imperial Tobacco Company in 1969. His first initiative was to change

the name of the company to India Tobacco Company—later abbreviated as ITC Ltd. He transformed the company from an indolent
perks-proud raj-style tobacco company into a multi-business (including paper and board, cement, hotels and exports, besides tobacco)
professionally-driven organization.

In the arena of public sector too, some trail-blazers who contributed
profoundly to professionalism in management do come to mind. One
such person is V. Krishnamurty. His bold, turn-around decisions and
strategies, and the missionary zeal with which he ushered in a purposeful work culture in Maruti Udyog Ltd, and later in Steel
Authority of India Ltd shall always be remembered with admiration
and gratefulness.

By and large, public sector organizations tend to be run in a typical
bureaucratic fashion—under the tight control of bureaucrats—leaving not much room for innovations or bold risk-taking decisions.
Until recently, these bureaucrats clung to—even took pride in—the
inverted concept that the most important purpose of an industrial or
business organization was to provide social services like employment
and other community services such as housing, schools, medical
facilities, etc., with little or no concern for economic viability.

All this has thankfully changed. The change cannot be said to have
come from a conscious synthesis of the three streams; it has come
about more because of the flux into which all industrial and business
organizations have been thrown. The reasons behind this flux are:

♦ the recent liberalization policies;
♦ the attendant realization that only the fittest shall survive; and
♦ the floodgates of competition being opened up on a global scale.

It is possible that this flux may break the barriers that had hitherto
kept the three streams separate, and it may produce a synthesis leading
to emergence of a mighty river of purposeful and dynamic management.

What is Meant by 'Professional' Managers?

Is there such a thing as professional management?

Management should be judged simply in terms of *whether it is
effective or not effective.* What use is a so-called professional management if it is not effective enough to achieve its targets, and be fit to
meet new challenges and create new opportunities? Therefore, the
question whether a management is professional or not is not all that
crucial. (Of course, it is an interesting coincidence that wherever

management is effective, it is anchored on professionalism practised by its managers.)

Professionalism, however, has great relevance—and is crucial—for managers. It is the managers who can be professional. And it is the professionalism of managers that holds the key to whether a management will be effective or not.

Let us first be clear about what is meant by 'effectiveness' in concrete terms. The effectiveness of management—or of a manager—connotes *two* primary factors:

1. It must lead to *desired results* that:
   ◆ deliver the goods;
   ◆ happen on time;
   ◆ are cost-effective;
   ◆ do not produce negative side effects; and
   ◆ go beyond the confines of the immediate problem.
2. It must be *on-going, self-sustaining and motivational.*

Now let us consider what makes a manager professional. A professional manager is one who has the following *ten* qualities:

1. Is guided in his work and actions by a set of core principles that are internally consistent and non-violative of good and legally sound principles.
2. Is consistent in the yardsticks he applies for dealing with people and situations.
3. Has a broad framework for analyzing, judging, making decisions and taking actions—that is, one who is not arbitrary and seasonal in his practice of management.
4. Has liberated himself, to the extent possible, in his decision-making, from the elements of:
   ◆ subjectivity;
   ◆ impulsiveness;
   ◆ guess-work;
   ◆ unpredictability; and
   ◆ economic or social irresponsibility.
5. Bases his decision-making on the elements of:
   ◆ identification of the organization's chosen goals and objectives;
   ◆ challenging his colleagues and subordinates for maximizing their skills and expertise in such a manner that they feel motivated to give of their best;

- developing his people to their highest capabilities;
- careful consideration of the economic and social consequences of his decisions both within and outside his organization; and
- strategic planning.

6. Has the vision to see beyond his own job or his decisions to the larger interest or good of his immediate community or society. He should also have the courage to articulate it, and strive for its implementation in spite of it being unpopular in the beginning.
7. Has a set of ethical and moral principles that he lives up to transparently.
8. Is willing to quit rather than 'submit' to or 'go along' with what he considers wrong or unethical or immoral or illegal.
9. Is open to criticism and willing to change his ways when he discovers that his principles are wrong or outdated. He has the conviction about his beliefs, but he is courageous enough to discard or change them once he is satisfied they are wrong or unsuited to the situation. He is not obstinate.
10. Seeks, at his own initiative, to enlarge his body of knowledge and enrich his fund of experience. He does this by honestly acknowledging that he keeps learning from others—be they his superiors, peers, subordinates or colleagues.

Let us recall the model of the peanut-vendor's management style. That simplistic model would crack up in the face of the highly complex and challenging modern-day management situations. But what is interesting and noteworthy is that the essentials of *what* is being managed do not alter much. What undergoes changes and keeps us on our toes is *how*—with what commitment, expertise, approach and finesse—they are managed; and this is very much dictated by the ever-changing situations around us. It is the quality of our 'managing' that enables us (or not) to introduce innovations and self-upgradation.

The need for professional managers is very real. In fact, it keeps growing. But let us face it: acquiring professionalism is not an easy thing for a manager. He has to undertake a great deal of self-discipline and 'unlearning'. The deciding factor, ultimately, is whether he wishes to upgrade himself into an effective (professional) manager or remain a mediocre, ineffectual manger who simply 'carries on'.

It is this difficulty that has given rise to a lot of cynicism as to whether professionalism in managers is a myth or reality. The irony is that what is very much a reality (the need for professionalism) has been so callously battered about that it has indeed begun to look like a pale and receding ghost!

From where, and how, has this battering come in? Most organizations are subject to great deal of pressure from:

♦ competition getting fiercer;
♦ products getting obsolescent;
♦ run-away prices leading to unmanageable cost of production; ever-increasing pressures for price escalation; and the two together, leading to shrinking profits;
♦ ever-increasing demands from employees and managers for higher emoluments, better working conditions—encouraged by competing organizations offering any price to entice good workers;
♦ the insatiable hunger of politicians for funds/donations and jobs for 'their men'.

Beset by these maddening pressures, most employers are forced to weave a web of expediency. Little do they realize, though, that even in the short run such expediencies start exploding like small time-bombs. Managers are left with little or no choice in deciding or acting on professional lines. Under such compelling pressures, how can a manager think of sticking to his professionalism? It is in this context that the question gets asked repeatedly: 'Is professionalism in management a myth or reality?'

Despite this, time and again it is being proved that there are no short-cuts to effective management. Any amount of time or efforts that we may squander in flirting with expediencies are simply lost, and the ailment keeps getting worse! The real issue is whether we are ready *now* to face the reality and internalize the lessons.

Professionalism: Is it Desirable and Possible?

Yes, it is certainly desirable and possible to promote and reinforce professionalism among our managers, in spite of the apathy—even disincentive—that plagues our managers on this issue.

It is desirable, because a manager—more than anyone else in an organization—needs continuing motivation to manage effectively. This motivation is an on-going fuel to his usefulness, and it cannot come merely from more money or promotions or job-security. The real fountainhead of such motivation is the manager's self-esteem, fed on his self-respect. This self-respect, in turn, comes from his contributions that are adjudged by most people to be truly worthwhile. If he settles down to the role of a mere 'fixer' and keeps dancing to the tune of expedient demands made by others or by situations, his personality as a person and a manager gets eroded. Eventually, he begins to slip down in his usefulness even as a 'fixer'! Ultimately, he is down to such a state that he needs to save himself from himself!

And, yes, it is possible, in spite of the apathy or disincentive from others and from situations, to be a professional manager. After all, even his employer who falls for expediency does so out of helplessness which arises from the fact that somewhere and sometime his managers too lost the nerve to act professionally. A typical case of blame being heaped upon the 'effect' rather than the 'cause'! Let us consider the case in greater detail.

Let's say the competition steals a march over a certain organization due to its superior cost-saving techniques or technology. All said and done, it is so because, basically, the concerned managers in the losing organization failed to be on their toes. Actually they could have helped matters significantly by simply remaining professional, that is, by merely keeping themselves abreast of the technological advancements or innovations in their field.

Another common situation is when labour indiscipline or low productivity compels the employer to give in recklessly to the demands of the union. The root cause, however, may be that in the past his managers shied away from dealing firmly and/or imaginatively with the first signs of such indiscipline among the employees! In all probability, the managers had ignored their 'professional' responsibility of convincing—or fighting if necessary—both their employer and the union against those small but significant aberrations.

And on almost all such baffling problems relating to human beings, it is the neglect or evasion of these seemingly small aberrations that leads to a torrent of problems which, later on, threatens to drown the organization itself.

Reinforcing Professionalism in a Manager

Right to Opportunities

The question that must be dealt with is: 'How and why should a manager take up a so-called professional stand when the other people around him are inclined or compelled to take expediency measures?

Why should he invite so much tension and risk on himself?' True, the managers today have far more opportunities for securing new, and better, jobs if they wish to. But despite such opportunities, they are reluctant to take a stand on 'professional issues' because they find themselves struggling between expediency and professionalism, between risking their comfortable relations with their bosses and adhering to tough professional decisions and actions. This ultimately compels most of them to succumb to the expediency-oriented dictates of his boss or employer and the situations surrounding them.

However, the long-term consequences of such expediency-based actions or decisions—even those which promise comfortable outcomes in the short-run—often end up, ironically, in the manager *losing the very job he had been protecting* while yielding to short-term expediencies. Decisions based on expediencies invariably prove to be self-destructive; and they erode the very foundations of the organization itself. Take a close, clinical look at any of the large or small public sector or private sector organizations that have gone sick or are gasping for breath. In the vast majority of such cases, you will find that they had been flirting with expediency-based decisions and actions. Initially, they might have had a spell of 'good times' till they started sinking under the weight of their own ad-hocism. Therefore, even for his long-term job-security and 'right to opportunities', a wise manager would do well by reinforcing the organization with his professionalism. This can be done by:

♦ displaying courage to disagree with expediency-based, unwise courses of actions whenever he is convinced that they will lead to undesirable after-effects;

♦ offering sound alternatives which, he has taken pains to determine, would be best-suited from a long-term point of view; and

♦ offering to undertake the task and the responsibility for accomplishing the objectives along the lines suggested by him.

In other words, professionalism requires from a manager a combination of *(a)* conviction; *(b)* the courage of his conviction, *(c)* competence in the field of his current assignments; and *(d)* his entrepreneurial risk-taking instincts.

A Conceptual and Actionable Blueprint

One of the fundamental prerequisites for professionalizing oneself is self-reliance in self-development. You must not go on waiting till your organization comes forward one day, saying 'OK folks, here is a plan which we shall now operate for developing you'. What we are talking about is self-development which reinforces professionalism in you. This kind of change must begin at home—and at the initiative of 'you', the home-dweller.

Much of what is suggested here are *actions that can easily be taken by you*. These are basically thought-starters which, hopefully, might spur you into self-developmental actions. In a way, these suggestions are the forerunners of what follows in this book, and these are the self-developmental actions that, collectively, will enhance your effectiveness as managers.

They consist mainly of your attempts to clear possible misconceptions or correct imbalances in the emphases on managerial attitudes and actions. These may well make all the difference between adhocism and professionalism in your role as managers.

Authority vs Power   As mentioned earlier, authority must exist and be used. Even your subordinates down the line desire that authority prevails and is exercised in their organization. Authority, however, has to be *earned*, not by the decisions taken by virtue of the exercise but by *the quality of the advice and wisdom culled out of mature experience* acquired over time. Your subordinates do 'judge' your directives in terms of *their* understanding of the issue and its solution; and their enthusiasm or lack of it in implementing such directives is in direct proportion to their judgement.

Authority, by the same token, should not be—should never have been—concentrated only at the top. It should reside and be used by your people in varying doses *down the line, commensurate with their knowledge, responsibility and dependability.* This implies a duty on your part to enable your people to enhance their knowledge, responsibility and dependability through promotion by you of participative decision-making and delegation.

'Power', on the other hand, is usually associated with concentrated authority used in a personalized and egoistic manner. When authority is imposed, it is identified as 'power'; and 'power' is always resented—and resisted whenever possible.

Efficiency vs Effectiveness   Greater the compartmentalization or structuring in an organization, the greater is its vulnerability to the tug of war between efficiency and effectiveness. Undoubtedly, everybody in an organization ought to be as efficient as possible. More important: the sum total of individual efficiencies must result in the overall efficiency of the segment or department to which these efficient people belong.

But when 'efficiency' comes to be practised as a cult or obsession, as an end in itself and in disregard to the objectives of the organization as a whole, the latter is in danger of being stifled; it needs to be saved from the stranglehold of its own 'efficiency addicts'! When each one—the production man, the quality-control man, the finance man, the purchase man, the personnel man and the like—goes around pursuing efficiency exclusively in his own field of activity, all we get is a bunch of 'efficient' men or departments—pulling the organization apart in different directions. *Efficiency for the sake of efficiency is just no use. The efficiencies in each sector must be harnessed together so that the organization acquires the much-needed effectiveness to enable it to achieve its goals and objectives, and to cope with challenges.*

One effective method for achieving this is to encourage widespread interactions between the people from various departments or disciplines within the organization. By opening the ducts—the narrow and unwarranted boundaries built around departments—you can provide to a majority of managers the total view of the organization. Once the managers are exposed to the larger picture, the urge and commitment to pool together the diverse channels of available efficiencies into one mighty river of effectiveness is bound to follow spontaneously.

Achievement vs Performance   Somehow, 'target achievement' and 'performance' tend to be generally regarded as synonymous. But that is not so—neither in their implications nor impact.

The following illustration may help to bring out this distinction.

Let us say, the all-India Sales Manager of a company secures an agreement from his two Regional Managers for an identical sales target of, say, Rs 10 million each, during the next 12 months. He leaves these managers alone to improvise their strategies, but keeps a watching brief over their progress. At the end of 12 months, both these managers rush to their boss, feeling justifiably elated at having 'achieved the target' and expecting a pat on their backs, combined possibly with significant rewards.

But the boss is very worried about one of these Regional Managers. During his regular tours, he had noticed that this Regional Manager had been flogging all the resources and systems and disciplines at his command. He had violated the financial and commercial codes and disciplines, and twisted the arms of the dealers to push so-called sales. As a result, what happened was that the dealers, under duress, had simply transferred the products from the company warehouse to their stores! And even more disturbing, he had driven his subordinates to breaking points. Their morale was now at the lowest ebb; and resentment and alienation among them were high. In other words, the total organization under him was about to crack up. But he was elated because his target had been 'achieved' !

The other Regional Manager had simply adhered to normal, healthy managerial practices. There was nothing very spectacular about his methods. He remained in touch with his dealers. And in accordance with his own assessment of the market, which he kept touring constantly, he helped his dealers to effect real sales by offering the right kinds and quantities of products at the right time. In addition, his style of managing was such that all the resources at his command were reinforced and enriched. Having participated in—and having met—the challenges, his subordinates were filled with a sense of achievement. They considered themselves a part of a closely-knit team; and they were motivated enough to willingly take on a similar challenge in the future as well.

It is obvious that the distinction between the two Regional Managers is the *style* of their performance, despite identical target-achievement. The case highlights with dramatic impact the fact that it is not only *what* you achieve, but *how* you go about achieving results that is equally, if not more, important. This illustration also brings home the lesson that great damage can be done where achievement of targets by hook or by crook is demanded or encouraged as an obsession, at the cost of the style of performance.

Target-achievement vs Efforts As a corollary, it should be emphasized that there is another very significant distinction that you, as a professional manager, must always bear in mind. This relates to situations where a subordinate is unable to achieve the target despite his best efforts in the proper style of performance. We all know that shortfalls in achievement are a common happening. Should you judge your subordinate only in terms of whether he has achieved the target? What about his tireless, honest, risk-taking efforts? Is your subordinate in control of all the elements of success? There may be many slip-ups or failures over which your subordinate has no control. It is important that you give due credit and recognition to your subordinate for the amount and kind of efforts he has made—even when he has been unable to fully achieve the targets set for him.

Delegation vs Abdication　One often talks about the time constraints under which one has to work. While you think that much of these pressures are imposed upon you by your boss or by the system, few realize how many such pressures are imposed by your own subordinates! They dump *upwards* tasks that they should be performing. And, amazingly, *you* are largely responsible for such a state of affairs! This is traceable to the 'do-it-myself' syndrome most of us suffer from. Your subordinates are usually good mind-readers; and they happily indulge in task-dumping in direct proportion to their perception of how much of a 'do-it-myself' addict you are. Therefore, you must consciously scrutinize the daily volume and kind of work you do to find out how much of it is flowing upwards to you through capillary attraction. It is best that you embark upon the practice of true delegation so that each one of you—yourselves as well as your subordinates—does a bit of the tasks belonging upstream, not downstream.

While doing so, you must remember that *delegation does not mean abdication*, that is, passing off all the tasks or the whole of a task to your subordinates in order to get rid of the work. Delegation presupposes determination of the following *three* questions:

1. What can be delegated?
2. Who are worthy of which tasks—in terms of their knowledge, maturity and dependability?
3. What kind of continuing help must be provided by you so that accomplishment of tasks by the delegatee becomes a *highly stimulating developmental* activity, generating all-round job-satisfaction and involvement?

By the same token, delegation does not consist of dumping downwards your unwanted, petty, routine, uninteresting chores. If the tasks delegated are of such kind—or they are done with these intentions—nothing could be more disastrous and demotivating for your subordinates. They would only see an implied insult or exploitation in such so-called delegation; and sooner than later they would rise in revolt.

Firmness vs Fairness   In the ultimate analysis, it is the quality of leaders in an organization that determines its effectiveness, its capacity to stand up to challenges and to the winds of change. Besides, it is this factor of leadership that holds the key to the success of the individual managers themselves. No one can take away their right to opportunities, notwithstanding the maddening present-day stresses and strains of management. But, for this, managers must strive for achieving true leadership qualities, and living up to them.

One of the most important ingredients of leadership—and also professionalism—is that you must practice *fairness coupled with firmness*. The popular notion is that fairness means being soft, accommodating, nice to people; and firmness means being tough, strict, difficult, saying 'no' most of the times. But the truth is that *it requires more courage and guts to be fair than to be firm*. Actually, fairness and firmness are simply two sides of the same coin; every time you try to be fair to one person, you have to be firm with half a dozen others who may try to prey upon you with their vested interests.

This conceptual and actionable blueprint is by no means exhaustive or foolproof and easy to practice. But the 'price' you have to pay for inculcating professionalism in yourself is that you must first embark upon self-development. And the pains you take for this now are invariably rewarded many times over by the cumulative benefits they bring to you in the future. You thus prove to be of immense value to your organization, apart from growing up in your self-esteem.

Conclusion

The *function* of management is age-old, and it permeates all human efforts to manage resources for providing useful products and services. It is the *study of management practices*, and experiments with the dynamics of human motivations which are relatively new—and growing. One perennial challenge that every management faces is that it must continue to find newer and more subtle methods of motivation for its employees.

The present industrial scenario is being spurred by the new opportunities from mounting global competition, a greater degree of daring entrepreneurship, the Indian government's liberalization policy, crowned by ambitions of some industries to go global. All these have led to a new wave of innovations in the field of management practices. Most of these innovations, though welcome, are actually in the nature of 'techniques and devices'. In the right hands, they can prove to be very useful for meeting the challenging situations of competition, expansion, diversification and customer expectations.

However, these 'invigorating' forces also impose upon modern management the most maddening demands, specially from competition, rapid technological advancements, assertive consumerism, government policies and, economic and social forces. Employers, owners or even top management find themselves benumbed by these demands, and fall an easy prey to the temptations of expediency in taking decisions of short-term relevance.

Can this tug of war between opportunities and demands promote 'professionalism' among our managers? Will true professionalism remain a myth or reality in the Indian management scenario?

The answer is 'yes' and 'no'. 'Yes' in that new orientations towards work, work-culture and customers, promoted by the new techniques and devices, will certainly promote a more professional approach among employees. 'No', if reliance is placed only on the current innovations of techniques and devices which, at their best, are merely cosmetic in nature. What our industry really needs today is in-depth professionalism. I am convinced that professionalism has become essential now, and is almost round the corner—due to compelling forces, if not by choice. The compelling forces are the new opportunities and the attendant challenges. To conclude, professionalism is a reality and is eminently desirable, even on pragmatic long-term considerations. In your enlightened self-interest, you have to fight to bring in, uphold and refine professionalism in your role as managers.

There is no such thing as 'professional management'. Management is either effective or not. It is only you, the managers, who can inculcate professionalism in your reflexes, and thus make significant contributions to your organization. It is these contributions that make your organization effective. For this purpose, you will have to internalize in your reflexes the innate values that have been discussed in this chapter. Unless you do that—and there are no short-cuts—you will not be able to stand up to the real tests and challenges of the new wave of opportunities.

The path to promoting and reinforcing professionalism among managers is not an easy one. The chances of success are proportionate with your tenacity and dedicated self-discipline. It calls for sensitive re-orientation of a number of your popular misconceptions, and courageous efforts for practicing the tenets of professionalism discussed so far.

There is no need to re-invent the wheel. All you need, for inculcating a deep-rooted sense of professionalism, is to call upon the old, well-tried, essential values of management. Of course, you need to integrate the new and emerging innovations shaped by today's realities with the orientation suited to the velocity and direction of the new winds blowing across the globe. If you position yourselves properly, and in good time, there is no reason why you cannot wrest your right to turn these challenges into opportunities.

TWO

The Winds of Change

CHAPTER OBJECTIVES

- Present the new trends in Indian management, including new indigenous innovations and experiments
- Show how these experiments, if they stand the tests, will establish not only contemporaneity in Indian management practice but also prove to be path-breakers for others

---

New Trends in Indian Management

A lot of bold and innovative management systems and practices are being adopted since the mid-1990s by managements in India. The first spurt of encouragement came from the government's 1991 liberalization policies. But the real determination for these innovations can be traced to the shock waves that rose from the brief period of recession following this liberalization. Another factor that left us with no alternative are the managerial and business challenges continuing to emanate from the growing number of multinationals positioning themselves in India. And to top it all, there are the mounting aspirations of many Indian industrialists to go global.

Let us scan the industrial-socio-economic scenario in India to get some idea of our strengths and weaknesses at this 'take-off' stage. The initial results have been encouraging. Even if some of them eventually turn out to be unsuitable, the important gain that would still be ours is that innovative re-thinking and actions have been initiated in our country; and they are most likely to continue.

The industrial sector in general has shown the best records since the 1980s. The overall production has risen by nearly 10 per cent in 1996 against 5.4 per cent in 1993–94.[1] The contribution from the agricultural sector has gone up by 7 per cent in 1996. The Gross Domestic Product (GDP) rose by 6 per cent in 1995–96. Foreign trade and balance of payments too were heartening for the third year in succession. Foreign exchange reserve has risen from $ 6.5 billion in March 1993 to over $ 21.79 billion in March 1996.

According to the World Bank assessment, announced in August 1996, India has 'fundamentally altered its development strategy' over the last five years—from a highly regulated and insular economy to a more open and liberal market economy. Its economic recovery has been 'rapid and robust'.

While these are heartening facts, there are some factors that do chasten our enthusiasm. While exports grew (by 18.27 per cent) to $26.23 billion, imports grew to $28.25 billion, thus enlarging the trade deficit in 1994–95 to $2.02 billion. Our fiscal deficit was high at 6.1 per cent in 1994–95 and threatens to remain out of control for some time. The real cause of concern is the government's revenue deficit—the difference between its revenue receipts and its non-investment expenditures. It used to be 2.5 per cent of GDP from the 1980s till 1992–93, but climbed up to 4 per cent in 1993–94 and 1994–95.[2] Meaningful fiscal adjustments have yet to take place.

There is little evidence that the poor have benefited in any significant manner. What is really needed is not so much the allocation of funds and resources for them, but effective improvement in the delivery system so that even small allocations produce optimum tangible results for the ultimate beneficiaries. But till early 1997, the ruling parties of the central and most state governments continue to remain caught up in political and tactical manoeuvrings, and have been unable to undertake effective measures in this direction.

Government services in areas that are vital to industry and business have also been disappointingly poor; areas like health, education, public distribution system, power generation and distribution and services to small-scale industries continue to suffer. And to top them all, there is the disgusting spectacle of scams with the chilling realization that what has come to surface so far may only be the tip of the iceberg!

Inflation, after an initial spell of decline has started to inch upwards—with a near two-digit figure in January 1997. The net result, as far as the common man is concerned, is that prices are rising by the week—never mind what index figures indicate.

One may argue that these figures depict only a passing phase. But still they—or the pattern they present—are very relevant. We have to reckon with the fact that industry and business shall always be confronted by similar factors in different permutations and combinations and one will have to find ways and means to deal with them and carve out their opportunities by tackling these constraints. Table 2.1 gives some important data from the period 1950–96.

TABLE 2.1: Some Important Data

	1950–54	1970–71	1980–81	1990–91	1992–93	1995–96
Population In millions	361.1	548.2	683.3	846.3	878.6	Approx. 900
Growth rate						2.2%
Birth-rate Per 1000	39.9	41.2	37.2	29.5	28.5	
Death-rate Per 1000	27.4	19.0	15.0	9.8	9.2	
Life expectancy		In years				
Male	32.4	46.4	50.9			61.5
Female	32.1	45.6	50.4			60.8
TOTAL	32.1	45.6	50.4			61.0

NOTE: Recent studies indicate that despite all our efforts, we are growing @ 49 births every minute! And we are adding the equivalent of Europe's population every ten years!

Meanwhile, and silently, the company–customer relationship profile has changed significantly. Six years after liberalization, the marketplace has suddenly become frighteningly competitive. Not only have new players including a host of powerful transnationals come into the country, there are more brands available than ever before in every segment of every market. The customer has undoubtedly emerged as the king. With the first flush of euphoric post-liberalization growth rates tumbling, corporate India's sales have risen by just 8 per cent while its net profits have fallen by 2 per cent over 1995–96. True, India still enjoys an improved (and 'interesting') external profile; true also that the tax regime has been simplified, and there has been a 'skillful and significant liberalization' of the financial sector, even though dominance of the public sector continues. But the stark reality of today is that virtually every company finds itself struggling for survival.

Befittingly, for the first time since India's independence fifty years ago, the customer holds the final verdict. He is already finicky about what he wants; he will now onwards buy only that which meets his every need and desire. The smart companies across the country are no longer talking about product or service quality; what they are trying to build-in are *relationships* with their customers with a view to delighting them! Companies, it seems, will have to maximize the value they offer for the lowest price because that is the only way they can keep their customers—and stay in business.

It is in this context that we must now take into account the innovative measures being taken by our industry and business. These are the contemporary chain of efforts devised indigenously by Indian management to meet the challenges, grab opportunities, and adopt state-of-the-art management practices and styles.

We must, however, understand that these management techniques are no magic mantras; they cannot—in or by themselves—solve all our problems. Any changes brought about without considering *(a)* the unique nature of the organization where they are to be tried; *(b)* its work-culture; *(c)* the thinking and temperament of its employees; and *(d)* the basic theme of the change-concept will yield little or no results.

The Stirrings of Change

Total Quality Management (TQM)

TQM[3] has come a long way during its seven decades of existence. Walter A. Shewhart, a physicist at AT&T's Bell Laboratories in the USA, gave birth to the management science called 'Quality' in the 1920s. He introduced statistical concepts into manufacturing systems. Since then, experts have been continuously mapping newer territories in their quest for quality. *TQM is both a goal and a path;* its journey is thus never likely to end. TQM is taking quality out of the shopfloor to encompass every conceivable activity in an organization, with the customer at the centre of all thoughts, processes and decisions.

The future seems to be characterized by 'metaquality' which will have four layers of 'quality workers'. One, doing the work; the second, improving the work; the third, improving the way work gets improved; and the fourth, improving how improvements get improved! The attempt is to involve all employees as members of all the four stages.

In our country, we have come a long way with regard to quality. During the fifty years since the country's independence, corporate India has been producing poor products. According to a study done by the Geneva-based World Economic Forum, India occupies a lowly 28th position on the 'price-to-quality' parameter in the *World Competitiveness Report 1994*. On the global bench-mark of TQM practices, the *Report* ranks India 38th—in a sample of 41 countries. While Motorola, the American telecommunications equipment manufacturer, is busy attaining 99.99997 per cent defect-free manufacturing, in India a colossal Rs 6,000 crore worth of products—five per cent of Rs 120,000 crore of industrial production in 1993–94—had to end up on the scrap-heap before they even left the factory gates![4]

But today, there is a consensus that a quality revolution is essential if our country is to survive. TQM has been 'institutionalized' in the work-culture and management style of a large number of organizations. According to a survey conducted by the Bombay-based Indian Market Research Bureau (IMRB) in December 1994, Indian quality today ranks between four and seven on a ten-point scale; and 82 per cent of the respondents (which included fifty-eight CEOs, directors and vice-presidents of firms employing more than 500 people) believe that we would catch up with the world in the next ten years.'

Here are a few examples:

Perfect Machine Tools (PMT) D.L. Shah, its founder and Chairman Emeritus, is the first man outside North America to receive the American Society for Quality Control's Lifetime Achievement Award in November 1994. He puts more faith on the following set of simple paradigms than on formal quality theories:

♦ product quality is what is perfect from the customer's point of view;
♦ the customer must be satisfied at all costs;
♦ instill a sense of pride in their work in the workforce; and
♦ empower people to develop their skills.

A mere 60-crore turnover company, PMT now—thanks to its quality upgradation—has an 86 per cent share in the automotive lathe machines market, 60 per cent of the computerized numerically controlled internal grinders market, and 80 per cent of the ophthalmic lens machine market. Shah never thought of quality as a philosophy until he started exporting machine tools in 1968. This export was a condition imposed by the Reserve Bank for special permission granted to Shah to pay for the imported machines after a lapse of six months. Once its importance dawned upon him and he put it to work, he and his organization became totally committed to quality. Here is how he ingrained 'quality' among all his employees:

- set a personal example of practising what you preach about quality;
- create the environment for innovation and personal development;
- instill in every employee a sense of pride in the work that he must do;
- invest in training people at all levels in quality theory and practices; and
- empower employees to go to any length to satisfy the customer.

To Shah, quality is more than just a management technique; it is a mechanism that can 'transform a human being and free him'.

Mukund Iron and Steel   After considering the merits and other aspects of several models for over a year, Rajesh Shah, the Managing Director of Mukund, and others in his team were convinced that no single quality model would fully suit their organization. Eventually they have established four pillars on which their quality edifice rests. They are:

- the Juran quality improvement process;
- the Japanese concept of quality circles;
- the European standard of ISO 9000 certification; and
- continuous training

They realized that each of these four models and methods was, by itself, eminently implementable while they were complementary to each other. But any one of them, in itself, was not all encompassing for them. Therefore, they decided to mix and match ideologies with the intention of synthesizing what may be called a uniquely Mukund way to TQM. They set up a separate body for implementing TQM: the Total Quality Council Secretariat (TQCS). This body does continuous monitoring of the quality drive, ensures mid-course corrections, guides other councils created for implementing TQM in the company, and manages Mukund's need-based training system.

The company has already started reaping the benefits of this movement, not only in terms of higher productivity with better quality, but also in enhanced employee satisfaction.

Modi Xerox   It believes that total quality can be achieved only by standardizing each and every one of its processes in the form of systems—from manufacturing to advertising, from training to customer service. By breaking down every activity into discrete, sequential steps, the company attempts to eliminate deviations from the norm. Rigid, documented protocols of procedure govern Modi Xerox's practices, banishing the possibilities of individualized or informal approaches. It believes that quality comes from maintaining these systems, irrespective of the movement of individuals in and out of the company.

Asea Brown Boveri (ABB)   A progeny of the Indian subsidiaries of the Swedish company, Asea, and the Swiss company, Brown Boveri, ABB was undergoing post-merger pangs in the early 1990s. The global focus of the parent organization was shifting from products to people. ABB formally embraced TQM in 1989 as a result of which customer-driven quality-orientation swept through the 1,300 operating units around the globe. One of the messages that came up loud and clear was that 'the importance of people was crucial to its success' despite the fact that this is a technology-intensive—not manpower-intensive—company.

ABB found itself having to cope with consolidation, liberalization and TQM almost simultaneously. Realizing that both its future and the fate of its total quality drive depended on its people, this power-equipment manufacturer decided to restructure its human resources development policies for quality. While institutionalization of teamwork was the obvious choice, this threw up several issues. How do you foster team-spirit in an environment where individualism was high? How do you reward employees when they are organized in teams? In resolving these issues, ABB has managed to pioneer a set of quality practices which they call: 'team resource development'.

Drastic changes were introduced to promote the concept of teams. Cross functional teams—about 130 in all—were set up, each consisting of about five or six members for building long-term relations with customers. Also, small-group activities were started to find solutions to shop-floor problems. This style of functioning helps, among other things, 'deglamorise titles and delink power from positions. It also helps individuals develop under peer influence'.

Arising from this core structuring, several HRM/HRD initiatives have been taken by the management. They are:

- ♦ snapping all direct links between performance and compensation;
- ♦ re-orienting appraisals to reward team—not individual—performance;
- ♦ awarding all the managers in each grade the same increment every year; and
- ♦ training senior managers to counsel employees in team functioning.

Their next goal is to refine and introduce the system to the shop-floor staff as well. The company subscribes earnestly to the philosophy that *when an individual wins, the company does not necessarily win; but when the team wins, the individual also wins.*

Indian Aluminium (INDAL)   The 838-crore INDAL was confronted by a raw material crisis that pegged it down to a production of only 50,000 tonnes against its annual requirement of 100,000 tonnes of aluminium. Its managing director, Tapan Mitra who took over in January 1991, decided not to impose a solution from the corner office, but to stimulate his team of workers and managers to come up with a plan for the company's survival and development. Senior managers fanned out presenting scenario-sharing sessions and asking the participants for solutions. This was a call for bottom-up quality movement!

Since the company would have to continue to buy its metal from the global market, the employees concluded that an export drive would have to be mounted which, in turn, would require that its products must meet international standards. Total quality was thus the inevitable requirement; and its adoption and acceptance hardly needed any strenuous proddings.

The 'quality route' emerged out of a brainstorming session involving sixty-two participants from various levels of the company in early 1992. Having spawned these ideas themselves, the workers went on to lead the move to institutionalize quality across all the plants and offices in the organization.

As a logical corollary, the company launched a competition between plants on how much waste they could eliminate through quality practices. Workers internalized the processes far quicker than they would have through normal training; and they generated savings of Rs 12 crore in 1993–94.

Similarly, INDAL initiated a customer–champion programme, designating individual workers to visit customers, and then to represent them on the shop-floor. Stunned by the feedback from the customers on poor quality, the workers started protecting their quality practices fiercely, assailing one another if they failed to meet standards.

Business Process Reengineering[5]

This is the hottest trend in management, and some organizations in India have already begun to reengineer their business. Done well, it delivers extraordinary gains in speed, productivity and profitability.

A former Massachusetts Institute of Technology professor, Michael Hammer, pioneered this movement through his essay published in 1990 in the *Harvard Business Review*, entitled: 'Re-engineering Work: Don't Automate, Obliterate'. Its central theme is that it is crucial to break away from the outdated rules and fundamental assumptions that underlie operations; the rules themselves have got to be changed. Today, business process reengineering (BPR)—popularly called 're-engineering'—is considered to be the most powerful as well as the most maligned management tool. *It starts from the future, and works backwards*—unconstrained by existing methods, people or departments. In fact, its practitioners ask, 'If we were a new company, how would we organize and run this place?' Its chief tool is a clean sheet of paper. It is actually a sharply-focused practice that can produce extraordinary benefits provided the following *four* fundamentals are adhered to:

1. It is process-centric. This tool concentrates on processes—the activities that convert inputs from suppliers into outputs for the customer. This refers to breaking from the past and changing the steps that go into manufacturing, marketing, accounting—even the presentations.

2. It is redesign-ruled. Modification will not do. One must start with a clean slate and lay out the steps of the various processes from scratch, the way you would like them to be.

3. It is radical. Reengineering will leave you with business processes that bear no resemblance to their earlier forms. It eliminates them altogether instead of simply trying to execute them more efficiently.
4. It is dramatic. It aims at burning away large chunks of expenses by half or even one-third.

One would tend to wonder whether Indian industrialists would even consider going in for such daring and dramatic changes. Besides, the predictable trade union resistance must not be forgotten or under-estimated. Nevertheless, the fact is that a number of well-known industries have already gone in for reengineering, and they claim to have benefited a lot from it. Some of the companies are:

Sundaram Fasteners   It was determined to upgrade its quality to world standards in order to export large enough volumes to offset its required imports. It focused on its manufacturing as the core process for ruthless reengineering, and came to realize that its manufacturing was clustered more around operations than around products. Reengineering transformed the process from being task-centric to product-centric. Machines were regrouped into two 'zones of autonomous production' (ZAP). Along with this, the responsibility for meeting customer requirements was shifted from the marketing department to the manager of each of the two ZAP modules. The results were tangible: 50 per cent improvement in adherence to schedules, increase in inventory turnover from four times to 20 times and a 25 per cent jump in productivity!

Hindustan Motors   It presents yet another facet of reengineering. At its earth-moving machinery division, the earlier manufacturing process could cater to only one kind of machinery. Being used for every category of product, it led to a less-than-optimum utilization of resources. What they now wanted was to create a manufacturing process for ten products. They needed the new manufacturing process to allow coexistence of different methodologies required for different products. And they needed this process to permit prioritization of orders according to customer needs. Now three mini plants have been formed—one each for dumper equipment, loader equipment and tract vehicles. And each plant has been divided into cells, each staffed with multi-skilled workers. Each cell is responsible for fabricating and assembling the entire product, and reducing delays that used to occur frequently. Work-in-progress has already been reduced by 20 per cent, and is expected to be cut down by another 30 per cent.

Siemens India   It too has gone in for reengineering for improving installation time and service quality of its hi-tech medical diagnostics equipment. Earlier, both installation and post-installation services were the responsibility of the same department. Any order received for an equipment was processed by forwarding its copies to the commercial and dispatch departments and to the customer. The former would then pass the order to the service department which, in turn, would check with the customer whether his site was ready for installation. There were too many interfaces and far too many people had to be involved. Reengineering has led to delinking installation of the machine from the service department. A separate project management team and a commercial and technical assistance centre (C-TAC) have been created. Now the sales order is sent directly to the project management team which handles all pre-installation work. And the C-TAC manages documentation, on-site technical assistance, etc. Service engineers now concentrate on their primary function of providing post-installation service. Installation time has come down from ten to three days, and the service engineers have enormously improved their response time to complaints and quality.

Union Carbide   It has used reengineering to scrape $400 million out of the fixed costs in just three years.

Managing Teams

One of the most distinctive changes nowadays on the shop-floor in Indian industries is the installation of team-based systems—also known as 'Quality Circles'. These can be said to have sparked off almost a revolution. By bringing together workers, supervisors and managers from different disciplines and organizing them into small teams, corporate India is radically altering its manufacturing process. As a result, factories are turning into team-based entities which, in turn, are:

♦ cutting costs;
♦ improving quality;
♦ boosting productivity;

- catalyzing innovations; and
- improving worker–manager relations.

Ever-increasing competition has spurred this metamorphosis. No longer is manufacturing best done by breaking a process down to its smallest, repeatable component, as 'Taylor's scientific management' had propounded. Increasingly, industrial organizations in India have begun to realize that workers, when placed together in small groups, can be far more innovative and productive than the sum of their individual initiatives.

A team is a small number of people with complementary skills. They are committed to a common purpose, performance goals and approach for which the members hold themselves mutually accountable. Functionally, teams operate better by choosing an internal coordinator rather than a hard task-master. The best teams are self-directed. Most of the successful teams work in a 'closed loop formation' that allows them to meet their goals quickly, disband and re-form as a new team to attain new goals. As a corollary, horizontal organizations are essential for team-led management.

There is growing evidence now that motivated teams—exotically called 'Kshitij', 'Aavishkar', 'Alpha', 'Delta'—are revolutionizing the workplace today. To be truly effective, teams must have few boundaries, and their members must be *empowered to take decisions,* and their decisions/recommendations must be taken seriously by the seniors and acted upon. Complementary skills are important. For example, a typical team would include a service mechanic (to appreciate the customers' complaints), a sales representative, a production-line man, a quality department representative, etc. Mere empowerment is not enough; top management's interest and responsiveness must be present, and visible to all.

Philips India Its CEO, H.J.J. Rensma, said that he would like to do away with the distinction between workers and managers; he liked to consider them as collaborators. Philips' 'small group activities' are part of a structured training programme where participants attend sessions on statistical modules, diagnostics and remedial actions. In addition, the company also runs training programmes called 'Human Relations at Work' where groups of 25 participants—including managers, executives, helpers and workers—play team games with the objective of winning by collaboration.

Titan Industries   Hari Rao, Vice-President of Titan Industries feels that 'workers' is too restrictive a term; it implies people from whom we just buy muscle power. In a way—and particularly in enlightened management circles in India—the days of assembly-line production are numbered. Instead, industries are replacing traditional tasks by team empowerment; and they are winning. An eight-member team, for example, was set up to improve productivity through workplace redesign. After two years of deliberations, the team suggested cavities in the workplace so that components are not dislocated while in use, special axle-holders for easy pick up, raising the workplace height by 10 cm for a more comfortable working posture, etc. The net effect was that cycle times came down by nearly 180 per cent, and the maximum production per shift rose from 1,346 to 3,773 watch components!

Modi Xerox   It was one of the first corporates to kick off team movement by setting up six continuous quality improvement teams in 1991. Now, team formation is so structured that the company has a Blue Book which defines the areas that cross-functional teams can attend to. One of the teams, called 'Ankush', tackled the problem that all the resistors, capacitors, diodes and transistors ended up having excess leg length after wave soldering. The team worked under two self-imposed rules: the solution of the problem must be within the control of the group, and it must not call for any additional investments. It found the solution by modifying the dies that shaped the pre-forming tool, and by removing a wrong kink. The net impact was that productivity improved by 687 per cent, leading to a time saving of 1,142 hours per year, and Rs 28,543 per year.

Cadbury India   In 1995 it set up small groups in its factories to enhance worker-involvement and ownership. The result is already visible: nearly all the bottlenecks that choke cost reductions or efficiency improvements are tackled by these inter-departmental teams. It sets annual targets for savings, efficiency and cost-control. If any bottlenecks are encountered in achieving these targets, eight-member teams are then set up to try and remove such bottlenecks. Members of such teams include managers who need not necessarily be the team leaders.

Videocon Taking a leaf out of Toshiba and Hitachi in Japan, it has instituted radical changes on its shop-floor. At its Aurangabad plant, workers have been divided into four independent business units which compete with each other in attaining targets.

TISCO It has set up more than 100, and TELCO about 2,000, 'Quality Circles' which is the common and closest ancestor of 'teams'. VOLTAS uses cross-functional teams as part of its quality control systems. In TISCO's forging division, each manager is required to involve himself in a team. This is based on the belief that existence of collaborative and positive relationships between workers and managers is important for the success of Quality Circles.

Delegation and Empowerment

Delegation is a well known tool and has been used in Indian industries and business for decades. Many organizations believe that this is the only way to 'empower' employees. In a way it is; but delegating authority and responsibility is not enough to make people *feel more powerful.* It must be coupled with the opportunity to exercise it. For example, an individual performing in an organization must be *in a position to take decisions in the absence of his superior.*

Empowerment[6]—a process being used increasingly all over the world and also in India—goes beyond delegation. In most cases, delegation remains a matter between an individual boss and his subordinates whereas empowerment is adopted *as a system* based on the philosophy that employees at almost all levels should be empowered to take decisions on behalf of their superiors—either when the superior is absent, or even when he is present and wants his subordinate to exercise his own judgement and take his own decisions. This is done to enhance the employees' sense of involvement with his functions and his organization. Empowering means making an employee feel more powerful—in terms of his competence, capabilities, authority for resource utilization, decision-making, and feeling responsible for his decisions and actions. Thus, empowerment, on the one hand, liberates decision-making and actions emanating from decisions from the stranglehold of bosses and the attendant delays, hesitations, and hardships to the end-users. On the other hand, the employees are enabled to develop themselves, innovate and take initiatives—for greater effectiveness of the organization. Empowerment takes place at three levels:

- individual level;
- team level (network of individuals); and
- organization level (network of teams).

The following are the pre-requisites of empowerment:

- delegation of authority;
- involvement of employees;
- providing adequate resources;
- providing development opportunities;
- trusting employees;
- offering useful criticism;
- sharing information;
- recognition and rewards; and
- empowerment of teams.

What is heartening is that delegation and empowerment are now being tried out, consciously and in a planned manner, by the CEOs at the corporate level. It has already shown convincing benefits in terms of heightened effectiveness, deeper and healthier relationships at the workplace and greater motivation for excelling past records.

Take the example of the Rs 7,500-crore Reliance Group which is currently undergoing an amazing transformation from tight owner-control to company-wide decentralization of authority and responsibility. Until two years ago, Dhirubhai, who built this group from scratch, and his sons, kept a very close control on all decisions, transactions and business and industrial thrusts. The owners have now re-invented their fundamental principles and systems of management; they are now systematically handing over day-to-day tasks of managing their megacorp to a team of professional managers. Nearly 100 key executives—styled *owner-managers* because they are reinforced with stock options—have been entrusted with this responsibility and commensurate authority. The family's withdrawal is proceeding rapidly; younger managers (the average age now is 35 against 42 five years ago) are increasingly occupying posts which were earlier held by retired public sector CEOs. Each business group is like an independent company, with the functional heads working like managing directors.

Nevertheless, while the family is withdrawing, it does not intend to fade away—not yet. In the first stage of delegating responsibility to their virtual CEOs, the Ambanis persist with a system of checks and balances that prevents unbridled authority accruing to a single manager. Indeed, the trick lies in a subtle change in the style of leadership. The top management must maintain an 'experienced presence' by providing direction and interest in the early stages of team-building and delegation, and slowly move to a stage where they become mere members.

The Reliance Group seems to be aiming at the following management goals:

♦ building a core team of young, multi-skilled, globally-oriented managers to lead the group;
♦ entrusting complete operational freedom to empowered executives sharing the corporate vision;
♦ creating a framework that shuns hierarchical structures and uses teams to accomplish tasks speedily; and
♦ replacing the ad hoc methods of the past with systems that can be followed independent of individuals.

Let us look at another case—of the Rs 240-crore, Madras-based Sundaram Fasteners Ltd (SFL). Started in 1966 with two machines and an equity of Rs seven lakh, it was fondly and personally nurtured by Suresh Krishna who continues as its CEO. SFL has the distinction of being the first Indian company to receive ISO 9,000, and of winning in 1993 the contract for supplying metal radiator caps to the $154.95 billion US auto giant, General Motors. Until the late 1970s, Krishna insisted and got all information—from daily production and shipment schedules, through marketing data, to cash flow. He believed in three ground rules:

♦ keep a close watch on what's going on;
♦ encourage your people to trust you; and
♦ trust them.

When SFL diversified and grew in the late 1970s by setting up a cold extrusion and powder metal plant and a second fasteners plant, it dawned upon Krishna that he had been operating on too much control and that he was an autocrat. He bartered his iron control for a determined corporate-wide decentralization and set about transforming his organization systems into becoming team-led, not CEO-led. And he is now a much more relaxed—as well as a much more effective—entrepreneur. His company's performance listed below speaks for itself:

- ◆ doubled net profits and trebled earnings per share in 1994–95;
- ◆ averted industrial unrest even when strikes paralyzed group companies;
- ◆ secured OEM status from General Motors to supply radiator caps;
- ◆ built the company into a total quality organization; and
- ◆ ensured that SFL was the first Indian company to get ISO certification.

Smartsizing

Smartsizing is being adopted by Indian companies in increasing numbers, with very heartening results—both in terms of healthier operations and better utilization of manpower. In simple language, 'smartsizing' means selling off a part of a company's unviable and unproductive activity to a better operator, ensuring as far as possible that the employees working in that unit are *retrained and redeployed.* Another important factor in smartsizing is that it is not an instrument for cutting down activities—a process known as 'downsizing'; *it is actually a process of discarding one set of activities for the purpose of ensuring growth in another set of activities.*

The compulsions for smartsizing originated in the 1970s when industrialists leveraged their licences to grow by venturing into myriads of unrelated businesses. Although most of the companies (which included multinationals as well) made money, they did not realize that some of those activities could prove to be hindrances when faced with free competition. Now many of these companies have been forced to chip and prune their activities to weed out the losers and, instead, to focus on their strengths. Some of the companies that have resorted to smartsizing are: Indian Oxygen Limited (now named British Oxygen [India] Limited), RPG Enterprises, Asian Paints, Hindustan Motors, Boots India, Godrej Soaps, Glaxo India, ICI, Ciba-Geigy, etc.

Take the case of Indian Oxygen: Mr S.S.Prasad, its Managing Director, confronted his senior managers with grim statistics; the company's net profits of Rs 5.35 crore in 1982 had dipped to a mere Rs 25 lakh in 1991. He asked his managers to do their brainstorming, and come up with *their* strategic-plan recommendations (although he did have his own ideas) for the company's survival.

The senior managers came up with the recommendation that the company should sell off the welding and explosives units since they were using obsolete technologies and were largely responsible for the company's losses. They further suggested that the money from the sale should be used not just for 'bottomline management' *but to strengthen the mainline activity, namely, the industrial gases operations, and to fund the voluntary retirement schemes for redundant employees.* This sale was to generate other savings as well. For instance, the welding unit ran up sky-high power bills which accounted for 65 per cent of the production cost of this unit.

This unit was sold to ESAB, a well-established welding equipment multinational company, which promptly modernized the plant and brought in the latest technology. It took over 1,600 (out of IOL's total strength of 5,500) employees who had been working in that unit, and has also turned them into more agile and productive employees. The sale-money was used to modernize 65 per cent of IOL's industrial gas manufacturing facilities. This modernization itself has given to IOL a reduction in power consumption by 25 per cent. IOL has also been receiving handsome share-dividends from ESAB, since it has retained part-ownership of the welding unit.

The result: the company's net profits have climbed up to Rs 13 crore in 1993–94—a jump of 85 per cent over its 1992–93 results. The company now plans to diversify into manufacturing hydrogen and carbon dioxide in Maharashtra and South India. Above all, all its 1,600 employees now with ESAB are doing well—thanks to retraining and redeployment. Redeployment has spread as a healthy contagion among the rest of the IOL employees, and has become a way of life there.

So we see here an interesting case of redeployment in reverse. Indian Oxygen went into what, in management parlance, is called 'smart-sizing'. One of the most important pre-requisites of successful smart-sizing is that every *chopping of unwanted activity must have the objective of corresponding growth, not shrinkage. Also, the recommendation for smartsizing must come from senior managers, and not from the Chief Executive.* The true merit of smartsizing is that it leads to all-round healthier growth, not to just a sell-off. And in the process, the employees concerned receive a new shot in their arms in the form of retraining and redeployment.

Judging the Boss

Another noteworthy trend in Indian management is that *many companies are asking employees to assess their seniors.* They hope that this will help executives improve their performance, and make them truly more effective.

This emanates from an old, deep-rooted desire in all of us to sit face to face with our boss and tell him, without fear of reprisal, as to what exactly we think of his style of functioning. All of us would like to tell our boss how and in what measure he unwittingly remains a pain in our neck, and how with a little variation in his style and approach, he could become far more effective! While fulfilment of such a desire would be asking for too much, particularly in the Indian context, a variation of this approach has nevertheless slowly been catching on in our corporate circles. It is called 'bottom-up appraisal' in which a subordinate records his perceptions of his boss as a manager and leader.

The main reason for Indian companies waking up to bottom-up appraisal is, again, the emergence of keen competition. One inevitable demand of competition is that each competing organization must perform better; and this, in essence, means each employee in the organization must be keen on progressive improvement in his performance. Companies have realized that this demand for better performance can be met only where conducive climate and culture are created and maintained. And this, in turn, depends on the individual style of the top-level managers, how they project and nurture it among their subordinates.

This system has been in use globally. (In all U.S. universities, the career and even the job-security of teachers depend largely on the 'appraisals' made by their students on their knowledge and teaching style). And now we have Indian companies that are using this system to help managers so appraised become better and more effective. Some such companies are briefly discussed below.

MIL (Mafatlal)   At MIL, the fluctuating performance of their textile operations had been a source of anxiety. A closer scrutiny revealed that there was *a significant relationship between the different managerial styles of unit heads and the units performance.* MIL—a company that was traditional and not too hot on HRD initiatives—decided to take a bold step; they sent twenty of their key people at vice-president and general manager levels to the Indian Institute of Management, Ahmedabad for a four-day workshop on managerial styles and organizational effectiveness. As a part of this workshop—and for the first time in MIL's history—each of the senior executives was assessed by ten of his peers and juniors. It was not very traumatic, though. Once it was felt, and accepted, that there does exist a correlation between the employees' performance and the functioning styles of their superiors, every senior participant was willing to know what his subordinates thought of him as a leader, with the intention of making suitable changes in his style accordingly.

Thomas Cook   Four of its senior executives were initially put through the routine of being appraised by their subordinates *as part of the company's global leadership programme.* These executives were the chief of the Indian operations—two directors and one general manager; and the appraisals were done by five subordinates and five seniors. Some of these executives were sent for further management training programmes.

Hindustan Ciba–Geigy   In October 1995, it too joined the other companies to attend a ten-day corporate structure programme, including sessions on 'situational leadership'. Top management of this company believe that managers must develop certain core competencies—one of them being *leadership*. (There is no such thing as 'the best' style of leadership. Successful leaders adapt their behaviour to meet the unique demands of varying situations; and in this context, it is essential for them to know what their subordinates think of their style of functioning, and how flexible they can be under different situations.)

Some of these companies have drawn up structured questionnaires that are filled in by the managers' subordinates; others like Eicher Consultancy Services prefer to do this informally. What is meticulously avoided is to pin down an appraised executive. What is always kept in the forefront is that this system gives a tool to the executives for their *self-development. The real objective is to promote an urge for change from within the executives.*

Caring for Customers[7]

The belief has been gaining currency that only corporate organizations close to the customer will survive the competitive 1990s. And one ideology that companies across the country—even the consumer-products public sector undertakings—are pursuing is C A R E: 'Customers Are Really Everything'! In a country where organizations have always taken customers for granted, this is a historic reversal of attitudes. The companies sold on this attitude are fast adopting a key survival strategy: don't just sell, *satisfy;* don't just satisfy, *pamper;* don't just pamper, *charm your customer.* And they go about doing so in the following ways:

Knowing what Really Makes Motivated Buyers   Today CEOs are personally going out of their offices into the marketplace—or inviting customers in—for obtaining first-hand knowledge of what motivates buyer behaviour.

Here are *five* examples:

1. S.M. Datta, Chairman of the Rs 4,500-crore Hindustan Lever group, used to personally visit retail outlets in different cities more than once a month.
2. Four times a year, C.Y. Pal, Chairman of the Rs 165-crore chocolate-maker Cadbury India, quietly circulates among buyers at various shops in numerous cities to obtain unfiltered information from the customer.
3. One Saturday every month, Pradip Kumar Dhoot, Director of the Rs 1,200-crore Videocon Group slips into his faded jeans and a crumpled bush-shirt, and travels second-class in the local trains in Bombay, chatting with fellow passengers in Marathi about television sets, audio products, and washing machines. He thus gets to know first-hand the consumers' needs and buying capacity.
4. The Rs 850-crore transnational Philips India regularly asks panels of housewives to help it design its domestic appliances.
5. The Rs 3,810-crore ITC Ltd has started setting up company-run retail outlets to come into direct contact with its customers.

Learning from the Customer   In addition, companies are beginning to *assess customer satisfaction.* This is, by far, the best strategy to increase company profits since loyal customers provide the following benefits:

- higher purchase volumes;
- impressive boost in extra sales due to word-of-mouth referrals made by satisfied customers for almost no extra cost for advertising; and
- the premium the satisfied customers are willing to pay.

In the wake of ongoing technological revolutions, products will keep changing fast, eliminating the very concept of product loyalty. Smart companies have now realized that it is not their products or product-lines but only the customer that will endure. The logical corollary of this trend is that tomorrow's survivors in the corporate world will be servicing their customer's needs—not just selling them TVs, VCRs, soaps or soups. Already, many consumer-item companies are inquiring from their customers about how they should design and price their products.

Here are *two* examples:

1. TVS–Suzuki's (a Rs 274-crore two-wheeler manufacturer) specially-constituted 'Task Force Scooty' probed the tastes of hundreds of potential customers through meetings at dealers' premises. This went on for 21 months before its 60cc 'Scooty' was launched whose specifications had emerged from such meetings with potential customers. Even after the launch, the task force spent two-and-a-half months talking to a total of 400 Scooty-owners, one at a time at ten days' intervals to assess their satisfaction levels. This feedback was used for further modifications in the Scooty.
2. Britannia Industries (a Rs 443-crore biscuit-maker) believes that the company must seek an insight into what customers think, and 'redesign its products, delivery and systems to offer value in function, image and service'. Its snackfood, Little Hearts—a puff-pastry combination which is radically different from Britannia's usual bakery products—grew out of an in-depth study of consumer tastes in Calcutta and Bombay. This has paid handsome dividends in terms of progressively rising sales of Little Hearts.

Generating Loyalty through Service   It is being realized by most consumer-product companies in particular that merely catering to what customers need is not going to be enough; *add-ons are going to become essential.* One such add-on is the quality of customer service which would be a factor of product differentiation. Thus has emerged the winning idea: *offer value additions that come to the consumer as unexpected benefits servicing an unarticulated need!*

At ITC Hotel's Welcomgroup Sheraton Towers chain in Bangalore, Delhi and Madras, guests are amazed to find a butler filling their baths, ironing their clothes, and making their appointments. It is the surprise element that gives the customers great joy.

On a rainy June night, one executive of Kalyani Sharp arrived at a customer's residence at 10 p.m. in Madras to install his newly-bought compact disc music system. The customer could not believe it! These little 'extras' are designed to provide more emotional than practical value in the service. Although these initiatives have so far been directed at affluent and socially more sophisticated customers, it is important to note that a new ground has been broken. Rather than merely supplying good quality products, a new direction has been taken in the realm of creating customer-loyalty through service. And this movement is bound to gather powerful momentum among common customers as well.

Empowering Employees for Customer Satisfaction It is only logical—and essential—that the working systems of companies aiming at customer satisfaction are almost turned upside down to empower the employees down the line to provide *prompt response and effective service whenever and wherever the customer approaches them.*

Steps have already begun to be taken in this direction among Indian industries and business houses. Employees must be empowered— irrespective of where they are in the hierarchy—to take decisions without looking for their boss if the customer has a problem.

Hewlett-Packard India requires from its employees that no telephone should ring more than thrice (because it could be a customer ringing). ANZ Grindlays, American Express Travel-Related Services, Mahindra & Mahindra have all taken concrete steps by reorganizing 'power pyramids' that encourage and enable employees to take suitable decisions at their levels. At Mahindra & Mahindra, shop-floor engineers visit their customers across the country twice a month where they videotape their interactions. Then they play back these recordings to their workmen for their education and to know what the customers want or complain about.

The latest slogan that has caught the fancy of marketing people in business houses is that customer 'satisfaction' is not enough; *Indian business has to strive for customer delight.*

Conclusion

We have presented above only brief accounts of some of the innovative efforts being made by Indian organizations. It is quite possible that many more—and bolder—experiments with management practices are being made nowadays which we may be unaware of. It is nevertheless clear that Indian industries have been taking bold innovative steps and are adopting seemingly unconventional practices for the purpose of enhancing the overall effectiveness of their organizations and employees. Indian industries are in the process of being liberated from the restrictive and protective policies of the government. They now have to contend with fierce competition that will grow both in its magnitude and sophistication. This, actually, is a blessing in disguise for indigenous management houses. They have been left to their own devices, and to carving out not only their own salvation but their destinies as well. Another blessing in disguise is the realization that 'borrowed wisdom, techniques or devices' for enhancing managerial effectiveness will not do for India.

'Change' in management techniques must not be rushed into because everybody is doing so. A suitable management technique should be selected only after understanding its principles and implications, and after a thorough examination of the ground realities and ramifications of the prevailing situation. It must be a three-stage process:

♦ it must start with a *need;*
♦ there must be clear set of *objectives;* and
♦ there must be a *plan.*

Take ISO 9,000 as an example. Not long ago, almost all companies were competing for this certificate. They did so not necessarily because they were sure that it would bring about operational effectiveness, but because they knew that it would provide a lot of publicity and mileage to their organization. A recent survey shows that ISO has not so far brought about the promised changes in the Indian industry.

Change is valid and implementable only when it is recognized as necessary and is shared, by the employees concerned. Efforts must be made to make the people at the operational level understand the philosophy and usefulness of the proposed change; only then can they accept the change and put it to productive use, yielding positive results. Major external threats, challenges and rapid environmental changes are all catalysts for change. A new challenging assignment or task can also spark off the much-needed change. Similarly, change can also occur when a keen desire is enkindled for positive developments.

In this context, it is heartening that our industries and business have risen to the occasion, and shown that they can devise their own solutions and methods; and they have gone ahead with that. In doing so, they have benefited from being 'late-starters', by learning from the mistakes and successes of others. Of course, only time and trials will tell whether these innovations and experiments will suitably cater to our needs; and it is quite likely that many of these new methods will fall by the wayside. There is nothing very alarming if some of these innovations do not succeed; what is important is that one has dared to innovate and experiment.

It has to be borne in mind, though, that what our industries and business have been busy with lately are only 'techniques and devices'; there has been little concern with inventing or stumbling on to new *principles* of management. Not that it matters much, since a large body of the core and well-tried principles have already been bequeathed to us by management thinkers and industries.

Let us now turn to examining some eternally relevant and useful principles.

THREE

Motivation: The Triumph of 'Inspiration' over 'Laboured Efforts'

CHAPTER OBJECTIVES

- Discuss the challenge of motivation as being the innate willingness on the part of employees to give of their best and to bridge the gap between laboured efforts and inspiration
- Show how motivation can be created and maintained through a balanced integration of rewards, fear of manipulation, encouragement and other such factors

---

Motivation: An Enigma

Whenever, and wherever, people are required to offer their services in exchange for compensation, a kind of tussle creeps in in most cases between 'laboured efforts' and 'inspiration' for doing the assigned tasks. At the lower end (of 'efforts'), people are urged upon to do their best in return for wages or, when required, they are manipulated through coercion or exploitation or fear. At the other end (of 'inspiration'), people are encouraged through incentives of higher payments, personal growth, recognition, better quality of life, challenges or exhortations to continue to put in better performance. However, the need for constant watch or cajoling continues with dogged persistence, no matter what the ambience or system surrounds human activity.

This has been true down the ages. Manpower was employed on a large scale, when the well-planned, geometric cities of Harappa and Mohenjo-Daro with underground sewers and vast granaries were built in ancient India during the thirtieth century BC, or when the pyramids in Egypt were built in the twenty-seventh century BC or the Great

Wall of China built in the fourth century BC, or later in the medieval period when the Taj Mahal was built in the seventeenth century AD. These countries were ruled by despots those days; and the workers on these projects had neither any choice nor even the promise of better wages or working conditions or better human relations. They worked—or in most cases were made to work—unquestioningly; and any kind of resistance by them was unthinkable. *Yet, their performance and zeal for giving their best could never be guaranteed.* History has recorded instances that, in spite of the 'fear' or 'no-choice' psychosis, the workers on these projects had to be coerced, exploited or punished in order to keep up with the desired targets of time and quantum of work.

The truth is that neither rewards nor fear nor manipulation nor encouragement through cosmetic recognition can, by themselves, ensure continuing and innate willingness on the part of human beings to give of their best. It is only a 'balanced integration' of these (and other) factors that can bring about 'motivation', which, in its true sense, signifies 'innate willingness on the part of the working people to give of their best and to continue to do better than their best—not only because of monetary rewards or greater degree of safety promised *but because such accomplishments are perceived by them as rewards in themselves!*

And it is this kind of 'motivation' which has the capacity to bridge the gap between 'laboured efforts' and 'inspiration'.

The enigma, however, is that from pre-historic days, motivation has eluded any set definition or formula or grasp. Scores of studies and experiments later, most managers still ask themselves—and others: 'How do we motivate our people so that they *continue, on their own*, to try to give of their best?' A corollary to that question would be: 'What do we do with an employee, or a group of employees, who have lost—or never fully attained—their motivation?'

No matter how daunting, this question is so basic for management—and so promising—that it simply cannot be ignored. Without sustained motivation, no management can be run in an effective and self-sustaining manner. Many innovative techniques have been tried over the ages to liberate organizations from the vagaries of human will: Different phases and movements of 'scientific management', of 'one best way', of 'human relations' etc., come to mind. One can also recall the periods when experts concentrated upon improving the efficacy of machines by inventing several impressive, labour-saving devices through automation and other fool-proof, waste-eliminating work-methods. Efforts have also been going on over a long period of time to bring about higher productivity and profits through mind-boggling technological advancements. Similar advancements on the marketing front are being made for enhancing organizations' profits through cost-reduction efforts, more imaginative marketing thrust and aggressive selling. These are being progressively accelerated with quantum jumps in sophisticated computer wizardry. But all the same, one also finds that management science has come full circle with the realization that a *continuing stream of motivation among employees is a must.*

The reason is simple enough. Any enterprise has to reckon with the management of its 'resources' all of which happen to start with the letter 'M':

- ◆ money
- ◆ materials
- ◆ machines
- ◆ manufacturing
- ◆ marketing
- ◆ media
- ◆ men

It is evident that all these resources, other than 'men,' are *inert*. They cannot do anything by themselves nor can they move anything into action or life. It is only the 'men' resource that has the capability to breathe life and dynamism in the other resources and make them productive or useful. But the resource 'men' itself may not necessarily become, or remain, productive to its full potential unless it is *primed* into a state of motivation. And this motivation can come only from men, i.e., the leaders, *through the alchemy of motivation.*

The Quest for the 'Mantra'

Several important, epoch-making studies, experiments and 'movements', have been conducted during the last 100 years to understand what motivation is, and how it can be ingrained in the employees. As a result, several highly educative, eye-opening and useful theories and principles have been enunciated. We shall dwell upon the essence of these theoretical models. Our main thrust here shall be to pierce through the maze of the available theoretical knowledge, and come up with some practicable suggestions as to what you and your organization can do to promote motivation among your people at work.

These 'movements' or studies have been categorized here under *two* broad 'input' headings:

1. Motivational inputs on, or from, the organization—the 'context' approach.
2. Motivational inputs on, or within, the employee(s)—the 'content' approach.

The Context Approach

Most of the experiments carried out at the turn of the last century were related to the work-setting, or job context rather than the content of the job. The underlying belief was that *if only the tasks to be performed could be made simpler or easier or more methodical,* significant improvement in workers' attitude towards their jobs could be brought about. Therefore, those experiments concentrated on restructuring the 'context' of jobs—imaginatively as well as methodically. Here are some examples:

At the turn of the last century, Frederick W. Taylor, father of 'scientific management' tried to increase production through more systematic work-methods coupled with the traditional supervisory assertiveness. In spite of his success, he was disillusioned with this approach since it left everyone feeling bitter. He then applied his well-known 'time-and-methods' studies based on the system of 'analysis and synthesis of tasks'. Under this system, each worker was provided with a card containing written instructions about each step he was to follow in sequence. Although it allowed little or no discretion to the worker, production improved significantly, and the workers could be paid much higher wages. And despite higher pay bills, there were benefits for everyone *because the size of the surplus was increased.*

It is, however, interesting to note that the deeper Frederick Taylor went into these experiments and the greater his successes, the more he came to realize that:

♦ 'a business is a system of human cooperation that will only be successful if all concerned work toward a common objective'; and

♦ a 'mental revolution' was necessary where 'both sides take their eyes off the division of the surplus . . . and together turn their attention toward increasing the size of the surplus.'[1]

Taylor primarily dealt with the 'context' of jobs, in consonance with the environment, including the workers' need-satisfaction level that existed at that time.

Then came the husband–wife team of Lillian M. and Frank B. Gilbreth who offered a refinement on Taylor's work. They strongly believed that there was always 'one best way' to do a task. They indeed demonstrated significant improvements in output, reduction in fatigue and cost of production, with convincing success. However, as in Taylor's case, their methods too were extremely rigid and methodical to be sustained.

The 'Human Relations' Movement

The next movement was led by Australian-born Elton Mayo. Although this too is concerned with the 'context' frame of work, it went deeper into *the minds and feelings of the workmen* rather than remain engrossed in the 'outer' structure of jobs and tasks. Started as a series of studies in 1924 at the former Hawthorne Works of the Western Electric Company (now AT&T Technologies), this movement is regarded as one of the most important breakthroughs in the evolution of motivation generation.

Mayo believed that the development of an informal group was a kind of indictment of the entire society of those days, since it was concerned only with economic self-interest, and treated human beings like insensitive machines. As a result, even the workers were conditioned to looking upon work merely as an impersonal exchange of money for work; to them work amounted to a kind of humiliation, entailing performance of routine, tedious and over-simplified tasks in an environment over which they had no control. This environment denied the self-esteem and self-actualization needs of the worker.

These experiments consisted of changing illumination levels, introduction of rest periods, reducing supervision to an extent that the employees worked with greater degree of freedom, and a close study of how the employees behaved in, and were influenced by, the group in which they worked.

Three significant lessons learnt from Mayo's experiments can be summarized as follows:

1. No simple cause-and-effect relationship existed between these measures and higher productivity.
2. The employees' positive response was not due to the introduction of better working conditions but due to the feeling of importance that the ongoing experiments provided to them and the freedom they felt in the absence of the old supervisory style.
3. The members constituted a complex social group with well-established norms of their own which regulated the day's output in terms of what the group decided.

The essence of these lessons is that *interpersonal relationships developed at the workplace—and not just pay and working conditions—is the most significant factor affecting productivity.*

It is obvious from the various studies and experiments that it is the *person*—what he perceives, what happens to his thinking and how his inner self is affected—that counts the most.

Therefore, let us now turn our attention to the *psyche* of the man at work.

The 'Content' Approach

The 'Need Hierarchy Theory', first published in 1943 by Abraham H. Maslow,[2] created quite an impact among the thinkers and researchers on motivation. According to this theory, people are motivated to seek satisfaction of *five* categories of their needs, in the following *ascending* order:

1. **The physiological needs:** The most basic needs are undoubtedly those for food, water, air and sex. When dominated by a particular need, a person tends to think that if only that particular need could be satisfied, he would be perfectly happy for the rest of his life, and will never want anything more. When there is reasonable availability of food, water, air, sex, the other higher needs emerge; and these, rather than the physiological hungers, dominate the organism. When these needs, in turn, are satisfied, again, new (and still higher) needs emerge; and thus the cycle goes on.
2. **The safety needs:** These needs manifest themselves as need for steady job with a long tenure, protection against unemployment and other kinds of hazards, desire for building up savings accounts and insurance of various kinds such as medical, unemployment, disability and old age, etc.

3. **The love needs**: Also called 'social needs', these are the love, affection and sense of belonging needs which raise their heads soon after the two 'lower needs' have been satiated. These are expressed in terms of friendship, affection, acceptance and inter-action with others on amicable terms. Serious maladjustments in a person occur when needs are denied or thwarted over a period of time.

4. **The esteem needs**: All of us have a need or desire for a stable, firmly-based high evaluation of ourselves, for self-respect, or self-esteem, and for the esteem of others. 'Firmly-based' esteem means that it is based on our *real* capability, achievements and respect from others.

5. **The self-actualization needs**: Self-actualization (the term was first coined by Kurt Goldstein) refers to the desire for self-fulfillment—to attain everything that one is endowed with and is capable of becoming.

Even if the first four needs are satisfied, we may still often (if not always) expect that a new discontent and restlessness will soon develop inside us! All of us, deep down within ourselves, have the desire to achieve our fullest potential, doing what we believe we are best cut out for. A musician must make music, an artist must create, a poet must write poetry. 'What a man can be, he must be!'

Maslow's need-hierarchy theory continues to exert a significant influence on current thinking and practice about motivation. Its managerial implications may be summarized as the following *five* points:

1. Motivation is generally determined by multiple needs; it would be an over-simplification to assume that only one factor accounts for motivation.

2. Managers must try to identify their employees' most important (or urgent) needs during the given period, and link need satisfaction to the desired performance.

3. A person's needs keep changing from time to time; and this should always be kept in mind while trying to cater to his needs.

4. Managers must bear in mind that what motivates one person may not motivate another; they must be sensitive to the differences in the satisfaction preferences of their employees.

5. Persons differ, and they need to be treated differently. Some need more encouragement, others more direction while some

want greater autonomy. But, by and large, people generally respond positively to being treated with respect and consideration.

The 'Two-Factor' Theory

This was another historically significant 'content theory', introduced in the late 1950s by Frederick Herzberg.[3] Extensive interviews and researches were conducted, and they brought forth evidence that the *factors producing job satisfactions were entirely separate from those producing job dissatisfaction.* That is, *although an unpleasant work environment might cause dissatisfaction, a pleasant work environment might not lead to job satisfaction!* This suggested that job satisfaction and job dissatisfaction are not simple opposites. And this is what led to the enunciation of a two-factor theory that *the opposite of satisfaction is not dissatisfaction, but rather simply 'no satisfaction'.*

Herzberg labelled the factors that produced job satisfactions as *motivators*; and he believed that these factors are directly related to *job content*, reflecting a need for personal fulfilment. Thus 'motivators' included:

♦ achievement;
♦ recognition;
♦ the work itself;
♦ responsibility; and
♦ advancement and personal growth.

He labelled the factors that were related to job dissatisfaction as *hygienes*, and found them to be related more to the work-setting, or job context, than job content. Hygienic factors include:

♦ company policies and administration;
♦ supervision;
♦ relations with one's supervisor and peers;
♦ working conditions; and
♦ pay.

A very thought-provoking conclusion reached by Herzberg was that only motivators *produce* job satisfaction, whereas hygienes merely *prevent* job dissatisfaction.

Herzberg was not nullifying, nor stating anything intrinsically different from what Maslow had enunciated. Maslow's five need levels can be reduced to Herzberg's two-factor theory. Herzberg's 'hygienes' roughly correspond to Maslow's three lowest needs; and his 'motivators' are roughly equivalent to Maslow's two highest needs.

Some Observations

Situations for All Times Cannot Remain Alike   At the time when the scientific management experiments were being carried out, the newness of those approaches, the 'never-before' feeling of importance given to the participating employees, were motivation enough for them. Therefore, the participants responded in manners that the researchers found to be rewarding. But try these on the men at work today. They will not even notice these inputs much less respond to them. Undoubtedly, it will be found that the law of diminishing returns will have robbed much of the glitter from these inputs.

All Employees are Not Alike   Not all employees would respond to the same extent to economic gains, pleasant working conditions, even self-actualizing opportunities.

No 'One Best Way'   The assumption is erroneous that there is one best way of either doing a task or motivating the employees.

Expectancy Level Keeps Changing   Employees will eventually cool off to one set of rewards, and keep moving on to the next expectancy level even where rewards and other kinds of stimuli are designed and provided to the employees in keeping with the expectancy theory.

Morale vs Motivation

Let us look at this issue in yet another way, in terms of morale vs motivation.

Morale is governed by the satisfaction or dissatisfaction of the *(a)* physiological, *(b)* safety, and *(c)* social needs, i.e., the *lower-end needs* as enumerated by Maslow or the *hygienic needs* identified by Herzberg. These are needs that can best be catered to by organizational efforts and inputs like fair or good wages, good working conditions, good human relations environment at the workplace. And these are the only areas in which an organization can make its contributions. But even when these inputs are at their best, all they can ensure is a 'feeling of well being' on the part of the employees. What, however, must be remembered is that *the employees continuing to feel fine does not guarantee that they will also continue to feel motivated to give their best to their jobs.*

The desire to give one's best, on an ongoing basis, can only come from *motivation*—not just from morale. Motivation is derived from *intrinsic factors*, which only good leaders of men, coupled with a supportive environment, can provide. What the leaders have to do is encourage their men to buoy up through the various hierarchies of needs towards a state of self-actualization where motivation begins, and continues, to flow from a state of mind. In this state of mind, a man's inner generator is set into motion, bringing forth a continuing stream of the will in him to:

- do better than his best;
- meet newer challenges;
- derive self-satisfaction by achieving goals or doing his tasks better; and
- build self-esteem, by realizing his full potential.

A very interesting conclusion that surfaces from the above is that the more the experiments and researches, the more pronounced has been the realization that it is the *person* who is the real focal point, and not the peripheral things like the context or the content of the jobs.

Thus, the truth keeps appearing and re-appearing—both as a result of, and in spite of—the various theories and experiments. The truth is that truly motivated people strive and work in response to some kind of internal wants or drives.

In quite a large number of cases, it may be found that not all employees want satisfaction of their needs beyond the social or self-esteem levels. In such cases, it should be better to leave them alone. But in quite a few cases, it is equally true that motivation begins to wane if satisfaction of progressively higher and higher needs is not available. In such cases, the organization or its managers have got to keep on innovating and improvising newer systems or challenges for feeding the ever-growing needs of the employees. In such cases, the organization would do well to orient its policies, practices and management environment in such a way that the employees are enabled to move into the arena of self-actualization. Once they do so, they do not need external stimuli. They are sufficiently self-motivated to realize their maximum potential. This is the state of being where the organization is liberated from the burden of having to go on providing motivational challenges; the employees' own, built-in, intrinsic stream of motivation flows on, and takes over...

Thus we see that the quest for a 'mantra' for motivation has brought us back to where we had started—the person himself! The more we keep this in mind, the better are our chances of finding the answer we seek.

Let us now address ourselves to what we can really do to motivate employees.

How Do We Motivate Employees?

It cannot be denied that money is a very strong motivator. But money *alone* is not good enough. When sufficient money is made available to an employee, he may begin to take it for granted, and the law of diminishing returns sets in relation to the motivating power of money.

Realizing that money alone is not always enough to motivate people, other incentives have been tried with varying degrees of success. These are: *participation in decision-making, job enrichment, behaviour modification of both the employees and their superiors, and other all-round organizational developments* to create an environment conducive to motivation among employees.

A well-balanced combination of inputs in the work environment and among the employees is suggested. These inputs could be on *three* planes:

1. 'Hygienic' inputs.
2. 'Structural' inputs.
3. 'Leadership' inputs.

'Hygienic' Inputs

As rightly pointed out by Herzberg, any starvation of hygienic needs leads to job dissatisfaction. These hygienic factors are related to the *context* in which jobs are required to be performed. To provide a positive context for jobs, there must prevail a clear evidence that the management is willing to provide—and reinforce—the extrinsic factors that take care of hygienic needs. These extrinsic factors are:

- ◆ fair wages;
- ◆ good working conditions;

- good treatment—including prompt conflict resolution, performance appraisal, counselling, etc.;
- safety at workplace;
- job security; and
- conducive social environment.

However, *two* things must always be remembered:

1. In most cases, satisfaction of these needs—even at an appreciable level—can bring about only a *temporary* spurt of motivation (if at all); it does not take too long for such motivation to dwindle.
2. When denied, these satisfactions may lead to dissatisfaction. But when provided, they can only be counted upon to *prevent* dissatisfaction. Expecting that they will lead to ongoing motivation (based on ongoing satisfaction of these hygienic needs) is asking for too much.

'Structural' Inputs

These are inputs which can be built-in by the manner in which the company and its managers 'structure' the functioning of the unit where the employees work. In other words, these are inputs which relate to—and give shape to—the very contents of the jobs.

It should be noted that a considerable part of the ongoing motivation is made up of the *job itself*—of how the jobs are structured, and of the style in which employees are invited to perform them. Many superiors try to motivate their employees through exhortation, through setting high personal standards and through well-meant close supervision. But this approach does not work; it often leads to irritation among the employees, and exasperation and frustration among the superiors.

Among others, *two* inputs have proved to be quite useful:

1. Goal-setting.
2. Job enrichment.

Goal-setting

This is a very straightforward technique. Apart from being more effective, goal-setting also holds out the promise of becoming a major mechanism for *toning up* the content of jobs leading to motivation among the doers.

The concept of goal-setting is not new. In fact, the task concept, along with 'time-and-motion study' and 'incentive pay', was the cornerstone of Taylor's scientific management. By the mid 1950s, the idea of goal-setting reappeared under a new name—management by objective. But this time it was addressed more specifically to managers. By the mid-1960s Gary P. Latham and Edwin A. Locke mounted a 14-year research programme to test and validate their findings on the role played by goal-setting in keeping employees motivated. The essence of their findings, published in their article, 'Goal-Setting—A Motivational Technique that Works', is summarized below in the belief that it throws some really interesting light on motivation:

Specific and Challenging Goals It was found repeatedly that those with harder goals performed better than those with moderately difficult or easy goals. Introducing a goal that is *difficult but attainable* increases the challenge of the job. Further, individuals who had specific, challenging goals outperformed those having vague goals such as 'do your best', because they made it clear to them as to what they were expected to do.

It has repeatedly been found that good pay and performance feedback led to improved performance *only when* these incentives led the individuals to set higher goals. In addition, a specific goal makes it clear to the worker *what* he is expected to do. And regular feedback on how, and how much, a worker is achieving as he goes along provides a sense of achievement, recognition and accomplishment to him. He can also know how well he is performing in comparison with others. These realizations were found to motivate the worker with a will not only to exert greater efforts, but also to devise better and more creative tactics for attaining the goal or, in some cases, even to exceed the goal!

Specific Goals Should be Coupled with 'Supervisory Presence' Another pre-requirement was that the supervisors must stay with the job and the workmen, and offer training and explanations whenever needed without, of course, 'breathing down the necks of their workers'. An extended experiment with some 300 supervisors conclusively proved that productivity remained high with the added benefits of low turnover and injury rate where specific, attainable goals were set.

Stimulating Competition

The story of how an implied challenge worked wonders is worth narrating here.

Charles M. Schwab was employed as the Chief of Carnegie Steel Corporation several decades ago on one million dollars a year salary—not because he was a wizard in financial or steel fabrication matters, but because he was regarded by Andrew Carnegie, his employer, as having a 'positive genius in handling men'. When one of the mill managers expressed utter helplessness in getting his workers to meet the production quota, Schwab asked the workers in that mill as to how many 'heats' they had done in that shift. When told 'six heats', he simply wrote a large '6' with a piece of chalk on the floor and walked away. The workers in the next shift found out what that '6' meant and who had written it, and saw that as a challenge. The result was that in every successive shift for the next few days, the number of heats kept going up; and soon that mill became the company's top producer. Schwab explained, 'The way to get things done is to stimulate competition. I don't mean only in a money-getting way, but in the desire to excel . . . . Throw down a challenge.'

But mere interest taken and shown by the supervisors is also not enough; they must involve themselves with the employees—not so much for how the work shall be done but what the work is about, and what are the problems and constraints that need to be attended to by the supervisors.

Goal-setting Must be Participative   People support what they help to create. Experiments were conducted with three groups of workmen. One where the goal was set through participative process, the other where the goal was assigned, and the third where they were asked to 'do your best'. The result was conclusive. The group that had done participative goal-setting almost always attained the goal in spite of the fact that they had voluntarily set significantly higher goals than the other groups.

The following *four* conclusions emerging from these studies are worth noting:

1. Specific, challenging goals lead to better performance than easy or vague goals;
2. Specific goal-setting, coupled with 'supervisory presence' (supportive and participative—not the 'policing' type), leads to goal-commitment and enhancement in motivation.
3. 'Participative' goal-setting is far better than 'assigned' goal-setting, although what really matters is that a goal is set, not how it is set.
4. Participation is not only a motivational tool; if practised with competent subordinates, it can prove 'educative' even for the superior in that it improves his knowledge and decision-making.

Job Enrichment

Job enrichment calls for redesigning the jobs in such a way that they hold more appeal for the job holders, thereby providing greater challenges leading to heightened work interest, greater sense of responsibility and importance and personal growth. This is believed to pave the way for motivation. Its primary requirement is that the redesigned job must be capable of 'turning on' the job-holders and providing excitement and commitment for performing better and better till they begin to attain their highest potential.

It is true that in some cases, job enrichment itself becomes a stimulus for rekindling the inherent need or desire of workmen for personal accomplishments. But mere euphoria and going into raptures over it (as many people do) is not sufficient. Researches have shown that job enrichment does not work for everybody. It may work only for such people who have strong needs, or desire, for personal accomplishment, for learning and developing themselves beyond where they are now.

In any case, job enrichment requires a lot of planning and strategy if its full benefits in terms of heightened motivation and better productivity are to be ensured.

A team of researchers comprising J. Richard Hackman, Greg Oldham, Robert Janson and Kenneth Purdy, published their findings in an article entitled 'A New Strategy for Job Enrichment'. These findings are summarized as follows:

Identifying the Employees As mentioned earlier, not all workers possess a strong need for personal accomplishments. Therefore, it becomes necessary to find workers who do possess such a need and what specifically are the factors that are most likely to 'turn them on'?

The following *three* were identified as the critical requirements:

1. Job holders should find 'experienced meaningfulness' in the jobs offered to them. They must perceive their work as *worthwhile or important* in terms of:
   ♦ skill variety demanded of them in the performance of their tasks;
   ♦ task identity, i.e., the degree to which they can participate in the completion of the whole or identifiable piece of work; and
   ♦ task significance, i.e., the degree to which the job has a substantial and perceivable impact on the lives of other people, either within or outside the organization.

   It must be noted in this context that jobs are jobs, and they must be done whether or not they appear to the job holders or others as important. Also, the management cannot possibly design all jobs in such a way that they appear equally important. But what is often missed is that the importance of a job does not come from its shape or size, but from what the doer himself packs it with—from the excellence and finesse and the commitment one puts into doing it. In this connection, the statement of Visweshwaraiyya, a great Indian scientist, engineer and thinker very aptly comes to mind; he had said: 'If your job is only to sweep, sweep so well that no one may excel you!'

2. Job holders should feel 'experienced responsibility' in regard to their jobs. They must believe that they are personally accountable for the outcome of their efforts. This, of course, requires that they are given sufficient *autonomy* —freedom, independence and discretion in scheduling and determining the manner in which they will carry out their jobs.

3. Job holders must be provided with the 'knowledge of results', i.e., ongoing feedback on *whether or not the outcomes of their work have been satisfactory.* Such feedback is best when it can be derived directly from the work itself.

Leadership Inputs

The 'hygienic' and 'structural' inputs depend to a large extent, on the intervention of the organization. This is based on the fact that the job itself can play a great role in keeping the employees motivated, provided it is designed properly and is continually redesigned in the light of the changing scenario of the job requirements and employees' 'needs hierarchy'.

However, it must be remembered that *motivation is primarily a matter of the employees' inner urges, their state of mind and their will to keep climbing up in their own self-esteem.* And this comes from convincing evidence that they are enhancing their capabilities and attaining personal growth. In this context, you have to remember that although 'hygienic' and 'structural' inputs are useful and necessary, they have their limitations. *They can only create the conducive scenario, not the miracle of motivation itself.* Those employees who are sufficiently and innately self-motivated will go forward irrespective of whether a conducive environment for motivation is provided to them or not. But such employees are few in number. The rest are divided into *(a)* those who would go forward once a conducive environment is provided to them; and *(b)* a large number of those who are borderline cases, that is, their capability to become motivated has been lying dormant and can be enkindled only when they are 'touched' by inspiring leadership.

Irrespective of the scenario, there has always been the need for the human input of leaders in an organization to play a role that is extremely dynamic and significant. What is emphasized here are the deep and lasting effects of interaction between immediate superiors and their subordinates. It would not be wrong to say that the positive atmosphere built by 'hygienic' and 'structural' inputs can be totally destroyed if the leadership inputs are faulty or disorganized. One can go so far as to say that *leadership inputs are more crucial for motivation than any other inputs.*

What I actually propose to do here is to offer to you some practical suggestions for the day-to-day, shop-floor, work-related interactions between you and your subordinates. This is done in the belief that what follows can significantly contribute to the building up of a positive environment of motivation among your employees.

Here are some suggestions for generating, and keeping alive, motivation among your subordinates:

1. *Do Your Best to Find Out What 'They' (your subordinates) Think*
   ◆ Get the right kind of information
     • What do they think about the work, your style of taking work, the workplace facilities, environment, etc.?

Watch Out for Hidden Agendas

Everybody has hidden agendas or specific individual needs that are often not apparent to their team members and colleagues. Hidden agendas aren't necessarily negative.

For example, one team member may be extremely ambitious, and is counting on using the team to further his ambitions. He is still committed to the objectives of the team but he'll design his performance to fit his agenda.

Another team member, for example, may simply want to devote less time to work and more time to his/her family.

Hidden agendas—positive or negative—influence the work of individuals in the team. Unattended, they can eventually undermine the team. Making an effort to acknowledge and understand the hidden agendas of others is the first step towards finding satisfactory solutions for both individuals and the team.

- When you take a decision, how do they tend to view it? Interested but hostile? Interested and involved? Disinterested? Totally indifferent?
- What kind of gripes, if any, have they been carrying?
- What are their plans about their tasks? What are their goals? Is there any congruence between their goals and the organization's goals?
- ◆ Gather information in the right way
  - Don't be evasive or secretive about the fact that you are out to gather information. Be straightforward in letting it be known that you consider it your business to know or find out as to what is going on at the workplace and also in the minds of your subordinates.
  - Don't, however, start a competition with them by appearing to mount a secret service. Be open and matter-of-fact. Make it clear that it is a perfectly straightforward effort on your part to know how things are; and that the more you know, the better would be your responses to your subordinates' needs and grievances.

- Gather the relevant facts over a period of time. Beware of irrelevant, misleading facts. Make mental notes carefully; don't jump to conclusions.
- Concentrate on the inner meanings and significance of what you find out. Look out also for under-the-surface facts. Try your best to come to objective, path-finding conclusions, leading to effective, corrective actions. Some of these corrective actions may even be directed upon yourself; have the courage to take the necessary steps to reform yourself as well.

2. *Tell Them What is Going On*
♦ Provide the right kind of information
  - Always give them the larger, total picture of all such plans, work-schedules, problems and the solutions being developed, etc., with which they are, or should be, legitimately involved.
  - Pay greater attention to issues that are of immediate concern to them, such as how they have been performing, how their efforts are affecting the quality, cost of production, time-schedule, safety, security, etc.
♦ Provide information the right way
  - Be frank. This will earn you credibility which is the most precious possession you need as a leader. Credibility not only makes communication easier and tension-free, but it also helps a great deal in securing enthusiastic support for difficult projects—a promising stepping-stone for motivation.
  - Be enthusiastic. If you are not, how can you expect to enthuse the employees with the will to try?
  - Be tactful—not only when you have to criticize, but also when you are giving an optimistic picture of things in the offing.
  - Talk—not at—but with your subordinates, making it abundantly clear that you consider them to be adult enough, and that you do value their views, even if they are different or opposed to yours.

3. *Make Life Easier for Them*
♦ Your subordinates expect you to provide them with a better quality of life at the workplace, particularly in terms of the following:
  - The work itself. Have you been doing your bit for introducing changes in the work-methods, skill-needs, work-simplification, so as to break the monotony in their work?

Let Enthusiasm Power You

Your enthusiasm—for a project, an idea, the direction you wish to provide—is vital if you want others to respond positively. If you are not excited, you can be sure no one else will be. But don't equate enthusiasm with exaggerated, loud proclamations. It must be a feeling that comes from within. You must believe in what you are doing or suggesting to others; you must believe in yourself; and you must really want to accomplish something definite, and definitely.

- What about the conditions under which they work—both physical and psychological? Can you do something innovative to make these conditions more congenial and motivating?
- What about the people—within their section and outside—with whom they are required to interact in the course of their duties? Do you pay attention to the tensions, stresses and any other difficulties your employees may have been experiencing, and putting up with silently?
- What about the personal worries of your employees—not only at the workplace but elsewhere too? Are you one of those people who put an embargo on your employees' personal worries, saying they are none of your business? It is a sad mistake, particularly when you wish to play the role of a 'leader'. Do try to *(a)* listen to them; and *(b)* do what you can about their personal worries. You will be amazed how much closer you and your people will feel to each other merely because you 'listen' to them, and how much and how easily you are able to resolve quite a few of their problems.

4. *Give Them A Goal*
   - *Set clear, challenging goals*
     Goals give you something to shoot for. They keep your and your people's efforts focused, and allow you to measure success. It is easy to drift if you don't set goals. Because no urgency is associated with it, you or your people could waste time. In the words of Harvey Macay, 'A goal is a dream with a deadline'.
   - *Concentrate on seeking agreement on the goals*
     Even in goal-setting, do not impose your goals; allow as much participation as possible within the time and cost frame.

♦ *Make them want to do it*

There is only one way to get anybody to do anything; and this is by making the other person want to do it. But how do you make people want to do something?

Give them a sense of purpose, a feeling that they are working toward an important goal. That satisfies a desire in all of us: the desire to be a significant contributor.

Getting Others to Buy Into Your Vision

- You must show by example that you are prepared to take risks to achieve your goals. You must live your vision—transparently, all twenty four hours. Mere pep talks, or brow-beating or threatening or even bribing them with promises of rewards will not do.
- Here is a very apt quotation from the *Bhagvad Gita*:

यद्यदाचरति श्रेष्ठस्तत्तदेवेतरो जन : ।।
स यत्प्रमाणं कुरूते लोकस्तदनुवर्तते ।।२९।।

It means: 'What a great man does is followed by others; people go by the example he sets.'

- You must 'build enrollment'—get your people 'buy into your vision'. It takes continual reinforcements with a convincing display of your commitment, the rationale behind your vision, its unquestionable advantages for the organization and your team-mates. It takes time to enroll people to your thinking, your vision, your fantasy, your dream. Above all, it takes efforts.
- As a good leader you would know that you get results by sending messages that say, 'We're in this together', 'What we are doing is valuable', 'You—my team-mates—are excellent and I depend on you with full confidence'.
- This will make sense to your people only when they see clear evidence that your words are backed up with actions. Give your people goals to shoot for. Recognize and praise them. Recognize not only the results they produce but also the efforts and their ingenuity—even when the results produced fall short of the agreed targets. Include them. Let them make decisions. Seek their advice.

When you show your people that you trust, respect and care about them, you will find motivated people all around you!

5. *Challenge Them to Achieve*

♦ Provide meaningful opportunities
- Pride grows when a crucial or difficult job is done well, *and* prompt recognition is given.
- Sense of fulfilment grows when the experienced employees are invited to groom—and succeed in grooming—the new or inexperienced ones into experts.

♦ Present challenges properly
- Be flexible; do not over-structure the tasks. Tell your employees *what* is to be done, in what time-and-cost frame; do *not* tell them how it is to be done.
- Your attitude should be transparent, and it should show that you anticipate success, not failure.
- Be realistic. Delegate only when practicable.
- Be honest. Explain frankly both the opportunities and the threats, safeguards as well as dangers.

6. *Appreciate What They Achieve*

♦ Know what merits recognition
Even when the overall results are not all that was projected or desired, there are several things related to the employees' efforts that must be taken due note of, such as:
- Their initiative;
- The difficulties they contended with;
- The risks to their own safety they may have taken;
- The loyalty they have displayed;
- The amount of hard work they have put in;
- The technical ingenuity they may have invested; and
- The resultant 'reliability' they have earned in the process.

In other words, always distinguish *achievement* from *efforts*, and remember that although all efforts are not always fully rewarded by achievement (of results), efforts, in their own right, deserve to be respected and appreciated. It is actually the appreciation of efforts that is the fountainhead of motivation—and, possibly, of achievement of results.

♦ Provide the right kind of recognition
- Praise given automatically, mechanically, thoughtlessly and without sincerity turns out to be counter-productive. The

recipient soon discovers or tends to think that his superior has been praising him for ulterior motives, or that he is being taken for a ride. This evokes suspicion or hostile responses.

- Therefore, praise only when the employee has made real contributions, over and above the ordinary level of performance. Do take care to somehow specify your reasons for praising.
- In your anxiety not to discourage your employees, do not accept half-done or poor-quality work done by them. Ask them gently but firmly to accomplish the job at the specified level.
- ◆ Provide recognition in the right way
  - Be prompt. Link performance with praise explicitly.
  - Be even-handed. Give praise both to the bright and the mediocre members of your team—if, and when, they do good jobs.
  - Don't get disproportional. Your recognition/appreciation must be in proportion to what your subordinate has earned.

Conclusion

So far we have tried to understand the nature and dynamics of motivation by looking at it in a wider perspective. We find that from the pre-historic days till today, motivation has been an enigma—neither easy to understand nor to practice. Yet it is such a powerful and dynamic factor in our life in general, and at the workplace in particular, that we cannot afford to ignore it or do without it.

Motivation reveals itself in many different ways; and there are so many methods that provide tantalizing promises of putting it into practice. The quest for motivation has taken us through various paths. From time immemorial, numerous methods have been tried, apart from the universally-tried method of rewards coupled with 'the carrot-and-the stick' approach. In recent times, these quests have covered all possible grounds, ranging from scientific management of tasks themselves to experimenting with the physical and mental 'context' of jobs. Several researches have tried to enter the psyche of working people in order to discover as to what it is that can motivate them, and keep them motivated. Valuable findings have opened our eyes to the fascinating interplay between an individual's reaction to *what* he is asked to do, *how* he is asked to do it, *how the work is presented* to him, and *what is the environment* in which he is asked to work. Researchers have also, very rightly, dug deep into *the nature and structure of work* in the belief that, if designed properly and infused with motivational character, *work itself can be a great motivator.*

Some of these findings are:

♦ workers are not motivated solely by money;

♦ effective supervision, i.e., supervision without policing and with an attitude of encouraging initiative and innovation in the employees, is an essential factor; and

♦ the informal work-group does generate a powerful 'group dynamics' which must be acknowledged.

We know now what *does not or cannot* motivate people, just as we also know that, in the context of motivation, satisfaction is not necessarily the simple opposite of dissatisfaction. We also know that satisfaction of one set of needs may provide a stimulus for possible motivation—but only for a short while, because soon different sets of needs would raise their heads. Thus, there continues a mirage-like chase between needs and their satisfactions in the whirlwind of which motivation gets blurred, if not lost.

It is this cycle (of satisfactions fading out with the regular emergence of newer needs) which brings us back, full circle, to the *individual.* It also underlines the fact that ongoing motivation flows from man's state of mind. It needs the energizing of man's inner generator which can bring forth a continuing stream of the will to give of his best—not necessarily for rewards and growth alone but primarily for enhancing his self-esteem. Such motivation can be enkindled by able *leaders* coupled with a supportive environment. The truth is that motivation is not a bag of tricks that would respond to gimmicks. It requires a very balanced and integrated approach, based on a synthesis of the various lessons that researches and experiments have bequeathed to us. It calls for *(a)* a lot of home-work by the organization on the 'hygienic' factors; *(b)* a lot of continuing innovations by you in organizing and offering work and tasks to the employees in such a way that they promote spontaneous motivation; and *(c)* leadership based on participative style of management and fairness that is transparent in its sincerity. All this pre-requires from you, the leader, a 'cleansing' on your own part till you emerge as a well-meaning, honest, sincere and painstaking superior, imbued with genuine interest in developing your subordinates to their highest potential levels. You must have more than a synthetic, work-related interest in your subordinates. Ongoing interaction on your part can fill your subordinates with professional excitement; and it is precisely this which motivation feeds and thrives upon. You as the leader must convincingly appear as your subordinates' philosopher, friend and guide.

FOUR

Delegation: Development and Motivation through Sharing

CHAPTER OBJECTIVES
- Discuss the developmental and motivational effects of delegation
- Show how delegation can prove to be a powerful instrument for creating and sustaining motivation

---

Introduction

Everybody talks about the practice of delegation and recommends it to others except, perhaps, to himself. Even those who practise delegation themselves, many continue to think that delegation is a 'respectable alibi' for dumping the dog-work on the subordinates. There are many who would delegate responsibility, but not many who would delegate commensurate authority. And, then, there are not too many who delegate at all in reality.

Common Misconceptions

Many managers use delegation as an instrument for drawing up *dividing lines* between the organizational hierarchies. Usually, the thinking is: 'Let the "lower staff" take care of the routine, lower-end chores, and let the "seniors" deal with important higher-end affairs involving responsibilities, authority, policy formulations or interpretations, issuance of instructions, important or importance-bearing tasks, etc.'

The responsibility for the prevalence of this kind of thinking perhaps lies with that age-old definition of a manager as 'one who gets things done by others'. In itself, there is nothing wrong with this definition. But it does lend itself to an erroneous interpretation, especially among those who are inclined to 'managerial laziness'. Such managers usually interpret this definition to mean any of the following *four* ways:

1. A manager is not expected to perform tasks himself; he is only expected to get others to work under his direction.
2. A manager should pick out assignments, stipulate the 'what', 'by when', and 'by whom' of the tasks, and then simply ask the chosen subordinates to accomplish the tasks.
3. The tasks assigned should be of a routine type, not requiring high level of skills or intelligence to prevent the job getting messed up by the subordinates.
4. As far as possible, authority should not be vested in the subordinates, lest they misuse it (nor should the assigned tasks be very important or highly visible, lest the subordinates steal the limelight or even make the boss redundant by accomplishing the tasks well!).

Reiterating the Concept Relevant to Delegation

To begin with and with due respect, it is necessary to restate the age-old definition of a manager: 'A manager is one who gets his things done by *letting* others do theirs'.

It is important to explain the emphasis attached to the word 'letting'. Perhaps the word 'getting' would have been a more natural choice, but the word 'letting' has been deliberately chosen to signify that even while delegating a task, the manager must leave enough freedom for the delegatee as to how *he* may choose to accomplish the delegated task(s).

The above variation in the original definition is meant to emphasize the following *two* things:

1. A manager does have a lot of work to do himself. First, he must plan how the total job under his jurisdiction shall be done. He then breaks it down into logical chunks of tasks to be done by others. Then he goes on to determine as to *who* should accomplish which tasks—*by when, within what quality and cost frames.* He has to *keep taking decisions* regarding each of these phases of task planning. That is why he has been placed in the position of a manager. This, in itself (together with planning, organizing, executing, getting others to do their tasks and controlling), constitutes more than a full-time, all-absorbing job for a manager!

2. Having planned and taken the required decisions, he embarks upon the next, more important and crucial task. The task of *seeking and obtaining the cooperation of others*, particularly his subordinates, for obtaining the desired results.

The 'profile' of present-day subordinates which a manager has to contend with constitutes the following *three* factors:

1. They are far more intelligent, perceptive, ambitious and self-respecting than the earlier generation.
2. They are more skill-and-knowledge-oriented, thanks to present-day technological and information explosions.
3. They have the same need, or respect, for authority as earlier counterparts, but with a difference:
   ♦ in terms of their perception, the authority must be exercised properly; and
   ♦ they would accept the authority, *in spirit*, only after critically assessing its rationale.

Motivation has attained great importance in the scheme of collaborative working. And, proper delegation does play a very powerful role in generating and maintaining motivation among subordinates, in addition to fulfilling its commonly-understood roles.

What does Delegation Connote?

What Delegation IS

Delegation has been described as the 'secret of executive sanity'. *An effective manager's total responsibilities are always much wider and bigger than his personal capacity to discharge them.* Therefore, it would be insane if he does not concede that he needs the help of others—not only casual or occasional help, but ongoing collaboration, which he can count and depend upon.

Delegation is an instrument for ensuring *optimum deployment* —with growing involvement, excitement and skill-development—of the existing manpower for accomplishing organizational objectives. It is also a process of 'empowering' an individual to act for another. *Cumulatively, the process of empowering leads to authority passing from a higher managerial level to lower ones.* But by doing so, the delegating authority does not reduce his own accountability; he continues to remain responsible for his own actions and those of his delegatees.

Delegation, then, is a *possible and promising management method to secure the sharing of tasks* in a manner that it:

♦ creates involvement and commitment for the tasks;
♦ generates heightened interest in performing tasks;
♦ leads to development of subordinates for higher tasks and positions;
♦ strengthens team-work and team-spirit;
♦ helps in accomplishing tasks; and
♦ offers freedom to the superior for attending to higher and more innovative tasks.

In a nutshell, delegation is an effective step towards the supervisor multiplying himself and developing his subordinates to their full potential. This leads to the proper deployment of personnel. And also adds up to the fullest attainment of organizational objectives.

Besides, the supervisor 'multiplies himself' not only in terms of creating replicas of himself who can stand-in for him when required; he actually multiplies *his own stature* by drawing upon the synergy generated by all-round growth in capabilities, self-confidence, team-work and team-spirit among his subordinates.

What Delegation is NOT

Delegation does not mean dumping downward of the unwanted, petty, routine, uninteresting or 'sticky' chores. It is not to be confused with 'assignments'. While assignment connotes tasks which are within the subordinates' area of responsibilities, delegation connotes tasks that come from the superior's area of responsibilities. Neither does it condone 'abdication' or the act of passing on to the subordinates all the tasks or the whole of a task in order to get rid of them.

Delegation is not exactly a synonym for empowerment. In most cases, delegation remains a matter between the individual boss and his subordinates where the accent is on *developing the subordinates* through the process of sharing responsibilities and authority. Empowerment, on the other hand, is applied throughout the organization as a conscious system. The accent here is on preventing any hold-ups in production or customer services. And for this purpose, the subordinates are 'empowered' to take decisions and actions without reference to their bosses, irrespective of whether they (the bosses) are present or not.

Delegation should not, generally, be done in regard to the following:

- the power to discipline;
- the responsibility for maintaining discipline;
- over-all control;
- the risky or 'lost' tasks; and
- duties for which the superior has been sworn to secrecy or trust.

The Pre-requisites of Delegation

Delegation must not be rushed into. A lot of care and wisdom are required for putting delegation into practice. Since delegation revolves around the subordinates, it calls for planning based on careful study of the skill and aptitude profiles of individual subordinates. The following *four* factors need to be predetermined:

. What tasks can be delegated and to whom?
. Who are worthy and ready—in terms of their skills, skill-needs, knowledge, maturity and dependability?
. What kind of training, briefing, authority-sharing, support and continuing help does a subordinate need from his superior?
. What can the superior do to present the tasks to his subordinates in such a manner that the tasks appeal to them as sufficiently and manageably:
    - challenging,
    - stimulating, and
    - s-t-r-e-t-c-h-i-n-g?

Why do Superiors Tend NOT to Delegate?

It is common knowledge that a very significant proportion of managers fight shy of delegating tasks—in the true sense of the term—to their subordinates. Though there exist a large number of superiors who delegate either the wrong tasks, or in the wrong way, or the wrong degree (almost gravitating to 'abdication' in the name of delegation). The reasons—both eye-opening and amusing—are not difficult to establish.

The blame for this ailment, however, lies with the superiors them selves! In most cases, they suffer from the 'do-it-yourself' syndrom for the following *seven* reasons:

1. They tend to believe that the subordinates will take much longe time to do what they can do much faster.
2. They fear that the subordinates may commit blunders, and th superiors do not wish to grant a 'licence' to the subordinates 't make mistakes at their (the superiors') cost'.
3. They may be compulsive perfectionists who are therefore froze into inaction as far as delegation is concerned.
4. They fear that ultimately they may have to redo the task; s why entrust the task to the subordinates when such an experimen entails double investment in terms of time and effort?
5. They are apprehensive that the subordinates may try to be difficul by raising questions like: 'Why should I undertake this additiona task?' or 'What is there in it for me?', and they fight shy o negotiating such questions.
6. In some cases, they are afraid that their subordinates may eve outperform them, and thus pose threats to their job security.
7. They also do not wish to recognize the fact that no one learn to do something without making some mistakes at times, an learning from such mistakes!

The truth may well be that not many superiors have either th expertise or the courage (in most cases the former breeds the latter) t take the risks involved in trusting their subordinates to do a task righ if only they are allowed and helped to do so. The result of thi ambivalence is that most organizations have *delegation operating fror bottom upwards, rather than the other way round*!

Steps Towards Effective Delegation

Attitudinal Changes in the Superiors

Delegation, like any other change, cannot be just switched over to on fine morning. In view of the constraints and hesitations of variou kinds described previously, delegation requires, on the part of th superior, certain attitudinal changes. These are briefly discusse below.

Decision-making The superior needs to realize that delegation is not just a matter of giving assignments to subordinates. It is actually a matter of both of them *sharing a duly selected interesting task*, which does not strictly fall within the ambit of the subordinate's normal duties. The purpose behind offering such a task is to stretch the capabilities of the subordinate by providing professionally stimulating opportunities in the belief that he will savour 'experienced meaningfulness' and 'experienced responsibility' while accomplishing the delegated tasks.

In such a context, the superior must, if necessary, change his attitude about decision-making; it should be one of *involving* the subordinate in the decisions relating to the task. The style should be *participative*, and the superior must try to 'sell' the decision (to the extent of adequately explaining *the why* of his decision) to the subordinate. Since the superior cannot, and should not, shirk his responsibility in taking his decision, delegation requires a very delicate balancing between 'awarding' and 'working out' a decision.

Result-orientation It is very easy to get carried away by the aura of delegation so much so that its real purpose may get diluted. The atmosphere of 'working together', 'forging an exciting relationship', involvement in decision-making' between the superior and his subordinate is sometimes so fascinating that their very exercise tends to become an end in itself. Sometimes, it is also seen that the superior is willing to make a number of compromises just to get going with the so-called formality of delegation.

What must never be lost sight of is the desired result—in terms of the required *quality, cost and quantum of the accomplishment*. The feeling of 'togetherness' in working is only a by-product; the real objective of delegation is upgradation of the skill and capability of the delegatee while he accomplishes the delegated tasks!

Therefore, the superior must chalk out in concrete terms—of course, jointly with the delegatee—the results they are going to be after; and conduct all reviews of progress in terms of the results. This pre-requires joint discussions for determining and adhering to:

- the primary functions;
- the key-result areas; and
- the targets

Inputs from the Subordinates

The superior should remember that each of his subordinates may b
at different levels of skill, capability, and his need for, and willingnes
to strive for self-improvement on these counts. They also may hav
different profiles of their overall strengths and weaknesses. Therefore
as part of his preparatory work related to delegation, the superior need
to draw up the strengths, weaknesses and need profiles of *each* of hi
subordinates. Though, initially, a little arduous and time-consuming
this home-work proves to be very valuable; it makes for prope
fail-safe inputs by the superior when he finally embarks upon delega
tion of tasks.

Specifically, he should draw up his plan of action comprising:

- preparation phase;
- planning phase;
- communication phase;
- audit phase; and
- appreciation phase.

Preparation Phase

Select the Tasks to be Delegated   Selection of the task constitute
the most delicate and crucial part of the delegation process. Eac
task you offer for 'delegation' holds within itself your 'message' an
the subordinates' perception as to whether it is being used for tru
delegation or with other motives. If the task selected is perceive
by the subordinate as a routine, uninteresting, unchallenging chor
below his level of competence, he may see it almost as an insul
It comes to him as an implied message that you do not think muc
of him, or he thinks he (the subordinate) can be 'taken for a rid
in the garb of delegation—which he will certainly resent. If, o
the other hand, the task offered appeals to him as one where hi
skills and capabilities are being challenged—and he is likely to im
prove his skills and capabilities by attempting to do that task—h
may look upon such a delegation as an *implied compliment*, an
may gladly rise to the occasion.

Therefore, you should try to *match* the tasks with the *existin
profile* of the subordinate concerned—in terms of his skill, capabilit
and need. In any case, with every task being selected, you must appl

the test whether, in relation to the subordinate concerned, the task is challenging, stimulating and stretching.

Having selected the task, you should break it down into small parts so that the delegatee may take his own decisions about them, and take over the responsibility for their accomplishment.

Decide Whom the Tasks are to be Delegated to Select carefully. Match the kinds and levels of decisions, actions required by the tasks with the present and stretchable levels of the delegatee's experience, expertise, dependability and personality. The following factors in the delegatee must be considered while you delegate a task to him:

♦ ability;
♦ knowledge;
♦ interests;
♦ experience;
♦ attitudes;
♦ confidence;
♦ development goal; and
♦ current work load.

Planning Phase

You should brief the chosen delegatee on the task(s) to be accomplished by him. While doing so, you should invite him to formulate his own plan of action—with helpful suggestions from your side if you are asked.

In order to do a proper and adequate briefing, you should take the following *nine* steps:

1. Explain the reasons and the importance attached to the task you have chosen for the delegatee.
2. Describe the project clearly in terms of:
   ♦ results expected;
   ♦ difficulties anticipated;
   ♦ the time frame;
   ♦ the cost frame;
   ♦ the importance of the task; and
   ♦ how the task fits into the overall, larger scheme of things.
3. Solicit the delegatee's views and plans about:
   ♦ the approaches he wishes to take;
   ♦ the schedules he thinks he will draw; and

♦ the resources and the kinds of support he would require.

4. Ensure that the 'delegatee' will have the required authority, time and resources before he embarks upon accomplishing the delegated task(s).

5. Be prepared and willing to allow the delegatee to make mistakes (but be watchful against blunders or disaster), since mistakes are an essential price for learning.

6. Plan on working upon each subordinate not just the 'high-fliers'. Here are some strong and irrefutable arguments supporting this idea:

   ♦ If normal or below-normal level of employees are ignored or neglected, you are unwittingly creating pockets of powerful demoralization and resentment within your team. This may well undo whatever the handful of your 'high-fliers' may achieve;

   ♦ In addition to this negative view, there is another point of view: It is rightly said that the best monument a manager can leave behind is the employees who 'flowered' due to his efforts and encouragement. And the real credit you can claim on this is when it turns out that today's efficient subordinates are those who, initially, were almost given up as too mediocre; and

   ♦ Even where there is one weak link in a team, it is that weak link, not the strong pillars, that inhibits the strength of the entire team!

7. Delegate authority, and give the required time and resources to the delegatee and not just the responsibility. How much authority—of what kind and with what limits—is to be granted? This must be predetermined by you. Similarly, you must plan and stipulate the time limits and the kind of resources which should be placed at the disposal of the delegatee.

8. Plan on delegating tasks in measured doses as both the delegatee and you are testing the ground.

9. If there are several delegatees in your team, you should set up an assignment chart so that allocation of tasks, and their follow-up, are done systematically. (Such a chart should show each delegatee's current assignment, special skills possessed, areas of special education or knowledge, and his current time-commitments.)

Communication Phase

Having done your planning, it is time for you to communicate—communicate all around and in all relevant aspects. Complete communication involves the following *six* factors:

1. What exactly do you want done—in terms of the tasks, and the standard of performance required.
2. Lay out the scope and authority and the kind of decisions the delegatee can take.
3. Also lay out the limits of his authority and responsibilities.
4. Furnish data to the delegatee on:
   ♦ cost control;
   ♦ quality tolerances;
   ♦ progress control; and
   ♦ parallel reports on other connected or competitive operations already completed or currently going on.
5. Tell others what you have delegated and to whom. Let others (who are accustomed to looking upon you) know clearly what authority and responsibility you have delegated. The decision-making prerogative delegated by you must be definitely and publicly conveyed; otherwise your delegatee will not have a chance.
6. Convince your delegatee by your continuous style of assistance that, on the delegated tasks, you are his working partner. To that end:
   ♦ treat him like an adult; do not breathe down his neck;
   ♦ tell him what to do—not how to do; and
   ♦ constantly engage him in 'What if . . .' games, but let him evolve his own solutions.

Audit Phase

This involves the following *four* stages:

1. Hold regular reviews with the delegatees on what has been accomplished and what has not.
2. Make sure that the required resources are made available. Discuss problems, obstacles encountered, and do the needful to facilitate things.
3. When mistakes do occur, do not revoke the delegation, or start performing that task yourself.
4. Consider rotating responsibilities, both by size and type, in order to enhance versatility among the delegates.

Appreciation Phase

Appreciation, for *transparently honest reasons*, is an important ingredient of the delegation process. You should take an active interest and note the progress being made on the project. You should also acknowledge the delegatee's efforts. Do not always concern yourself only with the results achieved. Even where there are some shortfalls in results, the efforts made may well deserve being taken note of, and you must *demonstrate that you are interested enough to notice the commendable efforts.*

However, do not accept unfinished, inaccurate, unprofessional or off-target jobs. Tell the delegatees without rancour as to why you are not accepting such jobs. Encourage them, and help them, to do their jobs at acceptable standards of performance (which you have already stipulated at the communication stage).

Show interest in the results, and reward the delegatees—more often, in non-financial, 'recognition-and-prestige' terms.

Never fall a prey to the temptation of praising where it is not due; this turns out to be counter-productive in the long run.

Always proceed on the basis that it is you who are accountable. Do not blame the delegatee for less-than-satisfying results.

Major Benefits of Delegation

After delegation has been in practice for some time, it begins to manifest its multi-faceted benefits. These can be felt at the level of the organization, the subordinates and the boss.

Benefits to the Organization

The organization benefits from delegation in the following ways:

♦ fuller and better utilization of available manpower—qualitatively as well as quantitatively;
♦ better and smoother accomplishment of the organization's task and objectives; and
♦ greater and more relaxed attention by the superiors to long-term vital issues.

Benefits to the Subordinates

Once the practice of delegation takes root and the subordinates are convinced that it is primarily for their development and attendant benefits, they begin to derive the following very significant 'satisfactions':

Skill Variety   A variety of carefully selected tasks offered challenge them to either refine their existing skills or acquire newer skills. Thus, enhanced versatility leads to greater confidence and professional pride in them;.

Task Identity   The opportunity and encouragement given to *complete* the tasks delegated to them stimulate a sense of responsibility for 'ownership' of an identifiable and completed piece of work.

Task Significance   It is easier and more apparent to see the impact an identifiable and complete piece of work done by them makes on the overall activity of the organization. This instils a feeling of 'significance' in the subordinates—both about the work done and the (significant) role played by them.

Autonomy   Proper delegation requires granting sufficient autonomy to the subordinates for scheduling their work and taking corrective measures, if necessary, in the way they work. All these give a sense of accomplishment to them which is a reward in itself.

Feedback   Again, under proper delegation, the boss does not simply fade out after he delegates a task; he is constantly there to interact with the subordinates as their 'facilitator'. One of the most important facilities he provides is giving the subordinates a constant feedback as to how they are doing on the delegated task. Such feedbacks serve the purpose of keeping subordinates on the right track; but an even greater significance of these feedbacks is that subordinates bask in the warmth of the feeling that their boss is truly interested in them, and is available for whatever facilities or guidance they may need.

The cumulative effect of all these satisfactions—in one word—is *motivation*.

The benefits to the delegatees can be summarized as follows:

◆ a feeling of being useful and worthwhile;
◆ professional excitement at matching their skills and capabilities with higher-level tasks;
◆ convincing evidence of continuous personal development—while contributing toward the achievement of the organization's objectives; and
◆ movement toward, and readiness for, higher assignments or positions.

Benefits to the Boss

Apart from the fact that the boss is able to 'multiply himself' through delegation, he derives several other, very important, benefits:

◆ a better and stronger team;
◆ a team that progressively becomes more cohesive, and develops true team spirit;
◆ stimulation among the subordinates of greater and increasing motivation;
◆ development of a true *guru-shishya parampara*—'a truly respectful and affectionate bond between the teacher and the disciple', under which the subordinates genuinely look upon their boss as their 'leader'; and
◆ development of personal loyalty for the boss, and a sense of belonging towards the organization.

Conclusion

Delegation has been a fashionable word in management circles, though, unwittingly, misunderstood and misused. In its name, practices have ranged from unwise dumping of 'dog-work' to 'abdication', to practically no effective delegation at all. The fact is that delegation has always been imbued with a powerful potential for effective utilization of the human resource in an enterprise.

However, delegation cannot be ushered in a superficial, off-hand manner. It is a managerial process which serves much deeper purposes than mere sharing of task burdens. Hence, it requires planning and preparation; and its implementation calls for an imaginative and delicately balanced approach. Any flaw in the preparatory phase can lead to *(a)* wrong use of delegation by you, the boss; and *(b)* an inimical perception by the subordinates that delegation is nothing but a hypocritical means for their exploitation. Therefore, you must, first, become clear about the real purpose of delegation. If necessary, you should reorient your thinking about your decision-making and management style. When you are indeed ready, you must practise delegation for developing both your high-fliers and mediocre subordinates. Such reorientation paves the way for a healthier approach to delegation before its implementation is undertaken. While delegating, you would do well to distill your plans through the phases of preparation, planning, communication, audit and appreciation.

Delegation is not merely a means of multiplying yourself (by developing a number of stand-ins to relieve you of burdensome tasks); it is actually a *multi-dimensional managerial phenomenon*. If applied properly, it can serve as an excellent catalyst for bringing about *(a) optimum and qualitative utilization of manpower, (b) upgradation and development—without tears—of the capabilities of your subordinates;* and *(c) ongoing motivation and team-spirit* in the human resource of your enterprise. It can also be used as an effective tool for freeing time for the superiors who can then utilize it for more innovative, future-oriented and vital issues or opportunities for the organization.

An important aspect of motivation deserves to be looked at in the perspective of delegation. We have said earlier that delegation is a managerial method for the subordinates 'sharing' some of your tasks. What really uplifts delegation from 'unjustified and exploitive utilization' of the subordinates is that it seeks to stretch and develop the subordinates' capabilities rather than simply get them to do the work assigned to them. It is this element of your 'selflessness' which puts delegation on a high pedestal. True, the subordinates may possibly look upon delegation, *in its initial stage of implementation,* with suspicion—even cynicism and resistance. But once they are convinced that delegation is being practised by you for the genuine purpose of enriching them, they might be filled with a warm feeling of appreciation for you, and for the process of delegation itself. The more they collaborate and the more they find themselves benefitting from delegation, the greater their loyalty to you and congruence with the project. This loyalty may culminate in the *guru-shishya parampara,* of early Indian civilization. The bottom line of this process is: *an ongoing reinforcement of motivation and team spirit!*

Delegation is a multi-dimensional management process which can provide significant benefits to an enterprise. It is too precious a tool to be ignored or misused.

Test Yourself

How Well Do You Delegate?

You can get a good idea whether you are delegating as much as you should by responding to the following questions. Please answer as accurately and frankly as possible.

How To Test Your Delegation Habits[1]

	Strongly Agree				*Strongly Disagree*
1. I would delegate more, but the jobs I delegate never seem to get done the way I want them to be done.	5	4	3	2	1
2. I don't feel I have the time to delegate properly.	5	4	3	2	1
3. I carefully check my subordinates' work without letting them know I'm doing it, so I can correct their mistakes if necessary before they cause too many problems.	5	4	3	2	1
4. I delegate the whole job—giving the opportunity for the subordinate to complete it without any of my involvement. Then I review the end result.	5	4	3	2	1
5. When I have given clear instructions and the task isn't done right, I get upset.	5	4	3	2	1
6. I feel my staff lacks the commitment that I have. So any task I delegate won't get done as well as I would do it.	5	4	3	2	1
7. I would delegate more. But I feel I can do the task better than the person I might delegate it to.	5	4	3	2	1
8. I would delegate more. But if the individual I delegate the task to does an incompetent job, I will be severely criticized.	5	4	3	2	1
9. If I were to delegate a task, my job wouldn't be nearly as much fun.	5	4	3	2	1

10. When I delegate a task, I often find that the outcome is such that I end up doing the task over again myself.   5   4   3   2   1

11. I have not really found that delegation saves any time.   5   4   3   2   1

12. I delegate a task clearly and concisely, explaining exactly how it should be accomplished.   5   4   3   2   1

13. I can't delegate as much as I would like to because my subordinates lack the necessary experience.   5   4   3   2   1

14. I feel that when I delegate I lose control.   5   4   3   2   1

15. I would delegate more, but I am such a perfectionist.   5   4   3   2   1

16. I work longer hours than I should.   5   4   3   2   1

17. I can give subordinates the routine tasks, but I feel I must keep non-routine tasks myself.   5   4   3   2   1

18. My own boss expects me to keep very close to all details of my job.   5   4   3   2   1

Total Score _____

Source: Adapted from Theodore J. Krein, 'How to Improve Delegation Habits', *Management Review*, 71, May 1982, 59.

Scoring Key

If your total score is:	*Your delegation...*
Between: 90 and 72	It is 'ineffective'.
Between: 71 and 54	Your delegation habits need substantial improvements.
Between: 53 and 36	You still have room to improve
Between: 35 and 18	You possess 'superior delegation skills'. Keep it up.

FIVE

Decision-making: Some Home-truths

CHAPTER OBJECTIVES
- Present decisiveness as an essential requirement for effective management
- Discuss the use of imaginative decision-making for motivation and team-building

---

The Imperatives of Decision-making

The Ubiquitous Nature of Decision

In any kind of enterprise, the human resource enjoys supreme importance. This, of course, is too obvious to require reiteration. But the predominant reason for its importance lies in the fact that it is the human resource that takes 'decisions' and it is the 'decisions' that breathe life into all other resources employed by an enterprise. Without decisions—whether they are day-to-day 'operational', or future-oriented 'strategic' ones—even the richest of the other resources could stagnate as lifeless monuments, and lead the organization to decay and extinction. The following *five* characteristics are vital to decision-making:

1. Decision-making is a key activity for all aspects and at all levels of management. Every aspect of management—planning, organizing, staffing, leading and controlling—requires decision-making and decisions. Similarly, decisions have to be taken at all levels by everyone up and down the line in whatever activities they are engaged in, notwithstanding the nature, magnitude and importance of the decisions they take. Even the decision 'not to decide' is one which requires to be taken and acted upon.

2. Decision-making is actually a part of the continuum of the 'planning process' which, in essence, determines an organization's objectives, and selects the future course of actions to accomplish them.
3. Decisions must be implemented; otherwise they would simply vegetate as *intentions*. Implementation requires *selecting* a course of action to achieve the objectives of the enterprise, and then *acting* upon such a course of action in collaboration with a host of other people. These too require decisions.
4. Finally, results achieved have to be *evaluated* by comparing the actual results with the 'hoped for' results. Evaluation also calls for decisions.
5. Above all, it is only through a convincing record of decisiveness that a manager upgrades himself as an 'effective' manager.

Decision-making permeates all aspects of planning. The need for planning arises from the fact that almost all enterprises are surrounded by an unavoidably changing environment and uncertainties that result from such environmental changes. The primary purpose of planning is to offset future uncertainties and thus minimize the risks surrounding the operations of an enterprise.

The first two stages of planning are:

♦ identification of objectives; and
♦ development of premises.

These too require decisions at every step. At the next stage, decisions are required even for:

♦ identifying alternative courses of action;
♦ evaluating alternative courses of action; and
♦ selecting a course of action.

All these call for decisions at every stage of planning, implementing and evaluating.

What is a Decision?

Decision-making is an act of choosing between two or more alternatives in order to solve problems, carve out or take benefit from opportunities—*all for the purpose of achieving desired objectives*. This identification and selection of alternatives can occur under conditions that vary dramatically—conditions of certainty, risk, and uncertainty. (More on this, later.)

What Decision?

When a manager takes decisions, what does he strive for? Is it the:

- 'best' decision;
- 'perfect' decision; or
- 'right' decision?

As mentioned above, decisions are primarily required to produce desired results—in situations that are surrounded by uncertainties, risks and sensitivities of the people. Ideally, all decisions, equipment and actions must be perfect regardless of the sensitivities of the collaborators. However, in the majority of our day-to-day decision-making exercises, we have to work under 'situational' compulsions. And these compulsions require us to seriously consider the 'acceptability' of our decisions, both by the implementors and those who will be affected by them. In view of these, it is not necessary—nor even possible—that the decisions must be 'perfect', let alone the 'best'. But the following three factors can be kept in mind:

1. What we need, in practical terms, is not the 'perfect' or the 'best' decision, but, by choice, the 'best-suited' decision—one that is best-suited to the overall situational considerations.
2. A decision-maker has got to reckon with the additional factors of:
   - situations that may have emotional, political or vested-interest overtones; and
   - prevention of misunderstandings about the very intentions and purposes of the decisions being taken.

   Even where the decision-maker is after the 'best' or the 'right' decision, he cannot afford to overlook the question as to *whose point of view* should his decision cater to:
   - the decision-maker's point of view;
   - the implementors' point of view; or
   - the points of view of those who are going to be affected by the decision?
3. Most decisions are neither right nor wrong; they are simply better or worse. Experience tells us that even a so-called 'worse' decision may yield better results if carried out enthusiastically and correctly

than a so-called 'better' decision carried out unenthusiastically and wrongly!

To sum up, decisions taken by the manager must *(a)* meet the situation—which may vary from place to place, time to time, group to group; and *(b)* be acceptable to as large a number of people as possible. This does not, however, mean that the decisions have to be taken by 'popular' choice.

Decisiveness vs 'Keenness for "Quality" in Decision'

Decisiveness is associated with persons having the courage to be 'conclusive' and free from hesitations when a decision is required. They do not like dilly-dallying, and would rather go ahead and take the decision quickly.

In one sense, our lives are a sum total of the decisions we have taken. It is not only *what* decisions we take but also *when* we take our decisions that determine the profile of our lives. There resides in every decision we take or are about to take *a crucial moment* when we must make up our mind.

'Keenness for "quality" in decision', on the other hand, is associated with persons who possess another kind of courage. They do not care if others decry their taking time on the decision at hand; they would go on deliberating until they are satisfied that the decision reached is indeed imbued with judgement, resolution and purposefulness.

Should the manager be more particular about being 'decisive' or about the 'quality' of the decision he is about to take? It is very difficult to give an 'either-or' advice. This is so because each approach has very strong merits; and the necessity for going in for one or the other is intertwined with complex requirements and compulsions of the situation surrounding each case. Nevertheless, it must be stated that you should be 'proactive'; you must take the initiative to spot an opportunity or foresee a problem.

And you should be in command by taking proactive decisions; otherwise, you will wait till you discover you have missed the opportunity or have been swamped by disaster.

The word proactive means more than merely taking initiative.
It means that as human beings, we are responsible for our own
lives. Our behaviour is a function of our decisions, not our

*conditions. We can subordinate feelings to values. We have
the initiative and the responsibility to make things happen.*

*If you are proactive, you don't have to wait for circumstances
or other people to create perspective expanding experiences.
You can consciously create your own.*

—Stephen R. Covey, *The 7 Habits of Highly Effective People*

Let us consider the following case:

Apple Computer introduced its pioneering, user-friendly Mackintosh Computer in 1984. The 'Mac' quickly became popular, and appeared likely to dominate the field. But Apple officials were reluctant to licence the Mac's operating system to other manufacturers, since they believed this would amount to giving up control of the product.

Meanwhile, Microsoft developed the 'windows' system for rival IBM Computers and for other compatible machines. Microsoft licensed its operating system to *whoever could pay the price;* and its sales boomed.

In September 1994, Apple finally licensed the Mac technology. But by then, most computer manufacturers were committed to 'windows', and only few customers signed up with Apple.

'Apple made the right decision', says financial analyst Douglas Kass, 'they just waited too long to make it'.

Deciding too quickly can bring disastrous consequences; delaying too long can mean missed opportunities. Often, 'when' you decide is as important as 'what' you decide.

Employers generally tend to expect decisiveness from their managers without realizing that wise decisions on some issues do need time, or that *if* they do require time, we must not rush them. True, you cannot ignore the pressures of work and time under which you are often required to take decisions. But lack of time to make a decision is not a good justification for making a lot of wrong decisions. You may be in haste to take a decision, but that does not mean you must take a 'hasty decision'. You may seldom find enough time to do things properly, but, by the same token, do not forget that you hardly ever can get enough time to do that thing again!

Decision-making is like dropping a pebble into a pond: it *will* make ripples. You have got to take into account what the size of the ripples is likely to be *before* you drop the pebble. Trying to remove the pebble with your hand will not only not stop the ripples—it shall only make them bigger!

Decisions by Whom?

Decisions of all sorts are taken all the time by different people at different levels. There are some decisions that are of the 'maintenance' type which rectify faults or solve problems or overcome obstacles. Such decisions merely ensure that the routine functioning of the organization is carried on unhampered. This is done by those who 'execute' things. These 'executors' too undoubtedly play a role in an enterprise. But the decisions that amount to contributions—those that are 'path-breakers'—are often taken by managers or leaders. This is not to deny that sometimes non-managers or 'executors' too do and can take such 'contribution-making' decisions. In fact, it is the 'contribution' factor of decisions that separates an 'executor' from a 'manager' and enables an 'executor' to achieve the stature of a 'manager'.

Your genius as a wise decision-maker lies in your ability to assess the overall situation correctly and then take the 'best-suited' decision (not necessarily the 'best' decision) that promises to fulfill the chosen objective. After all, the soundness or otherwise of a decision is soon tested on the anvil of the results. And the results must fulfill the 'hoped for' objectives of the organization.

There are, however, various kinds of mental blocks that inhibit the decision-makers. Some of these are described below:

Hamlet's Disease Some individuals are most reluctant to commit themselves to any course of action. This stems from their personality which is a prisoner of Hamlet's dilemma: 'To be or not to be...'

Compulsiveness Some individuals suffer from the opposite of Hamlet syndrome. They feel compelled to make decisions, to take action—often premature or immature. These are the people who believe in 'decisiveness' at any cost.

Consequence-anxiety For some, decision-making is extremely uncomfortable because they continue to be haunted by the fear of having 'guessed wrong'. Any decision which is less-than-perfect gives them great anxiety; they distort the consequences of any decision to such an extent that it freezes them into inaction.

'Do-nothingism' This is manifested in a disinclination to take *any* decision or a tendency to procrastinate. This disinclination has nothing to do with 'consequence-anxiety' or with any personal antipathy to action. The person simply remains blissfully unconcerned with what he is or is not doing.

As opposed to these ailments, the 'mentally healthy' manager finds a certain amount of *excitement* in decision-making, and approaches the process with zest, and the feeling that *his* decisions will meet the objective and are likely to be as good as anyone else's.

Risk vs Uncertainty Factors in Decision-making

In almost all cases of decision-making, we are faced with risks and uncertainties.

Risk implies that the alternatives and the likelihood of their occurrence are known but their outcomes are in doubt. Uncertainty implies that neither the alternatives nor their occurrence or potential outcomes are fully known.

Although it is highly unfeasible, a condition of certainty would mean that the decision-maker has access to perfect knowledge about the available *alternatives* and their *consequences.* The element of chance would simply not be there. But rarely is the future known with such perfect reliability, and a manager rarely makes decisions under such conditions.

Decisions under conditions of *risk* are perhaps the most common. In practice, decision-makers assess the likelihood of various outcomes based on past experience, research, and other information. It presupposes that similar situations or types of problems or opportunities have been subjected to decisions in the past, from which a kind of predictability, *in a given set of similar circumstances,* can be derived.

Decisions under conditions of uncertainty are unquestionably the most difficult. In such situations, a decision-maker has no knowledge on which he could even estimate the likelihood of various outcomes; and he has no historical or research data to fall back upon. Such situations generally exist when either a new technology or a new product is to be introduced. When the Dalmias first decided to introduce 'holiday homes' on a time-sharing basis, they must have been tormented by a lot of uncertainties since they were the first in India to offer a service based on totally unknown and untried idea. What really propels decision-makers in such cases are:

- complete faith in their 'idea' which gives them the courage of conviction;
- a gut feeling supported or not by the outcomes of analogical ventures by them or others;
- a certain amount of reliance on their risk-calculation; and
- a true entrepreneurial spirit urging them to take the plunge!

As a decision-maker, therefore, you have to reckon with the fact that you will have to decide in the face of information gaps; you will have to do the best you can with available facts or indicators. Under such circumstances, you can, to some extent, save the situation by taking recourse to either of the two methods suggested below, after you have made your decision:

Conduct a Test Run   In some cases it is possible for you to try out the decision short of full implementation. If the results are satisfactory, you may proceed with an all-out launch of the decision. Otherwise you can revise the decision.

Have Flexibility   It is desirable for you to develop a decision with 'branching' steps, like trying out, simultaneously, two slightly different versions of the same decision, and finally adopting that version which proves to be more satisfactory.

Steps in Decision-making

Regardless of their nature or significance, all decisions involve certain steps to be taken *in sequence*. Gone are the days when a leader could take a decision in the seclusion of his cabin, or draw upon his inspiration to come up with a decision all by himself. Today, every problem or project requiring decisions, has a plethora of information, knowledge, expertise, several angles for viewing the problem or its possible solutions, and large set of pros and cons for each alternative.

In this context, you must also be prepared for the knowledge-and-information explosion that will become even more pronounced by the turn of the century.

Intuition or inspiration based on long years of experience, though valuable in itself, is not going to be enough. Hard facts regarding a large number of variables have now become the primary basis for decision-making.

One imperative requirement for a modern manager is that he must be computer literate, so that he can position himself on the information highway. A decision-maker cannot operate on a 'stand-alone' basis; he must flow with the organization's information tide.

Stage 1: Decision-making

The various steps for decision-making can be seen as fitting into three main stages, namely, decision-making, decision-taking and decision-selling and implementing. This process—let us call it the 'chemistry of decision-making'—can be best visualized in Fig. 5.1:

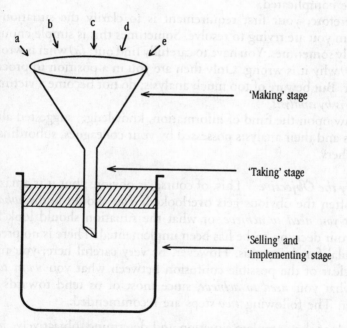

FIGURE 5.1 The Chemistry of Decision-making

The arrows at the top (see Fig. 5.1) represent the inputs. These inputs are—or should be—invited from all such people who are connected with the matter under consideration, and are in a position to contribute. They can be colleagues, subordinates, people from 'sister' departments, concerned outstation units, etc. The arrows marked a, b, c and so on denote the following inputs:

- ◆ information;
- ◆ knowledge or expertise;
- ◆ analysis of the information and knowledge gathered;
- ◆ generating alternative solutions; and
- ◆ scrutinizing the pros and cons of each alternative.

Analyze and Identify the Situation   There is a wise saying that it is more important to know the right question before attempting to find the right answer. If you don't know this, you may come up with a profusion of 'right' answers, but for the wrong questions—thus, ending up not only *not* solving the problem but making it more complicated.

Therefore, your first requirement is to clarify the situation or problem you are trying to resolve. Sometimes this is simple enough, but only sometimes. You have to carefully find out: *(a)* what is wrong; and *(b)* why it is wrong. Only then are you in a position to proceed further. But beware of too much analysis; do not become a victim of *paralysis by analysis.*

Draw upon the fund of information, knowledge, suggested alternatives and their analysis possessed by your colleagues, subordinates and others.

Clarify the Objective   This, of course, is obvious; but it is amazing how often the obvious gets overlooked. You should know *what it is that you need to achieve,* or what the situation should look like after your decision-to-be has been implemented. There is no precise 'formula' for doing this. However, be very careful here; you must steer clear of the possible confusion between what you *want to do* and what you *need to achieve,* since most of us tend towards the former. The following *two* steps are recommended:

1. Look at the complete situation and determine, objectively, *what needs to be done.*
2. Write down what you believe to be the real objective (since the act of writing down can clarify much of your thinking). This 'writing exercise' should be full of phrases beginning with: 'Why...?' and 'What if . . .?'

A natural spin-off from the above exercise is the consideration of the *factors* that will influence the choice of appropriate actions. You must reckon with the resources needed and available, the constraints to be tackled, and the implications that surround them and you. It is this identification of 'factors' that reduces the chances of your exclaiming later on: 'I wish we had thought about that before we went ahead!'

Generate Alternatives   You are now ready to generate alternatives from which the 'best-suited' decision may be chosen. It is impossible for a decision-maker to know all available alternatives. Therefore, you should mount a systematic effort to generate alternatives. Invite all those who may possess *(a)* information; *(b)* knowledge; and *(c)* the power of analysis relating to the problem or situation, and the objectives you need.

Identifying a reasonable number of alternatives may not pose much of a problem, but identifying 'good' and practicable alternatives does not come so easily. It calls for a certain level of creativity on the part of the participants. Creative thinking actually entails a daring mental effort, not one that is subdued or shackled by opposing voices such as: 'It's against company policy', or 'We wouldn't be allowed to do this' or 'It has been tried before' or 'We couldn't afford it'. New, bold and innovative ideas seldom emerge from such so-called logical thinking. (This is the premise on which a contemporary process called 'Business Process Reengineering' is based.)

The language and the spirit here are: First-person, plural, i.e., WE.

A couple of creativity techniques that have proved effective are: brainstorming and Nominal Grouping Technique (NGT). Their essential features are described below:

Brainstorming   Developed by Alexander F. Osborn, a principal of the New York advertising agency Batten, Barton, Durstine & Osborn, brainstorming remains one of the most effective techniques for identifying creative alternatives. Osborn coined the term to mean using the *brain* to creatively *storm* a problem.

The sole concern of brainstorming is *idea generation, not idea evaluation.* A group of six to eight members, drawn preferably from various disciplines (even different enterprises), is presented in advance with a brief description of the problem or situation to be tackled. Then, on the appointed day, each member is required to come out, within a stipulated time of few seconds, with his/her suggestion, one at a time. Every member is expected to speak out; no one is permitted to 'pass' their turn without offering a suggestion, howsoever far-fetched or impractical or even ridiculous it may appear on the surface. In some cases, the exercise has more than one round till enough alternatives have been offered. Thereafter, the participating members are invited to select the more promising alternatives for closer examination in terms of how much, and with what minimal side-effects, they can help in fulfilling the objective. In many cases, use of audio or video recording has proved to be very useful in that: *(a)* it ensures that none of the suggestions has been missed; and *(b)* it shows to all concerned the nuances of the conviction (or lack of it) with which the suggestions were offered. This kind of exercise offers the following choices:

♦ an idea or ideas that stand the tests could be admitted as 'options' to be further evaluated at a later date;
♦ ideas which, with slight modifications, could qualify as 'options';
♦ an idea, combined with one or two more ideas, could make a viable 'option'; and
♦ the ideas that can be rejected.

Brainstorming has been found to be very useful in the areas of advertising, all branches of the armed forces, commercial problems especially connected with competitor's challenges, cost-reduction, and encouraging voluntary efforts or sacrifices by individuals where the objective identified is eminently acceptable to the participants. However, brainstorming is a time-consuming exercise.

Nominal Grouping Technique (NGT) Developed by Andre Del-becq and Andrew Van de Ven, NGT is particularly useful in situations where individual ideas need to be tapped, but where a *group consensus is also desired.* It generally follows a highly structured procedure. It is conducted in the following *five* steps:

1. Seven to ten individuals of varying backgrounds and training make up a group where they are made familiar with the problem(s).
2. These individuals are brought together in a room at an appointed hour. Working silently and alone, each member is asked to prepare a list of ideas for solving the problem.
3. After a period of ten to fifteen minutes, members share their ideas, one at a time, in a 'round-robin' manner. A facilitator

records the ideas on a flip chart for all to see. This process continues until all ideas are presented and recorded.

4. A period of structured interaction follows in which members openly discuss and evaluate each recorded idea. As a result, ideas are reworded, combined, deleted, or added, as the objective may require.

5. Each group member votes privately, ranking the recorded ideas in order of assessed importance. Following a brief discussion of the outcome of voting, a final secret ballot is conducted. The group's preference is the arithmetic total of the ranked votes. This concludes the meeting.

NGT differs from brainstorming in two important ways: *(a)* it does not rely on the free association of ideas; and *(b)* it purposely attempts to *restrict verbal interaction*. As the name itself suggests, the 'group' role is only nominal.

NGT has been found very useful in a variety of enterprises. Its principal benefit is that it *minimizes the inhibiting effects of group interaction*, particularly during the initial stage. Moreover, NGT is *proactive*, rather than reactive, since it requires the group members to generate their own ideas instead of hitch-hiking on others' ideas. Its one shortcoming, like that of brainstorming, is that it is time-consuming.

Stage 2: Decision-taking

The most important thing about a decision is that it be taken! You as the decision-taker should obtain a perspective of the issues at hand in the light of your collaborators' contributions at the decision-making stage. Then you should distill this perspective within the ambit of your wider responsibilities, multiple linkages and understanding of the ripple effects it is likely to create. At this stage, you, as the leader, embark upon a lonely journey through a narrow tunnel since 'taking' a decision cannot be delegated, nor can it be done through a committee. Take a deep breath and choose one of the alternatives, or their combination, or an altogether different alternative of your own.

While in the preceding alternative-generating sessions, alternatives are considered and their number is narrowed down, the actual final choice of *the* alternative for decision-commitment has to be made by you, the decision-maker. It is you who have to own responsibility for your decision. If your decision succeeds, you share the credits with your alternative-generating-and-decision-implementing collaborators;

but in case it fails, you alone take the bullets! It is for this reason that you earn the stature of a decision-maker and, therefore, of the leader.

The language and the spirit here are: First person: singular, i.e., 'I'.

Evaluate Alternatives and Make the Choice

As the decision-maker, you have to do the final evaluation of the pros and cons of each alternative in terms of *your* own experience and judgement, and of the objectives set at the beginning. Such a choice may be made by you either intuitively or through scientific methods like operations research, etc. But one prime consideration that must preside over this process is that you should look at the 'possible-choice' option not only in terms of what it can do *to* you (in terms of the challenges, trials and tribulations you deal with), but also in terms of what it can do *for* you (in terms of achievement of the objective for which others are looking up to you). As this is your last chance to look at the options before you commit yourself to a decision, you should exercise an element of 'constructive caution'.

Since a perfect option is seldom found, you have to make the best-possible and the best-suited choice. This means either a compromise or 'balancing' or both. This is especially true in sensitive situations where:

+ improvement in morale of employees requires large cash injections;
+ cut-back on expenses entails the cost of upsetting some employees;
+ improvements in customer satisfactions impose difficulties of more or difficult operations within tightening expense budgets;
+ required reduction in budgeted expenses poses risks to safety standards;
+ improvement in maintenance standards threatens to slow down production rhythm;
+ improvement in quality standards imposes additional manufacturing costs; or
+ higher productivity poses threats of cutback in manpower.

A very important lesson that you must always keep in mind is that the so-called compromise should not be allowed to creep in while you are about to make your decision-commitment from the available options. Compromise(s), if any, ought to be left for the trial stage of implementation when flexibility is going to be required in varying degrees. The original choice must fall on the *right* option—that which is right for the enterprise's current and long-term objectives.

The following is what Peter Drucker has acknowledged as a 'lesson' he learnt from Alfred P. Sloan, Jr the Chairman of General Motors during his first big consulting assignment in 1944. While offering the assignment, Sloan told Drucker:

'I shall not tell you what to study, what to write, or what conclusions to come to. This is your task. My only instruction to you is to put down what you think is right as you see it. Don't you worry about our reaction. Don't you worry about whether we will like this or dislike that. And don't you, above all, concern yourself with the compromises that might be needed to make your recommendations acceptable. There is not one executive in this company who does not know how to make every single conceivable compromise without any help from you. But he can't make the *right* compromise unless you first tell him what "right" is.'

—Peter F. Drucker, *The Effective Executive*, 1966, p. 135.

To sum up, once the available alternatives have been evaluated, you, as a decision-maker, should select the one with the highest estimated probability of success. It is at this final step that a plan of action is adopted and the climax of decision-making takes place!

Role of the Subconscious When the moment of decision-taking arrives, you would do well to take a brief pause. There is still a lot of value in the old saying: '...sleep on the decision for a while. Do not rush out with a solution in haste!' This allows the subconscious to sort out various conflicting and baffling factors. It saves you from getting caught in the game of counting arguments for and against, and deciding on 'quantitative' lines. There are often ten reasons for not doing a thing, and only one for doing it; and qualitatively *the one reason for doing it may prove superior to the ten against!*

In order to tap this great potential for quality decision, the following *five* suggestions may be tried out:

1. Determine the *date* on which the decision must be taken.

2. Work back, say, four days from that date. (It should, preferably, include the weekend.)
3. Up to the fourth day prior, collect all possible and relevant information on the analysis, alternatives and their pros and cons. Then write down all the arguments—for and against, and ponder over them.
4. Then destroy the paper. From now on. whenever the topic of *this* decision comes up in your mind, push it back or, preferably, push it away.
5. On the final day, wait until it is time to take the decision, and then decide spontaneously!

This manner of decision-taking steers nicely between the laziness of not doing any analysis and the arrogance of insisting that inspiration has no place in decision-taking. It paves the way for *a good balance between logic and intuition, between the sermon of reason and the quiet wisdom of the subconscious.*

On arriving at your decision, commit yourself to take full responsibility for its consequences. The implication is that you must be prepared to either take all the blame upon yourself *if* your decision fails, or *share* the credit with your colleagues/collaborators if it succeeds! This unwritten commitment between you, the leader, and your collaborators comes into existence automatically, not only by the force of logic but also out of moral and motivational considerations. Above all, this ensures that you will continue to be accepted as a leader.

Stage 3: Decision-selling and Implementation

Selling the Decision   Having taken your decision, you cannot just go ahead and implement it. You have to first reckon with the following *two* considerations:

1. How to generate the best possible *enthusiasm* among those who would be called upon to implement the decision?
2. How to ensure that the large number of people who are going to be affected by this decision—adversely or favourably—*understand*, if not agree with or appreciate, the considerations on which your decision has been based?

Perhaps, the expression 'selling' tends to lend itself to a wrong interpretation. 'Selling' has been used here only to mean that everyone concerned is furnished with the *reasons why* you, the decision-taker, have chosen this alternative as your decision in preference to the other alternatives. If your collaborators accept your decision, well and good; if not, the skies are not going to fall. It is certainly not being suggested here that you have to bend over backwards to get everyone to applaud your decision. In reality, there is seldom a decision with which everyone would agree; and this is nothing to feel upset about. However, it is important that even those who cannot agree with you get a chance to *understand* your point of view—specially those who are likely to assist you in implementing it. If they understand why you have taken this decision, they will be better inclined to give it a fair chance in the course of implementing it—despite their personal disagreement with the decision itself.

You may find it uncomfortable to deal with your opponents. But that is more than outweighed by the certainty that the concerned people shall feel mad at you when they find out that you have taken them for granted on matters they have been involved with, or are going to be asked to implement, or are going to be affected by. Therefore, do explain your decision to them. When enough arguments and discussions about the rightness or otherwise of the decision have gone back and forth, you are finally entitled to say: 'We have discussed this enough; now let's go forward as a team and give this decision a fair chance by implementing it as best as we can.' In any case, your best 'selling point' is the unwritten contract: 'Credits *we* share, bullets *I* take!'

In cases where you are only a 'recommending' authority, 'selling' becomes essential. Someone else will have to be convinced that the decision is sound enough to be acted upon. You must do a good job of presenting your decision to him. Remember, even good recommendations fail to be accepted and turned into decisions if you do not present them properly.

Implementing the Decision As mentioned earlier, a decision simply vegetates as intentions unless it is implemented. Again, it is not simply the implementation, but *how* it has been implemented that makes the difference between a decision gone awry and the one that succeeded.

You need to take into account the following *three* situations:

1. All those who will be involved must be informed, and appropriate resources must be allocated.

2. Some implementors resist the plan because they aren't 'sold' on the decision. The best remedy is to involve them during the 'alternative generation' sessions—all the way up to the point just prior to your making your final choice. Thereafter, as mentioned earlier, you must 'sell' your decision.
3. Some implementors may resist the plans because they have not fully understood it; they would rather live with a problem they can't solve than use a workable solution they don't know!

During the 'selling' session, you should make attempts to let your team see the logic behind the plan. But for promoting implementation, you must clearly tell them what *they* are supposed to do. This means:

♦ developing and making known, the performance standards;
♦ establishing reporting relationships and frequencies; and
♦ determining deadlines for completion of activities.

It merits reiteration here that even a 'worse' decision has a better chance of yielding good results if carried out enthusiastically and correctly than a 'better' decision carried out without enthusiasm or improperly.

Here are some basic considerations required for implementing a decision:

Strategic Timing   One major decision is to decide as to when to implement the decision. The decision: 'not to decide yet' or 'not to implement yet' is also a decision. But you must promptly make it known to the people who are looking up to you for decisions;

Commitment   At the implementation stage, your team must be willing, or they must be helped, to finally put aside all hesitations or partial commitments to other courses of action. If necessary, you must finally *assert* your view that, like true soldiers, they should now fall in line and do their best;

Announcement   The way in which you reveal your decision to your staff or to all employees in the enterprise can make all the difference between its acceptability and its viability. Let enthusiasm power you. When a decision is stated with resolution, confidence and optimism, its chances of success are greater. Your enthusiasm is vital if you want others to respond. If you are not excited, you can be sure no one else will be.

Choice of the Doers Who gets to do what is a crucial factor. You should consider this not only in terms of the number of people but their quality, that is, their skill, experience, initiative, dependability, etc.

Who is Responsible for What? This must be very carefully determined. Not only for the top, but also for people down the line. Any confusion on this can lead to bickering, passing the buck, delays, mistakes, even 'derailment' of the whole plan. Also, the person with overall responsibility must be chosen and announced for everyone's knowledge and use. Among other things, this person must set up his own system for monitoring progress, removing bottlenecks, providing the required facilities, etc., so that uninterrupted implementation is ensured.

Required Facilities Everything from raw material to production equipment, money, authority, lines of command, reporting channels, deadlines, and cost-limits must be spelled out—and provided or organized by you. And there must be willingness on the part of the monitoring authority to remain flexible for adjustments as the process of implementation gets going.

Evaluation

The last, and very important, step in decision-making is to find out through a realistic, foolproof system:

- ♦ whether the decision has been implemented properly; and
- ♦ as to how the decision has turned out—whether its results are fulfilling the desired objectives or not. This, of course, should be undertaken some time after the decision has been implemented.

We can learn as much from success as from failure. A corollary to such evaluation is whether

- ♦ any difficulties in implementation are being experienced; and
- ♦ there are any grievances.

For this purpose, there must exist a monitoring system to ensure that the decision has *indeed been carried out.* This can best be done by the simple method of managers going around and seeing things for themselves. It is very easy to fall prey to obtaining, and depending on, reports. These can never give you any accurate idea of the 'feel' and the dynamics of the actual situation. It is best to walk over to the event rather than arrange for the event to walk over to you.

You should take due note if a feeling persists and grows that your decision has been a mistake. Either there is substance in this feeling, in which case you must make necessary adjustments in the decision—or there are misunderstandings, in which case you must clear them by mounting effective communication.

The tendency to hold on to a decision even when it is obviously defective can prove to be disastrous—both in terms of results going haywire and demoralization setting in among the people down the line. It is better to have a system whereby a wrong or defective decision can be promptly put right than to be obstinate about it—by hanging on to endless, unconvincing arguments fabricated to evade admission of a mistake. Please remember that the leader who can admit he is wrong, and is prepared to amend his decision, enhances his authority rather than diminishes it. (Of course, this should happen very infrequently.)

This kind of evaluation and corrective measures are critical not only to the success of the decision but also to that of the whole enterprise. It should be practised at all levels, from senior managers to the first-line supervisors. The best instrument for such evaluation is obtaining *feedback* all the time while implementation is in progress and results are unfolding themselves. Feedback provides a realistic measurement of the gap between the actual achievement and perceived opportunities, and of the practicability of the decision(s) taken. In case such a gap is revealed, you can make necessary mid-course corrections in the decision to the extent feasible.

Conclusion

The plan outlined here merely advocates that your decisions should be based on sturdy commonsense. This commonsense should permeate not only the decision being taken but also the objectives, premises and choices that are being considered. The implied advice here is that you should be *flexible to suit situations* because what you really need is not necessarily the best but the *best-suited* decisions. Instead of a stand-offish posture, you, the decision-maker, must engage yourself in a collaborative process. You should be open not only while you are deliberating upon *what* to decide, but even about 'selling' the decision you have finally taken. In short, you, the leader (or the decision-maker) must not seem to your people to be either unpredictable or too secretive as far as the *style* of your decision-making is concerned. Having taken your decision, you must see that *it is implemented, and implemented faithfully.* For this, you may have to exhort your implementors to keep aside their feelings about the rightness or wrongness of the decision, and to throw in their might to ensure that it is implemented in the proper manner and spirit.

Once the decision is implemented, you must 'walk over' to where the action is and obtain first-hand impression as to how it is doing. You must be open even at this stage to admit you were wrong if facts and developments demonstrate so. You should, in such a case, make amends in your decision rather than adopt an obstinate stand. You should be courageous enough to take the blame upon yourself if your decision has gone wrong, and large-hearted enough to share the credits if your decision has gone right.

These are the factors that may lead your team-mates to have faith and loyalty in you and your decisions. When such a state of faith is attained by you, even your not-so-good decision may have a chance of producing better results due to higher level of motivation among your team-mates than the so-called 'right' decision which could fall by the wayside if it is implemented without sufficient enthusiasm.

When you have succeeded in building such a team-spirit, decisions get upgraded to serve an even higher purpose than remaining only a cog in the wheel of planning. They take on an additional, effective role of throwing up or reinforcing your managerial effectiveness, your effectiveness as a decision-maker, and your becoming a potent motivator of your subordinates.

Test Yourself

Check Your Decision-making Skills[1]

When you face problems, do you usually try to act promptly, or do you delay as long as possible? When pressed for a decision, do you often act hastily, do you feel you function best when under pressure? Do you believe in consulting others, or do you consider it a sign of weakness? Do you often feel agonized both before and after making important decisions, or do you deal with such decisions calmly with no subsequent brooding?

The ability to make decisions sensibly, calmly, and with reasonable speed is helpful in any walk of life, and specially so for managers. One sure way to distinguish between good and inadequate managers is to observe the way they cope with decision-making. Effective and reasonably prompt decision-making is important to win the respect of one's superiors and subordinates.

To find out how well you deal with decision-making, please answer the questions that follow as frankly as possible with complete honesty:

Your Name ....   *Date* ....

1. Do you often try to avoid or delay making important decisions, and even hope that problems will go away?   Yes——   No——

2. When required to make a decision fairly promptly, do you become flustered, and fail to function at your best?   Yes——   No——

3. Would you consider it demeaning to consult your subordinates regarding a problem with which they have experience?   Yes——   No——

4. In deciding a complicated problem where strong arguments exist for either side, would you trust your 'gut feeling'?   Yes——   No——

5. Do you often wish that you didn't have to make any decisions?   Yes——   No——

6. When faced with a serious decision, are your sleep and appetite usually adversely affected?   Yes——   No——

7. Do you secretly dislike making decisions because you lack self-confidence? Yes——— No———

8. Are you uneasy even when required to make unimportant decisions? Yes——— No———

9. Would you fire a friend if his continued employment was against the welfare of the enterprise in which you hold a high position? Yes——— No———

10. When baffled by a problem within your jurisdiction, would you try to pass it off to others? Yes——— No———

11. At home, do you participate in all or most of the important decisions? Yes——— No———

12. Are you usually edgy both before and after making important decisions? Yes——— No———

Scoring Key

The most desirable response earns 4 points, the least desirable, 1 point.

Give yourself 4 points for 'yes' responses, and 1 point for 'no' responses to Items 4, 9 and 11 only.

Give yourself 4 points for 'no' responses, and 1 point for 'yes' responses to Items 1, 2, 3, 5, 6, 7, 8, 10 and 12.

A score ranging from 41 to 48 is 'above average' to 'excellent', and suggests a strong capacity for decision-making. A score ranging from 30 to 40 is 'average', while a score of 29 or lower is 'below average'.

SIX

Communication . . . Listening
. . . Communication

CHAPTER OBJECTIVES

- Offer practical recommendations on effective communication and stress on the importance of listening
- Discuss the issue of credibility and how this can be achieved by transparent conduct
- Suggest pragmatic steps to improve communication and enhance credibility

Introduction

There is an analogy that comes to my mind. At the end of a delicate laser treatment of my eyes, when I asked the eye specialist about any restrictions on reading or writing, he laughed and said the eyes keep functioning all the time—whether you use them or not. This triggered in me a chain of thoughts about the functioning of our senses. Of the five senses, it is only taste and touch which are put to use as and when we wish to; the remaining three senses—sight, hearing and smell keep functioning all the time whether we think we are using them or not! What about our brain and heart? Similarly, what about breathing and the blood-circulation in our body? They never go to sleep, irrespective of whether we think we are using them or not.

Communication too, is like these senses; it goes on whether we switch it on or not. Although we tend to think of communication in more prosaic terms like reports, memos, meetings, interviews, the fact is that nearly everything we do, say, wear, put on our desk or hang on our walls communicates a message! It is, indeed, the 'blood circulation system' in the fabric of any organization wherever information and ideas are in the process of being transmitted between individuals or groups of people. Try and somehow stop or restrict the blood circulation (or communication) in the body (or corporate) system, and you are bound to face atrophy or excruciating pain or complications of dangerous proportions!

Let us begin by restating the oft-repeated truism. All phases of management—planning, organizing, staffing and human resource management—depend on communication, from conceptualizing to executing and to feedback stages. And a manager's job, by its very nature, requires spending more time and effort on communication than on most other functions.

The top management first defines the objectives clearly, and then the component tasks to be accomplished by each wing of the organization. Within the framework of such objectives and targets, a manager down the line takes his decisions leading to a plan of actions, then goes about 'getting things done through others'. To do this successfully, he must resolve three different aspects simultaneously: *(a)* organizing, *(b)* communicating; and *(c)* securing cooperation. After a manager has decided what he wants done, and by whom, he still has to convey his decision(s) to his colleagues and subordinates, and enlist their cooperation. In fact, he needs to maintain ongoing participative communication during the 'formulation' stage with the intention of obtaining implied commitment from his would-be collaborators. The stage of conception and related decisions, and that of involving and securing commitment of the collaborators, are often poles apart. The process which can bring these stages together, and make them dynamic, is communication.

Although usually looked upon merely as a conveyor of information or instructions, communication, is essentially concerned with feelings and ideas, with morale and motivation. It is no exaggeration—and it bears repetition—that proper communication is the 'blood circulation system' in the fabric of an organization. Without it, even the best talents in manpower, the best of materials, money and technological resources could be rendered useless.

Figure 6.1 shows how the 'valves' in the 'blood circulation system' of communication operate in an organization.

Communication is the process—and the capacity of an individual or individuals—for conveying and receiving:

- information;
- ideas;

♦ feelings;
♦ attitudes;
♦ suggestions; and
♦ commands;

with the intention of evoking discriminating responses manifested in desired actions.

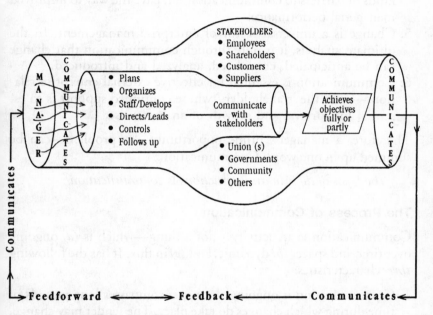

FIGURE 6.1 The Blood Circulation System of Communication

The Importance of Communication

How crucial and important is communication, especially for managers? Given below are *six* answers:

1. In any enterprise involving two or more persons, coordination of activities assumes great importance; and communication acts like the glue that holds the various people and work-groups together. It is, therefore, essential for the success of any enterprise.
2. Communication is not only vital in formulating and implementing enterprise plans, but is also the principal means of achieving the objectives of the enterprise. All decision-making, implementations,

follow-ups are information-processing-and-sharing activities which simply cannot be carried out without communication.

3. Managers cannot lead and motivate others if they do not have, and do not know how to use, the vehicle of communication.

4. Communication can be both the best opportunity or fatal weakness for managers if they do not use it properly. Therefore, an understanding of the process of communication and of different kinds of barriers to communication can pave the way to improved managerial performance.

5. Change is a universal factor of enterprise management. In the ultimate analysis, it is only through communication that change can be anticipated, considered, analyzed and introduced.

6. Communication is essential for effective external enterprise relations—with the 'stakeholders' whose continued support is so essential for survival and growth of an enterprise.

Therefore, a manager's prime opportunity—or problem—can be summed up in one word: Communication.

The basis of all human interactions is communication!

The Process of Communication

Communication is an activity—not a thing—which is *(a)* ongoing over time and space; *(b)* dynamic, and *(c)* in flux. It has the following *three* characteristics:

1. Communication is ongoing since it encompasses long periods of time during which changes do take place. The sender may change, the recipient may change, the nature of their relationship may change. Besides, changes may occur in themselves.

2. It is dynamic in that the sender may initiate a message which the recipient responds to in ways different from what was envisaged, leading to further modifications and desired or undesired responses, and so on. These responses and counter-responses create 'ripple-effects' which, if handled right, can create 'synergy' in the organization;

3. It is in a state of flux in the sense that we cannot 'freeze' the process of communication and isolate its starting or ending points. If a problem is brought up for discussion and advice, when does the communication begin? Does it begin when it is first talked about, or does it begin when the problem is first perceived as a

problem? Similarly, when does the communication end—when the discussion takes place or when the solution is agreed upon or when further reviews/actions are taken on finding out that the original solution does not work? And what about the back-and-forth interactions—much of it may be to sort out the distortions—that are triggered off?

The six elements, namely, communicator, message, media, recipients, decoding and feedback play essential and distinct roles—severally and collectively—in the success or failure of communication.

In any case, the process can best be illustrated as shown in Figure 6.2.

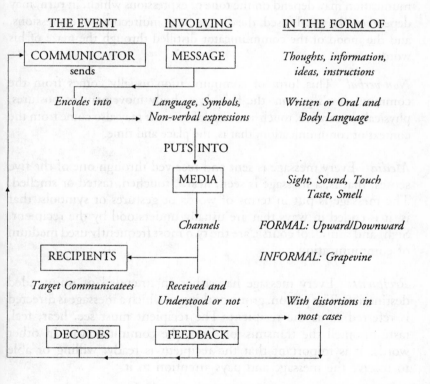

THE EVENT   INVOLVING   IN THE FORM OF

COMMUNICATOR MESSAGE   *Thoughts, information,*
  sends   *ideas, instructions*

  Encodes into   Language, Symbols,   *Written or Oral and*
                   Non-verbal expressions   *Body Language*

                 PUTS INTO

                 MEDIA   *Sight, Sound, Touch*
                             Taste, Smell

                 Channels   *FORMAL: Upward/Downward*

RECIPIENTS   *INFORMAL: Grapevine*

Target Communicatees Received and
                        Understood or not   *With distortions in*
                                            most cases

DECODES   FEEDBACK

FIGURE 6.2 The Process of Communication

Communicator The process of communication is initiated when the communicator has a message (i.e., he creates an idea, comes across an information or instruction, experiences an emotion), and then decides to share the content of his message with others. (Sometimes, the communicator may initiate communication unwittingly through actions at a subconscious plane like his facial expression, incidental touch, the clothes he wears, the way he walks, or even by being punctual or late for an appointment).

Message That which conveys meaning is a message. It is transmitted through both verbal and non-verbal media.

Verbal *Oral* communication depends not only on the words spoken but to a large extent on its loudness, softness, other inflections that may betray conviction, sincerity, concern or their lack. Verbal, *written* communication may depend on the tone of expressions which, in turn, may depend on the words used, the directness or indirectness of expressions, and the mood of the communicator distilled through the maze of his words.

Non-verbal This form of communication usually comes from the communicator's person: the face, eyes, body movement or postures, physical appearance, touch and tone of voice. It may also come from the context of communication, that is, the place and time.

Media Every message is sent and received through one of the five senses, that is, a message is seen, heard, touched, tasted or smelled. The message is put in terms of words or gestures or symbols, that is, it is coded in ways that are usually understood by the recipient. Sight and sound, of course, are the two most frequently used medium of communication.

Recipients Every message has either an intended or unintended destination. The person, group or thing to which a message is directed is referred to as the recipient. The recipient must see, hear, feel, taste or smell the transmission from the communicator. In other words, it is important that the recipient is ready, willing or able to receive the message and pays attention to it.

Decoding As mentioned above, messages are conveyed through 'codes' which the recipient tries to understand by interpreting or 'decoding' them in pre-determined terms. However, it is at this stage that a lot of the recipient's background, upbringing, level of knowledge, intelligence, perceptions, views on things and people come in, and they usually lend themselves to a whole lot of distortions. (Some distortions may creep in during the transmission itself of the message.)

Feedback　Effective communication can take place only when the recipient understands the intent and content of the message initiated by the communicator. Normally, the recipient acknowledges receipt and comprehension of the message by responding in some ways apparent to the communicator. When this does not happen, the communicator initiates other measures to obtain reliable information to ascertain the response actually evoked in the recipient. This response is known as feedback or 'return message'. It can be either verbal or non-verbal.

To sum up, communication is:

♦ any behaviour that results in the exchange of a *message* and its *meaning;*
♦ mutual exchange of facts, thoughts, emotions and opinions;
♦ a process of transmission of plans of actions, their implementation, and feedback; and
♦ a chemical process of influencing: attitudes, responses, morale and motivation.

mostly for evoking discriminating responses.

'Media' Effectiveness[1]

There has been an ongoing debate on whether the *written* medium is more effective than the *oral.* Actually, each medium is best-suited for specific tasks, as depicted in Table 6.1.

Written Media　When used appropriately, they offer several advantages, such as:

♦ **Note or Memo**
  • It is brief, but allows a tangible record to be preserved. It enables the writer to 'pre-think' what he/she puts down on paper.
  • The ordinary note or memo offers only a 'one-way' communication, and has no control or influence over the recipient at the other end. Besides, it is a rigid form of communication whose contents remain on record permanently.

However the latest computer-related E-mail provides a much better spectrum of expressions and feedback. One can obtain back-and-forth and instantaneous responses, together with the right feelings through symbols such as the 'smiley face', among others. E-mail is also flexible and informal.

TABLE 6.1: Effectiveness of Different Media

Type of Medium	Effectiveness	Examples
Written media	Most effective for transmitting lengthy and detailed material	Memoranda, charts, diagrams, bulletins, company newsletters.
Oral media	Most effective for communications requiring translation and elaboration to be understood by recipients with varying orientations and language skills. Also where spontaneous give-and-take of ideas is desired.	Face-to-face discussion, telephone conversations, lectures , conferences.
Multimedia	Most effective in situations such as settling work disputes, communicating oral/visual, written/oral/visual major policy changes and rectifying work deficiencies.	Written/oral, written/visual, oral/visual, written/oral/visual

♦ **Formal Report**
  • It can be comprehensive, and its material can be organized by the writer at his/her leisure. Its copies can be disseminated widely. The writer gets the opportunity to show the extent of his knowledge and writing skills.
  • It provides readers with the opportunity to understand the communication at their own pace.
  • It allows ideas to be conveyed over distance and time.
  • It is easy to store and retrieve for use while making decisions in future.
  • Being exact, it cannot easily be twisted either by the writer or the readers—at least in regard to what is already 'written down'. (Of course, it can lend itself to amazingly varying 'interpretations'.)

Oral Media   When used appropriately, they offer the following advantages:

♦ **Meeting**
  • It allows for two-way flow of communication, reinforced by non-verbal means such as body-language.
  • It promotes discussion and better meeting of minds—even several minds.

Of course, it is time-consuming, and at times it is difficult to keep the discussions on track.

♦ **Face-to-Face Conversation**
  • It promotes personal contacts during which a proper mood can be built up that is friendly and relaxed. However, some individuals may be subjected to undue pressure if faced with a powerful personality or a very senior/aggressive authority.

♦ **Telephone**
  • It offers speed and permits questions and answers. Since it does not involve visiting the person to be spoken with, the tendency to postpone a discussion is absent. However, generally there is no record of the conversation (except when modern gadgets are used to record the telecon).

On the whole, oral media have the following *four* advantages:

1. They are better suited to communicating feelings and ideas than written media because oral discussions provide maximum opportunities for interaction on the basis of both verbal and non-verbal cues.
2. They are particularly effective when rapid transmission of information and immediate feedback are desired.
3. They are specially appropriate for handling sensitive or confidential matters because discussions on ticklish subjects become easier due to the transitory nature of oral discussions.
4. They promote a personal touch that is difficult to achieve through written media.

Multimedia   Written/oral, written/visual, oral/visual, written/oral/visual transmissions employ different media consecutively or simultaneously to accomplish their objectives. For example, a face-to-face discussion on work problems might be followed by a written memorandum, thus 'putting on record' the means of overcoming problems that were discussed and concluded.

The effectiveness of a particular communication media depends to a great extent upon the type and purpose of the information being transmitted, as well as the circumstances and the types of individuals involved.

Channel Effectiveness

A clear awareness of the *power* as well as the peculiarities of the channels of communication is very important. Since, unfortunately, these are often not recognized, numerous communication efforts fail, despite sufficient preparations on other aspects.

Formal Channels

Downward and Upward Channels of Communication It is necessary to emphasize that communication from bottom upward is as important as the other way round. True, it is fashionable among managements to claim that they practise 'bottom upward' communication, in the same breath as 'top downward'. But in practice, very few organizations make conscious efforts to *(a)* 'open the ducts' from top downward in the true sense; and *(b)* deliberately and tenaciously seek truly representative glimpses of what is happening at the ground level. In many cases where efforts are initially made to do the above, the required follow-up and determined efforts to see that these practices are continued wither away somewhere along the line. In such a state of affairs, the management remains deprived of essential feedback on what is happening and what are the feelings of the people down the line.

Even 'top downward' communication is (mis)understood by many managers to mean a flawless system by which the management's announcements go down undistorted. They either mistake their announcements for communication or believe they are too busy to bother beyond making their announcements. Thus, such organizations go on taking decisions and implementing them, in a world of make-believe where there are plenty of right answers for wrong questions.

Eclipse of the Sun
(The Operation of the Chain of Command)

The Colonel to the Executive: 'At nine o'clock tomorrow there will be an eclipse of the sun, something which does not occur everyday. Get the men to fall out in the company street in their fatigues so that they will see this rare phenomenon, and I will explain it to them. In case of rain, we will not be able to see anything, so take the men to the gym.'

The Executive to the Captain: 'By order of the Colonel, tomorrow at nine o'clock there will be an eclipse of the sun; if it rains you will not be able to see it from the company street, so then, in fatigues, the eclipse of the sun will take place in the gym, something that does not occur everyday.'

The Captain to the Lieutenant: 'By order of the Colonel in fatigues tomorrow at nine o'clock in the morning the inauguration of the eclipse of the sun will take place in the gym. The Colonel will give the order if it should rain, something which occurs every day.'

The Lieutenant to the Sergeant: 'Tomorrow at nine o'clock the Colonel in fatigues will eclipse the sun in the gym, as it occurs every day if it is a nice day; if it rains, then in the company street.'

The Sergeant to the Corporal: 'Tomorrow at nine the eclipse of the Colonel in fatigues will take place by cause of the sun. If it rains in the gym, something which does not take place everyday, you will fall out in the company street.'

Comments among the Privates: 'Tomorrow, if it rains, it looks as if the sun will eclipse the Colonel in the gym. It is a shame that this does not occur every day!'[2]

The imaginary, but very realistic, exercise in oral communication reproduced above will open your eyes to the unbelievable extent oral messages can get distorted. It should also provide a great deal of humour!

Two-way communication—in its right spirit—has become all the more essential, especially in view of the changing work scenario. Increasing number of employees (even the so-called 'blue collar' ones) are now 'knowledge workers', influenced by vast technological developments and information explosions. They are more conscious of their rights and more zealous about a better quality of life at the workplace; they also crave for being better informed.

Communication with, and Among, Management Staff   Another aspect
—often neglected—is whether the top management maintains adequate and real communication with, and among, the members of
management staff themselves.

This question is prompted by the top management's assumption
that there already exists enough communication between them and
the other levels of management staff. They are lulled into such a belief
because they do usually consult the next level of managers on problems
or opportunities, and for generating alternative solutions. Another
reason for the top managements complacence is that whenever a
decision is about to be announced, the other level of management staff
is the first batch of people to be informed. Their thinking is: 'Let's
concentrate on improving our communication with non-manage-
ment staff (since communication with management staff, of course,
takes care of itself).' Therefore, top management often react with
disbelief and chagrin when the above question ('Is there enough
communication with, and among, management staff?') is posed to
them.

What is amiss in the above-described situation is that while management staff are certainly enabled to 'know' the facts and decisions,
hardly enough efforts are put in to 'sell and make them understand'
the issues involved, and to offer the 'why' of the decisions taken, in
their total perspective.

It should be remembered that management staff from the middle
level downwards are the focal points for disseminating and interpreting—downward or upward—all vital information and policies of the
management. They are the ones who ensure that the information
generated or passed on from one individual or group is received by
others with minimum distortion and evokes the desired reactions, as
far as possible.

How can the management staff fulfill this vital role unless they are
part of the two-way communication between the top management
and themselves, and among their peers? A manager is like the negative
in a photo-development process. If the image on the negative is not
sharp enough, no amount of tricks or superior quality of chemicals or
photographic paper used in the dark-room will produce a good print.
And as the communicator, negotiator or guide with the employees
down the line, can a manger do justice to his task (of communicating
up and down the line) if he has to carry an unclear picture in his mind?

Informal Channel

Communication Through the Grapevine   Every organization has its informal channels of communication. While the formal ones largely work through the organization's set of rigid chains of command, the informal ones, spearheaded by the 'grapevine', are far more flexible and dynamic; and they move in all directions. The grapevine is a natural offshoot of the informal relationships that prevail among the employees. Many think of it vaguely as the 'rumour department' of an organization, since it thrives on: *(a)* spreading information without any responsibility for accuracy; and *(b)* the natural urge among people to invent their own explanations for, or read too much into, matters that are not clear to them. However, rumour is often based on facts not yet revealed or made known clearly. The interesting—or disturbing—thing about the grapevine, though, is that any item picked up by it instantly becomes 'hot news' which people are only too eager to devour; and it gets hotter as it does the rounds. Why is it so effective? When news about matters that affect people's lives is withheld altogether, or is not reported clearly and promptly, or reaches them in trickles and in conflicting versions, people are not going to wait or be kept on tenterhooks. In the absence of authentic information, people tend to accept or believe what they wish to; they simply come up with some plausible explanations for any mysterious matter. And the version they will most likely come up with will be the one that either feeds their fantasy, or confirms their suspicions or fears.

Let us look a little deeper. While the formal systems of communication may occasionally break down, the grapevine can always be counted upon never to fail; it keeps operating speedily and powerfully! The question that should really be asked is not who is in on the news, or how it moves so fast and far and wide, but what is doing the rounds and why? In fact, it is a sign of health that employees at the workplace indulge in informal shop-talk, indicative of the fact that they take interest in their jobs or matters related to their jobs, the people they work with, and the company they work for.

Is the grapevine only a peddler of gossip, scandals and half-truths? Or does it—or can it be made to—perform a legitimate function as part of the overall communication process? Experiments with the grapevine have proved that it can play a role complementary to formal channels of communication. With an imaginative approach, its power can be utilized by the management for transmitting the 'desired' message with speed and effectiveness. Above all, it can serve as a barometer of what is ailing the employees, and what can be done about it.

Whether viewed as an asset or a liability, it is important for managers to understand the grapevine and its power. Since it is always present, speedy and largely accurate, managers should make effective and imaginative use of it as an alternative means of transmitting information.

Breakdowns in Communication

The worst assumption you can make about a message just sent or received is that it was received as intended. So many things *can* go wrong; therefore, you should assume that something or the other *will*. Barriers in communication are always there, and they have the capacity to distort the messages beyond recognition if care is not taken to minimize their distorting effects. This we can do only when we are aware of what kinds of barriers, and from which quarters, we have to contend with.

The complexity of this aspect of communication can be gauged from the fact that barriers can creep in in the following shapes:

♦ barriers in the communicator;
♦ barriers in the message;
♦ barriers in the media;
♦ barriers in the recipients;
♦ barriers in feedback; and
♦ barriers in the context.

Barriers in the Communicator

Here are *four* of the common erroneous assumptions held by communicators:

1. Some people assume or believe that:
   ♦ communication flows from them only when *they* choose to do so. But in reality, there are other unconscious or unintentional cues emanating from them that also send out signals, often

conveying the opposite of, or different from, what they think they communicate;

◆ all messages are verbal. But there are vast number of messages they keep sending out through the non-verbal media;

◆ words have intrinsic, and fixed, meanings. Actually, meaning lies not in the words, but in the people. Words mean whatever the people who use, or hear, them want them to mean;

◆ the recipients are passive receptacles of their messages. Actually, whenever they say something, or communicate in other forms, complex *reactions* are evoked in the recipients in unpredictable ways.

The communicators must understand who his recipients are—especially in terms of their motivations, attitudes, intellectual levels, etc.

2. Many communicators, specially the impervious ones, do not realize the value of feedback. They thus remain oblivious to the world around them.

3. Some communicators pre-judge what is being stated to them, jump to conclusions, and then rush out with 'solutions or directives'. This has the effect of shutting off the communication itself.

> *...and the greatest mistake. . .is judging before I understand, and acting before I really understand either the big picture or another person. Once the collective monologue begins, you start investing more and more of your ego into your convictions and into your own need to be understood. The other just isn't listening.*
>
> —Stephen R. Covey, *The 7 Habits of Highly Effective People*

4. Then there are some communicators who do not care whether proper understanding is being achieved. Worse still, they intentionally indulge in obfuscation, that is, sending out confusing messages because that is what they want, either to create the impression that they are profound or to trick the recipients for some reason.

Barriers in the Message

Words mean different things to different people—especially when the sender and the recipient have different views of life and the world.

Words are simply labels we use to describe or symbolize our personal view of reality. One study reports that for each of the 500 most frequently used words in the English language, the *Oxford English Dictionary* records an average of *twenty-eight* separate and different meanings![3]

And this is further complicated by the fact that, besides simply serving as labels, words are capable of evoking a vast array of emotions that may bias the interpretation of a message.

Then, there are difficulties arising from non-specific phrases. 'As soon as possible', for instance, may mean to some: 'when you have time, you may do this', and to some others: 'drop everything and do this'.

To further deepen the problem of understanding words, there are the jargon, slangs, colloquialisms. These are developed both by the 'occupational experts' and members of the 'informal social groups' in an organization—either to simplify and speed up communication or to enhance their sense of belonging within the group and to impress outsiders. Just listen to the 'lingo' your children use. Almost every traditional word you and I know has been given an abbreviated or more 'hip' sound. It would only be after a few days' efforts on your part to 'tune-in' that you would be able to recognize their expressions! These do add to a sense of puzzlement not only among 'outsiders' but sometimes even among the 'insiders' who are not yet fully initiated into the group.

Yet another problem of communication is the constant tug of war between the spoken words and the non-verbal expressions. Often there is a conflict between what the words seek to convey and what the non-verbal expressions end up conveying simultaneously! Our eyes, hands, facial expressions and body posture serve either to support or contradict our words.

Even when no words are employed, our non-verbal expressions convey distinct messages (about which we usually remain oblivious). Some examples:

S.No.	Posture or Behaviour	Message Conveyed[4]
1.	Sitting on the edge of the chair, or leaning towards the other person	Eagerness or attentiveness
2.	Wringing hands or fiddling with pencil, etc.	Either nervousness or deliberate ignoring
3.	Nodding the head	Agreement or encouragement
4.	Failing to attend a meeting in spite of oral support	Deliberate ignoring or contradictory behaviour
5.	Arriving late at the workplace every morning	Job dissatisfaction or bad personal organization
6.	Sitting far away from other people in a meeting	Desire not to participate, or superciliousness or inferiority complex
7.	Failing to recognize the significance of how something is being said	Lack of personal belief in what is being said

Verbal and non-verbal cues interrelate to create a total message.[5] In face-to-face communication, only seven per cent of the content of a typical message is transmitted by words; the remaining 93 per cent is transmitted by non-verbal expressions: tone of the voice (38 per cent), and facial expressions (55 per cent).

Barriers in the Media

You should decide whether your message should be sent orally or in writing. Inappropriate choice leads to misunderstandings. For example, it is wrong to transmit a large series of complex and important numbers over the telephone, since chances of errors are too great. Similarly, it is wrong to provide a message in writing if its contents are so complex or contentious that a preparatory discussion is necessary.

Barriers in the Recipient

People hear what they want to hear, and see what they want to see. This is conditioned by cultural background, bias, poor listening habits, emotional state or differing perspectives. Let us briefly discuss these:

Our Cultural Background   Our cultural background and past experiences with people and the world around us give shape to the meanings we attach to words, gestures and trends of events. These add up to a storehouse of pre-conceived notions; they goad us to hear what we want to hear, not what the other person is saying!

Poor Listening This is another recipient-caused barrier in communication, which is very common. It includes *(a)* not hearing what was said; *(b)* hearing only part of what was said; and *(c)* hearing information incorrectly.

One of the causes for poor listening is your emotional state.

Research suggests that a typical person listens at about 25 per cent efficiency only.[6] The main reason for this is that most people talk at about 125 words a minute, whereas they listen and understand at about four times (480 words) that rate. Thus, while the speaker goes on speaking, our mind can wander and think about many other things.

Differing Perspectives If the communicator and the recipient do not share the same perspective about the message, it is most likely to lead to misunderstanding. This is usually found between different functional groups, such as accountants, marketing people, production people, quality control people, maintenance people, etc.

Barriers in Feedback

Since feedback itself is a message, it suffers from the same causes of misunderstanding that apply to any other message, as discussed above. However, there are two special problems that are linked with feedback:

♦ if feedback does not follow the original message quickly enough, its value is lost; and
♦ if it is not specific enough, its relationship to the message that triggered it in the first place will not be understood.

Barriers in the Context

Messages do not occur in a vacuum; they occur in a context—of space and time. Experience tells us that the 'when' and the 'where' of communication do influence the 'how' of communication. Every single communication can—thanks to barriers—trigger off *six different messages:*

+ what you *mean* to say;
+ what you *actually* say;
+ what the other person *hears*;
+ what the other person *thinks* he hears;
+ what the other person *says*; and
+ what you *think* the other person says.

Some Suggestions for Ensuring Better Communication

The accent should be on *persuasion*. In simple words, it means that you transact your sessions with the communicatee in such a manner and spirit that he accepts—willingly and independently—what you had set out to suggest or recommend. (This is very different from 'manipulation' under which the communicator cunningly leads the communicatee 'up the garden path' into thinking that what he has accepted is his own view whereas it is actually that of the manipulator.)

The most important element of persuasive communication is *good listening*. Much of communication depends on listening *empathetically*, not so much on talking. It deserves emphasis that: 'One communicates the most when one listens more than one talks.'

Effective Listening

A graffiti on a London bulletin board once had an excellent piece of wisdom. It read:

> *Smart people speak from experience*
> *Smarter people, from experience, do not speak.*

And I would like to add: 'They (the smarter ones) listen!'

> *...reach deep inside and sublimate your need to be understood, and really work to get into the frame of mind and heart of the other. It's listening empathetically, and having the discipline and patience to simply hold your tongue. It's constantly relearning the anatomy lesson that we have two ears and one mouth, and we should use them accordingly. (Only one of the three holes closes!)*
>
> —Stephen R. Covey, *The 7 Habits of Highly Effective People*

It has been estimated by researchers that a typical manager spends about 80 per cent of his waking hours communicating in one form or another. Out of this, about nine per cent of his time is spent in writing, 16 per cent in reading, 30 per cent in speaking, and 45 per cent in listening. Yet of all these skills, most people pay very little attention to building up their listening skills.[7]

We have already enumerated poor listening as one of the serious barriers to communication. Let us see here what havoc it can play both with the communicator and the communicatee if both are poor listeners.

♦ In the case of a 'poor-listening' *communicator* :
  • he can never get adequate information and feedback;
  • therefore, his communication, at best, can only be a shot in the dark; and
  • in the end, he either fails to put across what he wants to or what does get across is distorted beyond recognition.

♦ In the case of a 'poor-listening' *communicatee:*
  • he never gets to know or comprehend even simple messages; his own emotional or other filters distort the message;
  • interested parties can use him as an easy prey to their motivated distortions; and
  • avoidable and unfortunate tensions, and misunderstandings continue to dominate the scene.

The prime responsibility for building up a good listening culture lies with the communicator. Good listening can be promoted in the following manner:

Take Care of Your 'Body Language'   Merely saying that you believe in 'open door' communication, and that anyone is free and welcome to come and tell you whatever he wishes to is not enough. People will feel like coming to you to share information or to unburden their thoughts and worries only if you show that you really *mean* what you say about open-door communication. This is eloquently manifested by the interest or indifference you show to others in the course of your communication with them (through your spoken responses or body language).

You must acquire a convincing reputation that you do pay attention when someone comes to speak with you.

Go for Perceptive Listening Listening is not accomplished solely through what is being said. Try to concentrate on:

+ *how* something is being said;
+ what is *not* being said; and
+ the *body language* of the speaker.

This habit of 'extra-sensory' listening can open up to you a whole lot of information much vaster than what you can get from only the spoken words.

Facts, while obviously important, are not the only thing to listen to. Subjective data, such as thoughts, feelings, ideas, opinions and beliefs, also provide important information.

When it is Your Turn to Put Across Your Message

Set the Stage You can do this if you:

+ create a pleasant, business-like setting. A quiet, comfortable office is one of the best places to establish a good communication environment;
+ minimize interruptions. Limit telephone calls and visits by others so that your focus is on your communicatees; and
+ pick a good time when both you and your communicatees are neither too tired nor overburdened with other worries or diversionary thoughts.

Take up Your Proposals When They are Ripe Examine the following questions critically and candidly:

+ is the proposal fully developed?
+ even if your people accept it, is it possible to act on it *now?*
+ are your people prepared for acting on it *now?*
+ even if the proposal is adopted now for action, will it conflict with other projects already under way?

Listen—and Learn
Nobody is More Persuasive Than a Good Listener

Listening is the most important communication skill. It's even more important than good presentation or writing skills.

- Why is it so important? You can't know everything. Listening to others is the best way to learn. Since you are not sitting on top of a mountain, and thus not getting a bird's-eye view of what you ought to do, your next best bet is to find out by listening to others. Train yourself to listen to others a lot. Listen to employees, customers, friends and critics. You may choose not to act on any or some of their views or suggestions, but at least hear them out.
- Listening is an active sport. It is important to listen to—not just hear—what others say. When you're merely hearing, you're thinking about other things, or what you'll say next. Active listeners, on the other hand, concentrate. They question and prod. They give thoughtful, concise responses; they lean forward to show interest; they smile, frown when appropriate, and keep looking the other person in the eye.
- Listening empowers. Attentive listening in an atmosphere that encourages frank and courageous expression of views and suggestions leads to a sense of belonging among the employees who are listened to. Gradually, they become chastened with a sense of responsibility about what they say, specially when they see that some of their suggestions are being taken seriously and/or being acted upon. Ultimately, the organization gets 'empowered' by useful ideas that emanate from such 'listening-based' communication; also, the employees feel empowered since they are 'listened to' with respect and attention.

If the answer to these questions is 'yes', your proposal is probably ripe enough for being communicated with your people.

Lead the Communicatees to Your Point   For this you must remember the following:

- a desirable pre-requisite is that communication between you and your people should be an ongoing process—not one that you switch on only when a crisis appears or an important announcement has to be made. Such a practice creates an atmosphere of 'relaxed interactions'; and relaxed interactions make it much easier for you to share even difficult messages with a greater degree of equanimity and acceptance;

♦ take your time, especially when you are trying to get across new or complicated concepts;

♦ unfold your ideas bit by bit; don't spring them on your people without a preamble or proper conditioning; and

♦ a good technique is to ask questions and invite questions and comments on the ideas or issues you wish to talk about. Provide freedom to them to speak frankly, and gently guide them to think and speak constructively.

Don't Make the Issue Bigger Than it Really is It may be that:

♦ in your anxiety to inject importance or enthusiasm among your communicatees, you fall a prey to the temptation of painting a larger-than-life picture of the issue at hand. Be matter-of-fact; neither minimize nor exaggerate;

♦ the temptation to exaggerate—to stretch the benefits or minimize the problems—becomes strong when you have a particularly difficult proposition to get across. You must never do that. Instead, you should frankly and realistically admit the difficulties and risks as you perceive them. This may attract greater attention from the communicatees, and may even motivate them to try and meet the challenge!

♦ messages about proposals or projects get exaggerated or distorted when passed from one group to another. Therefore, communicate personally, to the entire group of concerned individuals.

Tell the Whole Story You will find:

♦ it is far wiser, and more efficient, that you yourself give out the correct and adequate version, with proper emphasis of your choice. If you don't, the full, and possibly the distorted, version is bound to come out eventually—thanks to the grapevine;

♦ if you believe that some part of your message is likely to be unpopular, be sure to give that portion your meticulous attention, and to communicate that fully and honestly—without any attempt to gloss over it or to lighten it. Such frank disclosure creates greater credibility for you, throws a challenge to your people, and may, possibly, secure their commitment to meet the challenge;

There is a time to speak and a time to keep quiet. There are things to tell and things not to tell. But it is an excellent rule to practise frankness in all dealings and association with others, whether in business or socially. The frank person treads a firm bridge crossing a river, while the secretive person charily steps from stone to stone.

—B.C. Forbes, quoted in *Readers' Digest.*

But do Accentuate the 'Positives' You are Positive About   What is most important is that:

♦ you do firmly believe in what you are trying to convey to your people. Any lack of conviction on your part is bound to reveal itself to the searching eyes and ears of your people; and

♦ be sure to lay out the long-term benefits you are positive about, while you tell your people about the unpopular actions or results related with the proposal.

Give the Communicatee His Say   Especially when some 'heat' has been generated while you are communicating, you may feel like cutting off your communicatee in order to put across your own point of view. But a calmer and more persuasive approach is far more effective. You must:

♦ keep yourself open to accepting the communicatee's views and suggestions if they merit such attention; however

♦ you will do well to insist, in a gentle but firm manner, that the discussion must take place in a rational, unemotional spirit and tone.

Itemize the Message, and Back-track   If you watch carefully while communicating you will find that:

♦ it helps the communicatee to comprehend and remember your message if you break it up in clear-cut items;

♦ you can note whether your message is going across to your communicatees by watching their expressions. You can thus adjust your style of speaking, and your body language. Accordingly, you should vary your style: the pitch of your voice, the sequence of the message, your body signals, etc.;

♦ if you feel you are not getting across, or you have not got across fully, repeat your message in such ways that occur to you to be better. Try to anticipate objections, and 'cover' them in your communication before they are actually voiced. This saves you the botheration of 'rescuing' your message from battering, and goes a long way in making your message more acceptable.

Project Yourself Into Your Listeners Mind You must project yourself into the susceptibilities of your communicatee in order to understand his difficulties and hesitations, and to anticipate how he is going to react to your message.

Get Inside Their Skin

Whether you're trying to sell a product, please a customer, motivate an employee, or get along with someone, you'll do better when you put yourself in the other person's shoes. To begin to do that, ask the following questions:

- what experiences does the other person bring to this interaction?
- what is the other person trying to achieve?
- what is the other person trying to avoid?
- who else does the other person have to answer to? and
- what will it take the other person to consider the encounter with you a success?

Don't fulfill people's wishes blindly, but do what you can.

Be Sensitive About Timing Your communication of authentic facts must precede—not follow—the garbled versions thrown up by the grapevine. Once people get hold of the garbled versions, the task of clearing misconceptions and convincing people about the correct facts becomes stupendous—sometimes a losing battle.

Obtain Nuances Getting factual reports is only one part of feedback. What is more important is to obtain the nuances, true and hidden meanings, feelings and beliefs behind the facts being reported.

Feedback

The single most important method for ensuring good communication is feedback.

Communication without feedback is like a shot in the dark. When we seek feedback, we may, in many instances, be shocked at the kind of impact our so-called effective communication has made on the communicatees. However, feedback cannot be had just for the asking. It requires creation of an environment based on mutual trust and freedom as perceived by the communicatees for speaking out the truth to the communicator.

Feedback must be two way—from you to your people and from them to you. One most important precondition for promoting and sustaining two-way feedback is that *you* take the initiative of being frank and open. The more *transparent* your people perceive you to be in your intentions and statements, the more willingly they will open up to you. Authentic feedback sharpens your sensibilities—even while the communication session is in progress—as to *what* and *how* to communicate! It opens your eyes to whether you have communicated at all; and if not, it tells you what you should do about it.

In other words, feedback helps us in modifying *what* and *how* we say things in terms of the 'real time' responses we get from our listeners. It leads us to greater accuracy, credibility and effectiveness in our communication.

Feedback also automatically promotes multi-directional communication—upward, lateral and downward, thus fulfilling a very important pre-requisite of good communication.

Grapevine

Most of the so-called rumours can be traced to a breakdown in communication. Every day—in a dozen different ways—what the superiors say (or fail to say) shapes and colours their subordinates' opinions on matters that concern them, or are of interest to them. If answers to the related queries are not made available to them in adequate measure, or promptly enough, the grapevine is only too eager to oblige.

GOSSIP: The only thing that travels faster than E-Mail
—Angie Papadakis in *Readers' Digest*, April 1995.

Sometimes difficulties are created by too much confidentiality—even when the matters may be of great concern to the people down the line. Bosses should closely re-examine their judgement about confidentiality. They must ask themselves: are they overdoing this confidentiality stuff? This should, in turn, depend on how much of the information can be disclosed. Otherwise, the grapevine is going to churn up a garbled version anyway. The more open you are, the more others will believe you, and the more *they* will open up.

For attacking a rumour, the best bet is not to attempt to kill it, but to reach its causes and tackle them. Sometimes management can 'use' the grapevine by consciously injecting its side of the story by making it appear as a 'leakage' through seemingly 'careful carelessness'. Such leakages are devoured with relish—and thus they serve the not-so-ignoble purpose of balancing the mischief against the truth of the story!

Interpersonal Factors

Climate, Trust and Credibility No matter how efficiently you use communication techniques, they will still not produce the desired results if the interpersonal elements are not conducive. These interpersonal elements comprise climate, trust and credibility.

Climate relates to the relationship that exists between you and your subordinates which, in turn, depends upon how you treat each other, and how this reciprocal behaviour is interpreted. This combination of attitudes comprises the climate of interpersonal relationships; and it can either promote, restrict or distort communication at the workplace.

In the final analysis, communication is a give-and-take relationship between the communicator and the recipient; it is meant to produce a reciprocal effect on both parties. A major characteristic of all such relationships is trust. Distrust and suspicion between the parties can only lead to defensiveness, and inhibit open expressions. In such situations, even innocent and straightforward messages are looked upon with bias, and reactions to such messages are overloaded with counter-biases. The ultimate effect is that the chances of effective communication get nullified.

Closely related to trust, credibility refers to the *perceived characteristics of the source of information*. These characteristics may or may not be possessed by the source of information but, what is important, they are *attributed* to that source by individual recipients of the

message. In other words, the credibility of a source of information i
recipient-determined.

The characteristics that are the essence of credibility are: honesty
competence, forward-looking attitude and inspiring leadership
When a communicator is perceived as trustworthy, knowing what h
is talking about, dynamic and sincere, and having a sense of direction
others will see him as credible. And when he has credibility, peopl
are likely to comply with his requests, advice or instructions.

Credibility is one of the most vital ingredients of successful inter
personal communication. It can often cause insurmountabl
problems too. When you communicate, often your people do no
listen to your words or read your message; they primarily assess you
record of the actions and conduct to see the extent of gap, if any
between what you preach and what you practice. Only if your peopl
find that you can be trusted—or if their *perception* of you is on th
whole positive—will they take note of your current communication
Otherwise, no matter what the content of your current message, o
the excellent communication techniques you may apply, nothing shal
register in the minds of your people. In fact, the more you try, th
more hostility and derision you are likely to evoke if you do not enjo
credibility in the eyes of your people.

Express an Interest in Others   Part of any communication strateg
is showing an interest in others. People respond positively—the
can't help but respond—when you show you are sincerely intereste
in them. Smile at them. Learn their names. Remember their birthday
In fact, the more interest you take in others, the less bothersom
you may find your own problems.

It is not only wise but necessary that you take a candid view of th
interpersonal factors associated with you and your environment, an
do something to bring these factors to an acceptable level if you wis
to emerge as an effective communicator.

Conclusion

Communication permeates every aspect of management. In fact, it
inherent in every process where human beings interact. It is a proce
that goes on, on its own—irrespective of whether you will it or not

No amount of resources, plans of actions or efforts can be made dynamic without the alchemy of communication.

However, 'proper' communication, that is, a message reaching its target without distortion and evoking the desired reaction, is not easy. It is very delicately balanced on numerous equally delicately-balanced factors. Most of these factors are related to the imponderables of human behaviour and psychology. The challenge to you as a communicator lies in your adopting within your ongoing management style an integrated synthesis of these delicately-balanced factors.

Communication is not just a question of ensuring that your information or instructions are conveyed up or down the line in precise terms. It has very much to do with feelings and ideas, with morale and motivation—on both sides. It is certainly not merely a matter of your perfecting only the techniques by which messages can be put across.

In order for communication to play its real role of ensuring understanding and motivation among people for contributing their best, it is essential that all facets of an organization are based on clear, and clearly-speltout, objectives, and on sincerity of purpose. It also requires mutual trust. There must exist an innate faith in the trustworthiness of the superiors in the organization.

For this, it is not necessary nor possible that a honey-moon relationship must exist among people at various levels. In fact, you could be tough negotiators, hard task-masters, and you may sometimes have to engage yourself in trials of strength. All that can be understandable and acceptable—and can even be conducive to effective communication—as long as there is mutual trust between you and your people about the intentions and integrity on both sides.

It follows naturally that, after all the song and dance about perfection in the tools and techniques of communication, the credibility of the communicator as perceived by the communicatees is the very essence of communication.

Test Yourself

How Do You Rate As a Listener?[8]

Few virtues are more prized and less practised than good listening. This checklist, though certainly not complete, will help you gauge your own listening habits. Try to answer each question objectively.

When taking part in an interview or group discussion, do you:

S.No.		*Usually*	*Sometimes*	*Seldom*
1.	Prepare your self physically by sitting facing the speaker and making sure you can hear?	( )	( )	( )
2.	Watch the speaker as well as listen to him?	( )	( )	( )
3.	Decide from the speaker's appearance and delivery whether or not what he has to say is worthwhile?	( )	( )	( )
4.	Listen primarily for ideas and underlying feelings?	( )	( )	( )
5.	Determine your own bias, if any, and try to allow for it?	( )	( )	( )
6.	Keep your mind on what the speaker is saying?	( )	( )	( )
7.	Interrupt immediately if you hear a statement you feel is wrong?	( )	( )	( )
8.	Make sure before answering that you have taken in the other person's point of view?	( )	( )	( )
9.	Try to have the last word?	( )	( )	( )
10.	Make a conscious effort to evaluate the logic and credibility of what you hear?	( )	( )	( )

Scoring Key

On Questions: 1, 2, 4, 5, 6, 8 and 10:

For 'Usually'	give yourself	10 marks
For 'Sometimes'	give yourself	5 marks
For 'Seldom'	give yourself	0 marks

On Questions: 3, 7 and 9:

For 'Usually'	give yourself	0 marks
For 'Sometimes'	give yourself	5 marks
For 'Seldom'	give yourself	10 marks

What Your Score Means

A score below 70 indicates you have developed some bad listening habits.

A score of 70 to 85 suggests that you listen well but there is room for improvement.

A score of 90 or above means you are an excellent listener.

SEVEN

Dynamics of
Interpersonal Relations

CHAPTER OBJECTIVES

- Discuss the relational aspects of human resource management, focusing on how managers remain buffeted by inter-relational onslaughts
- Analyze the sensitive spots in workplace relationships
- Discuss the problems of 'difficult' subordinates, peers and the boss

---

Introduction

On his journey toward effectiveness, a manager depends upon several back-ups. Some are infrastructural such as well-balanced plants, machineries, technology, work-place facilities and manpower. These are provided by the owners of the enterprise. But several others are integral to the manager; these the manager acquires on his own—by learning from others, and from his own experiences distilled through grappling with problems and opportunities. He tries to put them in use through decision-making, communication, delegation, leadership, etc. But no matter how 'efficient' the manager may be in using the managerial tools, he can reach 'effectiveness' only when he obtains cooperative and collaborative support from his fellow employees, comprising his subordinates, his peers and his boss.

Within an organization, people fall into different 'structures' of relationships. The 'work structure' defines who is expected to do what. The 'authority structure' defines who directs whom and is responsible for what. The 'status structure' determines one's rights and liabilities. The 'prestige structure' defines the extent to which one may enjoy deferential behaviour from others. And the 'friendship structure' defines the informal relationships which people may have with each other. Each of these structures has an impact on the interpersonal relationships at the workplace. Where these are, on the whole, negative, they lead to emotional disturbance, general loss of motivation and, ultimately, even a rejection by the person of his own self-esteem, his own self!

The Profile of a Typical Manager

Typical managers, in a way, remain in a state of suspended animation. The environment in which they function is one of a 'conditioned equilibrium'. A tenuous balance is maintained due to the multiple, and mostly maddening, forces pulling each other in various directions—the demands of subordinates, bosses and peers. Most of the managers usually feel highly constrained and squeezed from all sides due to the following reasons among others:

1. Their superiors want high standards of performance. Their subordinates clamour for the fulfilment of their ambitious, self-seeking and nagging demands. And between these two, the managers are often hemmed in by a spate of (uninvited) sermons and 'specialist' advice from their superiors as well as outsiders.
2. They are torn between the multitude of demands on the one hand and not enough authority—or not enough freedom to use authority—on the other.
3. The subordinates are usually competent, but they seldom work with motivation, or anywhere near their full potential. As a result, greater part of the burden of accomplishing tasks falls upon these managers.
4. They are often pulled into meetings with the boss or subordinates; and most of these turn out to be a drain, if not a waste, of their time.
5. Despite the organization's high-tech information system, managers rarely get to know the *why* of the developments or of the important decisions. Although they may know *what* is going on, or is going to be done, sometimes they come to know of even routine developments—and decisions—from their subordinates! And the irony is that such lapses are not intentional; they are simply manifestations of others taking them for granted.

Of course, this description is not universal; but the variations in their permutations and combinations are indeed universal. The unfortunate outcome of these situations is that a significant gap persists between their performance and potential as well as that of the department, in addition to straining interpersonal relations.

Authority vs Influence

This problem is only a manifestation of an age-old tussle between authority and influence. Has authority alone ever worked in the sense of establishing self-sustaining systems?

Even in the days of despots or all-powerful rulers, coercive authority had to be used at every twist and turn in order to obtain the desired efforts on the part of those who were 'governed' by such authority. But the effect of authority was always short-lived. History is witness to the unbroken chain of proven facts that such 'power' used in any form and at any time has always been resented, and rebelled against whenever possible.

Authority is the legitimate right to command the subordinates' or followers' actions, thoughts, opinions or behaviour. It is, however, different from power in the sense that normally it is not used despotically. It is granted by others, or created by a person for an understandable purpose which is obvious to all concerned.

Influence motivates others to produce results due to appealing reason and personal examples presented by someone, without direct use of force or command.

Managing by authority implies direct control and manoeuvre for obtaining desired results—with, or without the willing cooperation of others. Managing by influence, on the other hand, hinges on willing cooperation of others emanating from their getting convinced about the rationale of the desired results. A manager's influence also depends on an ongoing—perhaps, growing—belief on the part of the subordinates that he can 'deliver the goods', and that by following his lead the subordinates can benefit in several ways—irrespective of whether the leader occupies a high position or not. What is important in the sphere of influence is *stature*, not status.

We know that a vast number of people genuinely believe that use of authority—in an explicit or implied manner—is essential. Authority continues to be required and desired, even by the contemporary rights-conscious breed of employees. But the 'manner' in which it is used determines its success or failure. It is successful where it is *not* rubbed in. The person who is successful in the use of his authority does his home-work to ensure that his propositions are backed by logic, reasonableness and natural appeal. One good test of successful use of authority is that it does not have to be enforced—or used frequently! Whenever authority has worked well, it has always been used in a more subtle manner. The name of that 'manner' is influence.

The 'boss' image has now become obsolete; it has been replaced by the 'leader' image. The usual impression is that a shop-floor 'executive' manager is endowed with a great deal of authority (and power) over a large number of subordinates. This contrasts with, say, a back-room scientist in the R&D department who usually has no subordinates. But if we carefully study how each of them actually gets things done it would (but should not) come as a surprise that both of them rely more upon their influencing powers than upon the 'authority-profile' bestowed upon them by the company's organization-chart.

In dealing with interpersonal relations, the first step for a manager therefore, is to understand the gap that separates his authority from his influence. You as a manager use only a *fraction* of the influence you are capable of. A manager is never without influence, whether he is conscious of it or not! When you consciously use only a part of your influence, the remaining part that you do not use still affects your work, in the sense that you are in any case using that part unconsciously—either less effectively or counter-productively.

However, influence must not be confused with manipulation. Manipulation is a cunning, premeditated move by which the manipulator 'tricks' the other person into saying or doing things in the belief that that is what *he* wants, whereas it is actually what the manipulator had set out to achieve. Influence is genuine; manipulation is counterfeit in its content.

Let us, therefore, note that *(a)* managerial effectiveness should rely more on interpersonal relations; and *(b)* interpersonal relations should rely more on influencing than on authority.

Some Pre-requisites of Interpersonal Relationship

1. A golden rule about interpersonal relationship is that the initiator must treat others with dignity. And before he can treat others with dignity, *he must be deserving enough to treat himself with dignity* if he does not possess sufficient and transparent self-respect the respect he shows to others might be mistaken as flattery. And his self-respect can be derived from—and can thrive only on—his possessing enough ingredients for positive self-regard.

which he can build up through the following efforts for self-development:

- he should *objectively* recognize his strengths and weaknesses. Having recognized them, he should continue to strengthen his strengths, and weaken his weaknesses;
- he should never permit complacence in regard to his knowledge, skills and overall competence. He must be up-to-date and willing to learn new developments in his area of expertise; and
- he must strive for creating a strong relevance and mutually-satisfying linkage between his capabilities and the needs of the organization he works for.

2. He must be prepared to *accept people as they are, not as he would like them to be.* And then, his approaches toward them should be conducive to building such bridges of understandings and feasible adjustments on both sides that they would finally lead to establishment of an 'influential' relationship.
3. In his efforts to please others, however, one tends to vary his roles according to what one thinks others want him to play. He thus becomes different things to different people. In doing so, he loses touch with himself, whereas it is important that *he must remain himself.*
4. He must always be *non-evaluative and objective* in his day-to-day dealings with the people he interacts with.
5. When required, he should *confront issues*, not people.
6. He must show people the same *courteous attention* that he expects from them.
7. He must foster an environment of *openness and trust.*

A Manager's Approach Towards his Subordinates

Establish Open Communication

The key to establishing an influence-oriented relationship, obviously, is open communication.

It is interesting that almost all managers today would like to claim that they believe in open communication. But a closer examination of the actual situation invariably discloses that subordinates *rarely* feel free to communicate with their bosses. Merely saying that you believe in open communication is not enough; your actions, body language during the interactions, and the actions and attitudes you adopt later on must convince your subordinates that you do mean what you say.

When adequate two-way open communication is lacking, your subordinates are usually reticent about disclosing their opinions and suggestions about the organizational problems encountered at their level. They may silently 'hear' your well-intentioned instructions, but they may not 'listen' to them for taking any action. Thus, they may fail to execute the task properly because they are either unsure about how to go about things or they disagree with your instructions. This amounts to the task getting sabotaged—though unwittingly.

To sum up, your approach towards your subordinates must be based on:

♦ truly open communication from you;
♦ your manner of actual interactions evoking confidence among your subordinates that your claim for openness is genuine; and
♦ the results of such communication proving, over time, to be mutually trustworthy and beneficial.

Here are some suggestions—some of them have been discussed earlier—for concretizing the above requirements:

Listen More Than Talk   The more you listen, the more you learn, and, therefore, the more you know *what* really you need to say, and do.

Do not Rush out With Your Own Diagnosis and Prescription

Find out first what the real problem is, and explore *with* your subordinate till you get to the bottom of the problem. Check the temptation to 'play the doctor'; lead your subordinate, with helpful goading, into diagnosing as well as finding out practical solutions on his own.

Curb Your Tendency to Highlight Only the Handicaps and Shortcomings (both in the infrastructure and in your people)   If you fail to do so, you may lose sight of the strengths and assets that are available among your subordinates, and you may be perceived as a pessimist or a cynic. This militates against creation of harmonious or trusting relationships between you and your subordinates. If, on the other hand, you remain equally aware of the strengths and assets (as you should be of the handicaps and weaknesses), you would stay more balanced, and would most likely feel the urge to build further on the assets and strengths. And, you should involve your subordinates to such an extent that *they* come up with their own suggestions for improving themselves.

It is these kinds of interactions that go a long way in establishing congenial relationships based on truly open communication, without anyone having to beat any drums about it.

Always Provide the Rationale

This is a natural corollary to open communication. A proposed project and its related decisions are likely to proceed well when *prior* conscious efforts are made to provide to the concerned people the logical basis of the project or the decisions. In order that the concerned people feel involved and committed, the rationale should be 'sold' to them. This step leads to involvement which, in turn, paves the way to commitment (even when there may be disagreements in some cases).

Provide Role-clarity

Everybody talks about the desirability and essentiality of role-clarity; but few managers are able to provide it. This is so partly because people do not know how to go about it in practical terms, and partly because clarifying roles seems like an onerous task—even a threat. I offer here a somewhat unconventional plan which is simple to implement, and may convince you that it involves no threat. It involves the following *five* stages:

1. Invite your subordinates, one at a time, preferably at a time when the departmental climate is relatively free from tensions or misunderstandings. Put them at ease by telling them at the outset that this is a 'man-to-man' chat for promoting clearer understanding about the jobs people do in your section/department.
2. Invite your subordinate to put himself mentally in *your* position and then tell you what he, from your position, believes are the roles, objectives, priorities, authorities, opportunities and constraints of:
   - your boss (that is, his boss's boss);
   - his boss (that is, you);
   - himself (as visualized by his immediate boss, that is you); and
   - his own subordinates (as understood by him).

3. Because of its sheer unconventionality, it will initially require some cajoling on your part to get your subordinate to open up. But once both of you get started, it will yield a rich harvest of eye-opening 'discoveries'. You will find amazing gaps between your and your subordinate's understandings about the roles that people are required to play as seen through your subordinate's eyes. The crucial part of this exercise is that you must fill in the gaps in such a convincing manner that your subordinate gains a new understanding about: *(a)* the goals, and priorities the various members in your department really seek; *(b)* the opportunities and constraints they have to contend with; and *(c)* the canopy of authority and responsibilities they possess.

4. During this period of interactions, a certain 'chemical reaction' is set into motion. After his initial surprise (even disbelief), your subordinate's skepticism and resistance toward you may dissolve considerably, once he is convinced that you are serious about ushering in a new kind of down-to-earth role-clarity that he can understand and live with.

5. The subordinate may ultimately believe that the roles clarified as a result of your interaction with him are true. Once that belief sets in, your subordinate gets a 'helicopter view' of the inter-dependence of roles operating in the entire department, and he begins to see for the first time the significance of *his own role*. This in itself has a great potential for filling him with a new sense of responsibility and commitment which, in turn, leads him toward playing his own role properly.

Seek Agreement on Targets and Standards of Performance

This is a logical extension of the role-clarity exercise suggested above. When the manager and his subordinates interact in a cohesive and participative spirit for setting their targets and standards of performance, a closer tie based on involvement for *shared purpose* can set in at their subconscious level. Inherent in such an interaction is also the challenge for achievement. When this challenge is met, the resultant exuberance may further bind them together. This is also the stage at which the manager acquires a valuable measure of influence on his subordinates.

Setting targets and standards of performance are usually associated with achieving objectives. But they have been suggested here in the context of interpersonal relations as well—in the belief that work itself is one of the best catalysts for bonding interpersonal relations.

Practise Delegation

Three aspects of delegation which are important in this context are the following:

1. Each delegated task must have an element of challenge for the subordinate's current level of knowledge and skill. The performance of such a task should 'stretch' him and result in his development.
2. The subordinate must be allowed sufficient independence for working out his own ways and means for accomplishing the task within the agreed parameters of quality, cost and time.
3. Each assignment must lead to the subordinate's progressive 'independence' from his dependence upon his leader.

The relevance of the above suggestions are derived from work-related 'relational' dynamics—arising from sharing of tasks, responsibilities and authority. Again, these intangible benefits do add up to enhancing the influence of the leader over his subordinates.

Some Other Measures

Some other very potent, though seemingly indirect, measures that you should apply are aimed at enhancing the subordinate's self-esteem. These are the following *four*:

1. Take a close look at whether your subordinates feel you are unapproachable. If yes, do your best to remove such an impression. Make yourself accessible. Consider moving closer to your subordinates' work area. Walk over to where the action is rather than expect the 'work' to come to you. But do it gradually; your sudden and frequent visits to your subordinates might be misinterpreted by them to mean that you are unhappy with their working and you are checking up on them.
2. Take time for informal chats with your subordinates. Share some of your personal interests. These help to unfreeze the subordinates, and they begin to feel closer to you.
3. If your subordinates wish to discuss their personal problems with you, be willing to listen—and help them to the extent you can.

However, do not undertake responsibilities for which you are neither trained nor capable.

4. Offer recognition to your subordinates, not only for the results they achieve, but also for noteworthy efforts they make (irrespective of whether they fully achieve the targets or not). Recognition should not hinge upon, or over-emphasize, monetary rewards only—although monetary rewards need not be barred. Such recognition can be in the following forms:

♦ certificates or plaques—with or without cash rewards;
♦ mention at staff meetings, or in the company's newsletter;
♦ assignments to more important or prestigious tasks;
♦ job rotation on important jobs;
♦ more consultation with the subordinate on planning, problem-solving, opportunity-generating matters; and
♦ nominating such subordinates to important seminars and/or on conferences for representing the company.

What About 'Difficult' Subordinates?

One of the most exasperating and demanding features of a manager's job involves his dealing with 'difficult' subordinates. They may be recalcitrant, careless or well-intentioned-but-destruction-prone individuals. These people call for a well-organized approach. They cannot be shouted down or wished away. You can try some of the following approaches with them:

Clarify the Issue   You must first try to understand as to *what* has made the particular subordinate a 'difficult' person. This must be done with a dispassionate frame of mind, without any anger or bias on your part. While taking the necessary corrective measures, you must take a good look at yourself and correct your own style where required. Such an exercise can lead, in quite a few cases, to adjustments resulting in easy and smooth improvements in your interpersonal relations.

You can also try to identify as to which of your people are: *(a)* 'difficult people'; and *(b)* 'people with difficulties'. Keeping this in mind, when you go into the 'what' of the problem, you may even find that there are several cases where individuals started out with difficulties and ended by becoming difficult people!

Some Adjustments in Your Own Style Before you set out to: *(a)* cater to the needs of your people with difficulties; and *(b)* deal with your difficult people, there are a number of things you have to do to your own style of management that would contribute toward minimizing the difficulties you are facing with your subordinates. *Five* such approaches are given below:

1. As explained earlier, you should give more importance to what your subordinates have—and build up on that, rather than depress everybody (including yourself) by moaning about what the subordinates don't have. You should *build* on your subordinates' assets and strengths, and involve them in this exercise.

2. Every time you take a decision that has the potential of affecting a number of people including your subordinates, it is advisable that you consult with them to ensure that all the possible difficulties are out on the table. While you may not be able to—nor do you have to—accommodate everyone's needs, consulting them offers the benefits that: *(a)* difficulties that do crop up are no surprises; *(b)* difficulties that can be avoided are taken care of beforehand; *(c)* all the people who are consulted feel that you do have concern for them; and *(d)* therefore, they are, by implication, committed to the decision that is finally taken.

3. Where you do not set higher standards in your own skill, knowledge, conduct, and behaviour, you cannot expect or get better standards from your subordinates.

4. Generally, we tend to brand an employee as difficult just because he does not conform to group standards in behaviour, attitude, dress, etc. But mere non-conformity does not make an employee difficult; he should be regarded as 'difficult' only when he, or his behaviour, interferes with the progress of his work, or with the work others are doing, or spoils the image, reputation or services of his department or company.

5. If your interpersonal relations have been fairly good (that is, you have been enjoying your subordinates' closeness due to open communication), it should be relatively easier for you to identify those who have difficulties, as distinct from those who are difficult. You should also be able to discern as to what their difficulties are. With this ground work done, you can easily build up your agenda as to what kind and degree of help you should provide to each of your subordinates needing help.

*The 'inside-out' approach to personal and interpersonal effec-
tiveness means to start first with self; even more fundamentally,
to start with the most inside part of self—with your paradigms,
your character and your motives.*

*The inside-out approach says that private victories precede public
victories, that making and keeping promises to ourselves precedes
making and keeping promises to others. It says it is futile to put
personality ahead of character, to try to improve relationships
with others before improving ourselves.*

—Stephen R. Covey, *The 7 Habits of Highly Effective People*

Catering to 'People With Difficulties' People with difficulties are
usually those who: *(a)* have shortcomings in their skill, knowledge
or self-confidence; *(b)* suffer from over-powering personal or other
problems that do not allow them to work or behave properly; or
(c) are poor in their interpersonal relations.

These people *need help*. But the help should be offered *with
understanding*. Great care should be taken to ensure that your manner
of helping them does not make them feel humiliated—even by
implication.

Another thing that must be ensured is that each incident of help
must lead them toward *self-dependenc* they should progressively feel
liberated from the help-giver. This implies that you must not play
'daddy' to your subordinates; you should help them see the crux of
their problem in an objective light. Your advice should lead them
toward alternatives that are practical and encourage them to try out
the one that appears best to them. You must not take over the burden
on yourself.

Dealing With 'Difficult' People

Such people also deserve to be handled very carefully and with great
understanding.

For one thing—and as mentioned earlier—many of these people
may initially have been 'people with difficulties'. If you go deeper into
their case-histories, you may find in most cases that initially they had
some innocent questions or points of view which no one cared to
answer or take note of. Those developed into a 'complaint, and still
later, got transformed into a simmering grievance. The result: these
persons started carrying a chip on their shoulder which soon became
a fixture in their personality.

Let us go through this very simplistic but instructive allegorical story: 'A Complaint's Lament.'

A Complaint's Lament
If only a complaint could speak, it would have spoken like this:

It is not pleasant being a complaint. Nobody really likes me—neither the employee who expresses me nor the Supervisor who hears me!

I wasn't always a complaint. Initially, I was only an innocent question which the employee asked his Supervisor. If the Supervisor had answered me adequately or properly, I would have happily spent the rest of my life as an 'answered question'.

But no, that was not to be. I wasn't answered. What is more, the Supervisor didn't even think much of me because I was so innocent and harmless in my youthful days. He laughed me off. So, I grew into a 'complaint'.

Right now, I am still willing to be resolved. Being a 'resolved complaint' wouldn't be too bad because, then, I shall settle down as a 'happily resolved complaint' (which would be far better than being battered around as a complaint, isn't it?) But it doesn't look like I will be resolved. The Supervisor is still not taking me seriously. The employee believes that the Supervisor has been ignoring me. Well, there appears only one fate in store for me now. I am now going to grow into a 'G r i e v a n c e'. A formal written grievance. And then the fire-works shall begin!

I do believe that I deserved a better life than being turned into an unpleasant grievance. After all I had started out simply as an innocent question. You can't find fault with that, can you? Even when I was compelled to become a complaint, there was still a chance that I could be spared the unpleasant role that awaits me, now that I shall become a grievance. But I guess, when there are poor supervision and human relations, 'questions' are allowed to turn into complaints, and complaints into grievances.

All I would like to say now is: 'I wish I had been born in a better work-unit where such unfortunate things are not allowed to happen!'

Such cases in particular deserve to be handled very delicately. You have the obvious duty of trying to 'open them up' with your own openness and empathy. In case you succeed and get to know the cause for their recalcitrance, you can try to remove the misunderstanding or unfair treatment involved, if any. While doing this, you have to maintain a very delicately-balanced attitude. While you do indicate your willingness to be as reasonable and flexible as possible, you must not give the impression that you are out to appease this difficult person. Such an impression would only encourage the person into thinking that 'being difficult' pays, and thus whet his appetite to become even more difficult. You must strive after leaving no doubt in the person's mind that you are seeking to straighten out things *to help him*, because you do believe in being 'reasonable', and not because you are weak or helpless before him.

Armed with the above attitude, you may wish to try the following *four* steps with your 'difficult' person—*in the order in which they are mentioned:*

1. Try to find out—first, by your own observations and, later, by discussing with the person concerned—as to *what the real cause of the problem is.* Be as objective as possible. Refuse to be put off by the person's hostility (which may even be deliberate). In case the hostility exists because your misjudgement of the person had put him off, remove it as gracefully and ungrudgingly as possible. If it is the person who has misunderstandings, try to remove them. There must be convincing evidence to show that you *really* mean it.

2. Even in cases where the person has compelled you to get annoyed, try—difficult though it is—not to give vent to your feelings before others. Once you let it be known to others that you are terribly annoyed, the battle lines are already drawn and it becomes a battle of obstinacy on both sides. In fact, it can serve as a fuel for the difficult person to take pleasure in annoying you. In any case, the chances of resolution of the problem in a reasonable manner are minimized if you allow your irritation to show.

3. In case the person happens to have a point of view not in accord with yours, and he happens to hold on to it rather strongly, be patient. Do not force him to agree with you even when you believe that you are right. Agree to disagree—for the time being, but only on matters relating to opinions or points of view, and not on the required accomplishment of tasks for the department. This will soften the rigidity, and later developments may bring

him round to your point of view if you have really been right all the time.

4. If none of these approaches works, you have no alternative but to get tough with him. Time has come to let him understand who is the Boss. Get tough about the tasks that have remained unaccomplished due to his recalcitrance. Clarify what those tasks are, spelling out the required standards of performance. Offer the assistance you are expected to extend, and insist on spelling out the time by when the task must be accomplished. Once again, use exhortation, emphasizing that he must not allow his controversy with you to hamper the department's work-plans. Do not raise your voice, be gentle but firm, and leave him in no doubt that you mean business. If he still persists with his intransigence, and fails to accomplish the allotted task, then make *this failure* to accomplish his task as *the issue*. Use whatever disciplinary steps you consider necessary, and you are empowered to take. But make sure that the disciplinary steps you initiate will stick. Any boomerang on such steps (due to interference from 'higher ups') can prove disastrous for you—not only with regard to the difficult person but with your position vis-à-vis the rest of your subordinates.

Tulsidas, in the epic, *Ramayana,* written some five centuries ago, has said: 'बिनु भय होहि न प्रीति'. It means: 'Even love does not survive without fear, i.e., mutual respect!'

A Manager's Approach Towards his Peers

Dealing with peers is perhaps more delicate and tricky than dealing with 'difficult' subordinates or the boss. Peers are one set of people who can, at 'the drop of a coin', as it were, be supportive or detrimental, friendly or hostile, easy to get on with or difficult to fathom. The reason behind such mercurial behaviour-patterns is that each peer is extremely zealous of his independence and prestige vis-à-vis the other; he is very sensitive even to an implied one-upmanship by another peer. Underneath the friendly surface, there flows an almost perpetual current of competition, laced with potential jealousy and envy. Therefore, one must tread very carefully on the ground of interpersonal relationships with peers.

Sign on a Company Bulletin Board

This Firm requires no physical fitness programme. Everyone gets enough exercise jumping to conclusions, flying off the handle, running down the boss, flogging dead horses, knifing friends in the back, dodging responsibility, and pushing their luck.

—*Readers' Digest*, August 1995.

Howsoever tricky and daunting this relationship may appear, there is no getting away from the necessity of nurturing interpersonal relationships with your peers. Positive, productive relationships with peers are essential for ensuring support, information and proper utilization of resources. In the ultimate analysis, it is the collaborative, inter-functional task-performance which becomes essential for achieving targets.

Suggested here are *three* measures each manager would do well to adopt with respect to his peers:

1. You must come across as a team-member, not as a competitor. This requires that you should 'invest' your efforts and time on building relationships with your peers *as individuals*—not merely as collaborators on the work to be done together.

 Some practical suggestions toward this objective are as follows:

 ♦ Identify the existing relationship with your peers
 - Rate the quality of your existing relationships with the peers you interact with regularly—ranging from 'very good' to 'very poor';
 - Then identify what are the specific barriers or problems in your relationships with *each* of your peers, and determine what specific steps you should take to improve them; and
 - Give yourself a time-bound plan for effecting the proposed improvements. Review, and continue with more efforts if necessary till the desired result is achieved.
 ♦ Establish open communication
 - Listen more, speak or emphasize your point less;
 - Give adequate weightage to the peer's views, his suggestions and the difficulties that he may present;
 - Empathize with him; look at the issues or problems from his point of view first. After your peer is satisfied that you have

given due weightage to his views, you may offer yours for his consideration, and then go in for a mutual appreciation and acceptance of one or the other or a modified version. Rely more upon the rationale behind the views than on any subjective aspect; and

- Don't rush matters at this stage. It is crucial that mutual appreciation is established, because this is what is going to set the tone of your relationship for the future as well.

2. You should promote competition between yourself and your peers for meeting challenges—not for seeking prominence. This will foster a healthy team-spirit which, in turn, contains the promise of reinforcing your interpersonal relationships.

3. You must be forthcoming and generous in your appreciation and praise whenever your peer does a truly praiseworthy job, or makes a praiseworthy effort. However, never try to use praise as a gimmick by offering it insincerely for unworthy work or efforts.

The above inputs will go a long way towards making your peers more receptive to you. It will lead to the emergence of a very relaxed relationship between you which will foster an atmosphere of greater willingness on the part of your peers to volunteer information, provide feedback, offer timely warning against mistakes and pitch in beyond the narrow boundaries of responsibilities, to ensure that the work gets done.

In fact, the test of a good interpersonal relationship between peers is that they provide feedback to each other without reservations, that such feedback is accepted without reservations, and that all concerned act upon the feedback without reservations.

A Manager's Approach Towards his Boss

Why Cultivate Relations With the Boss?

In some quarters the following questions are often raised:

- Why should we worry about *our* relations with our boss, about his pleasures or displeasures with us?
- is it not enough that we do our jobs well? or
- If at all, isn't it more important for our boss to do something about *his* relations with us since he is the one who needs our motivation?

Such attitudes are typical of the contemporary breed of employees with their new-found assertiveness and the bright young MBAs, particularly at the time they join an organization.

But the obvious is often ignored. What such people miss is that they too are bosses. No matter which level a person is at, he is both a boss and a subordinate at any given time! Therefore, he cannot escape the truth that all relationships are based on *equal stakes from both sides,* and each relationship is *a two-way affair.*

The truth about any manager is that for effective performance, he is constantly 'selling' his efforts or services to his:

+ fellow workers;
+ customers;
+ suppliers;
+ subordinates; even
+ community.

Then, why should he be so touchy or sensitive about 'getting along well with his boss'?

There are two broad reasons why you must get along well with your boss: one, because you need your boss's support, and the other, because the boss needs the support of his subordinates. One of the most important imperatives of this support from both sides is the creation and maintenance of congenial relations.

The higher a manager goes (or aspires to go), the more necessary—as well as tougher—it becomes to 'sell' himself to his colleagues at vertical and horizontal levels. In that context, congenial interpersonal relationships provide significant help toward ensuring managerial effectiveness.

It is largely through his boss that a manager becomes 'visible' to other senior people in the organization, and thus gets an opportunity for further advancement. However, his chances of being noticed are greatly enhanced if his boss himself is a 'successful' executive, since success does command appreciative attention. Thus a successful boss carries enough weight to take care of his as well as his subordinates' 'visibility' in the organization. Such a boss is often able to secure privileges, rewarding opportunities, better working facilities, greater recognition, and better chances for promotions and other kinds of career advancements for himself and his subordinates.

If, however, the boss is or remains ineffective due to lack of support from his subordinates, the advantages would have to be fought for by the members of his team individually in a posture of continual confrontation. There is a saying—one that is very apt for this situation: 'It is better to contend with a strong enemy than to depend upon a weak friend.'

> *Too many people work under insecure leaders whose paranoia stifles the growth of everyone around them. A leader who runs scared fills the environment with tension, hostility and tentativeness. He batters the self-esteem of his people, frightening them just as he is frightened. He kills incentive in the very people he must motivate in order to achieve his prescribed goals. This kind of manager can cripple an organization, and is a leader in rank only.*
>
> — F. G. Buck of IBM

I hope you have begun appreciating the substance behind these 'home-truths'. It is in your interest to contribute your best to make your boss successful. While the boss's need for help from you on technical or work-related skills and expertise may vary (from boss to boss, or from situation to situation), the one help every boss needs—constantly and as a crucial factor for his success—is a congenial, tension-free, collaborative relationship from you, his subordinate. Therefore, you must make every effort to build a healthy interpersonal relation with your boss in your own enlightened self-interest!

What is being suggested here is not that you should curry favour with your boss or seek to minimize his displeasure. Nor is it being suggested that you should turn yourself into a 'yes-man' of your boss. All that is being recommended here is that a manager must make himself *compatible* with his boss. For this purpose, he should make a beginning by first trying to know his boss:

+ what is his personality make-up?
+ what makes him tick?
+ what are his pet allergies?
+ what are his current objectives, targets and priorities?
+ what are his constraints—organizationally and personality-wise?
+ what does he expect from you? and
+ apart from what he may expect from you, in what ways can you be of real help on his critical issues and problems?

Once you understand and appreciate the above factors, you can easily work out a relationship with your boss which does not compromise your self-respect and wisdom.

Various 'Types' of Bosses[1]

An attempt has been made here to describe some typical kinds of bosses. These word-pictures are by no means exhaustive, nor do they describe a boss exactly or completely. In fact, most bosses are made up of characteristics drawn from more than one type described below. Similarly, it is quite possible that the same boss may pass from one type to another (or to a combination of different types) with the passage of time, or due to force of circumstances. All that is intended here is to make it easier for you to identify which general picture fits your boss, more or less—and, better still, to understand what kind of a boss *you* yourself are!

In addition to identifying the type your boss may belong to, you can work out your own strategies for: *(a)* dealing with him; and *(b)* embarking upon a 'relational' campaign for bringing him around to a tension-free working arrangement with you that may lead to greater effectiveness on both sides. These descriptions are action-oriented. It is certainly not intended that you must succumb to, or helplessly accept, the vagaries and whims of these types of bosses. What strategies you would work out, though, cannot be 'prescribed'. This has to depend upon so many imponderables, including your and your boss's personalities, and the relational climate prevailing *between* you, and *in* the department.

The 'dominant' boss:

- ♦ takes quick decisions and does not care to offer the rationale behind his decisions;
- ♦ rejects back-talk and suggestions;
- ♦ half-way acceptances like 'Yes, . . . but . . .' are not tolerated; and
- ♦ insists on having convincing enthusiasm and full support from his subordinates.

The 'administrator' boss:

- ♦ is a great believer in talking about leadership, planning, coordination, direction, team-spirit. . . ;
- ♦ wants his staff to follow directions explicitly;
- ♦ beating previous records within the department, or competition with other departments are his favourite sport; and

♦ subordinates' suggestions are welcome—but only as suggestions.

The 'teacher' boss:

♦ usually puts his subordinates on their own, but loves to watch and treat them as his pupils;
♦ would rather praise and encourage than criticize; takes mistakes calmly if admitted and his help is sought; and
♦ though easy-going, he can be quite stern as a disciplinarian when required; at such times, he expects submissiveness from his subordinates.

The 'specialist' boss:

♦ loves to indulge in long, technical discussions;
♦ is precise, literal and sets high standards for himself and others;
♦ is more interested in results than in credits;
♦ but is reluctant to take on steps along unchartered lines, especially if he sees uncertainties and prefers familiar techniques, tools and details;
♦ is skeptical about sudden or spontaneous 'inspiration'; and
♦ often ends up being more interested in how something is done than in whether it works.

The 'social' boss:

♦ sometimes uses flattery or sweet talk to get others to do his work;
♦ has no time or patience for details or routine work;
♦ loves meetings, and meeting people—preferably over extended lunches on the company's expense account;
♦ who you know is more important to him than what you know; and
♦ is not averse to knowing about, or even indulging in, office politics.

The 'seniority' boss:

♦ obeys, and wants others too to obey, all rules unquestioningly;
♦ knows the job, and the methods, by heart;
♦ frequently goes into raptures about 'how things used to be done';
♦ owes his present status mainly to the length of his service, hence does not like changes or innovations;
♦ admires 'plodders', distrusts brilliant or flashy subordinates; and

♦ security and unblemished record during remaining service period and good retiring benefits later are his main concern.

Establishing Greater Compatibility With the Boss

The most important thing is to *develop empathy with the boss*. For this you must take the following *four* steps:

1. Youmustmakespecialeffortstounderstand'empathetically'whatthe current problems or constraints your boss is faced with. You should considerwhatsupportorfacilitiesyoucanprovide,atyourlevel.
2. You should then have a sincere and friendly chat with your boss, as tactfully as possible—to identify what both of you consider to be his current work-load and problems.
3. Then you should volunteer the specific actions you can initiate to provide effective help to your boss. You must be very careful about the tone and attitude inherent in your dialogue lest you sound condescending. Otherwise, your dialogue can create a greater schism by aggravating distrust or hurting his pride.
4. You should then go ahead and act on the plan in such a manner that: *(a)* the boss's difficulties are eased; *(b)* he is enabled to become more effective, more relaxed and, thus, more self-confident; and *(c)* he begins to appreciate the support he is receiving from you and, thus, begins to rely increasingly upon you as his true friend.

This is perhaps the best way to become compatible with your boss in a mutually self-respecting, easy and transparently sincere manner.

Additional Steps for Improving Relations With the Boss

The efforts suggested above are *boss-specific*. They are more useful for mending fences with your boss or correcting faulty ideas in you, if any, concerning your relations with your boss.

What I now offer is a *general approach* you should adopt for the positive purpose of *starting off* on the right foot with *any* boss. These are *dual-purpose* suggestions: they are useful not only for those who *have* a boss, but also for those of you who *are* a boss.

Cherish Your Boss

♦ No one is perfect—neither the boss nor the subordinates. But everyone has some good points worth emulating. *Recognize those* good points in your boss, and adopt or adapt them in your style.

Help Your Boss

♦ Refrain from wasting his time:
  - seek his advice only when you must; and
  - when you do, go prepared with the problem duly identified and after having considered alternative solutions; don't just throw problems in his lap.
♦ Welcome delegation from him:
  - accept delegation of challenging tasks—*even ask for them*, and give your best to accomplish them;
♦ Keep him informed:
  - don't present surprises—not even pleasant surprises. Tell him what is happening, or not happening, and also tell him how you are tackling them.

Be on his Side—Transparently

♦ Let your actions convince him that *you are on his side:*
  - your outstanding performance alone is not enough to encourage him to rely on you. You must support him, in his presence as well as in his absence.
  - When you must disagree with him—on work-related or ethical issues—do so by all means, but privately, in frank discussions with him. Be sure, however, to present your contentions with sound reasons, in a dispassionate manner, and in the spirit of a well-wisher, not as an antagonist.
    If he does not agree with you, at least refrain from criticizing him publicly.

Never Stab him in the Back

♦ If you do, you will lose your best potential champion in one stroke!
♦ If you fail in your attempt to harm him, either you will have to leave the organization or your life with him is going to become miserable.
♦ If you succeed in your attempt to harm him, you will not necessarily benefit. There is no guarantee that you will get your

boss's position. But what is guaranteed is the reputation that you are treacherous.

♦ Your boss's successor may be worse—*to you* in any case; and he will never trust you.

♦ Others too will never trust you; no one will want you in his team—not even those who may have encouraged you to stab your boss in his back!

Above all, Enrich Yourself as a Boss   The best way to feel for your boss, and to get along well with him, is to view the overall situation by visualizing it as a problem between you and your subordinates, and by asking yourself how you would function. In other words, try and make yourself a good boss.

♦ Look after your people:
  • build team-spirit among them;
  • motivate them to take on challenging tasks;
  • delegate, guide, train, help; and
  • stand by them if they make mistakes
♦ As a result, bring them up to a state where you get your jobs done by letting them do theirs.

> *See to it that you are the best employee, and you will find you have the best bosses.*
>
> —Guillermo Fuentes, *Readers' Digest*, April 1995

Making yourself a good boss is the best way you can offer real help to your boss. As a good boss of your own subordinates, you are, in effect, offering a good team to your boss, and a good tradition to your department as a whole. Cumulatively, all these give your boss a very good chance to succeed. When your boss is successful, he will be in a much better position to help you and everybody else in his team!

And What do We do With a 'Difficult' Boss?

It will not do to evade or wish away this issue. In quite a large percentage of cases, managers' style of functioning, their psychology, their attitude toward life itself are warped, merely because they happen to have difficult bosses they do not know how to deal with. Many managers run away from their difficult bosses; they either seek transfer to other bosses, leave the organization, or benumb their sensitivity and try to coexist as indifferently as possible. The problem with such a resigned attitude is that there is no guarantee that the managers concerned would either 'solve' or 'escape from' their predicament; they may well find themselves jumping from the frying pan into the fire!

The frustration or annoyance that difficult bosses cause in their subordinates is enormous. It drives the 'victims' to lengths that can cause both concern and 'painful amusement'! This can be gauged from the fact that a Delhi-based management consultancy company, The Learning Curve, has recently hit the market with 'stress toys'.[2] The range consists of stress balls, voodoo dolls, desk dart boards, punch bags and hate diaries which can easily be carried in a briefcase. A stressed individual can 'punish' these toys with punching, hitting, stabbing pins, etc. so that his frustrations and anger against his boss can be released. The name of the person towards whom the aggression is to be directed can be pasted on the toy—to make things more realistic. According to the head of the company: 'Using it is like giving a suitable reply to an offensive action or causing harm, without actually hurting—a win-win situation for an apparent loser.' The concept of stress toys is very popular in the West, but it is appearing in our country for the first time.

A real-life case from one of the famous multinationals I worked for comes to mind. One of the young, bright management trainee officers was undergoing a lot of stress due to the obstinate 'policing' and humiliations his boss had let loose on him. This bachelor Trainee had to hire a new domestic servant. When the candidate mentioned the salary he would like to have, this Trainee offered him an additional Rs 20 per month—on two conditions: from the day he joined, his name would have to be 'XYZ' (which was the name of the Trainee's boss); and secondly that the Trainee would shower him with the choicest abuses every day when he (the Trainee) returned from his workplace.

The finale came one day when the Trainee's boss came to visit him at his flat—actually to verify whether the Trainee was really sick or not. The Trainee happened to be out at that time. Suddenly the boss was stunned at hearing the choicest abuses being addressed to him by name. At that moment the Trainee was ascending the stairs to his first-floor flat—oblivious of the fact that his boss was sitting there!

What is advisable, therefore, is that, like all other managerial problems, you should objectively analyze the causes behind your boss's belligerence, and try to tackle them—with courage and tact.

Here are some typical situations, and suggestions for dealing with them:[3]

When He Won't Listen to You   Usually his reasons for not listening to you are that, to him, your presentation is disorganized or your opinions are half-baked. Ask yourself ruthlessly: 'Could this possibly be true in my case?' In any case, try and inculcate the following habits in your discussions with your boss—or for that matter anyone:

- clarify, at the outset, the purpose of your discussion;
- be brief in defining the problem so that the other person can see the real issues—fast;
- your facts must be well-organized, and in logical sequence;
- your presentation should highlight aspects that you know are of special interest to the other person; and
- be sure to offer alternative solutions—do not end up by presenting the problems only.

When He Won't See You   You have to prove that the time he spends with you will be beneficial to him. The steps suggested earlier ('When He Won't Listen to You') apply here too. Additionally, you have to get across a short message, maybe on the telephone or through a brief, one-sentence remark to him when you run into him. This message must: *(a)* arouse his interest; and *(b)* highlight the benefits that can be derived by his seeing you.

When He Bypasses You   This happens in many cases. The boss steps right across and interacts directly with your subordinates. A distinction must be made here between 'reference for information' and 'reference for action'. The former is all right; there is no need for serious objection to the boss seeking information directly. Maybe he is in a hurry, or maybe, he wants to verify facts in a subtle manner. Let him. Once he sees that you are mostly up-to-date and correct in the information you furnish to him, he will stop going directly to your subordinates.

But his 'reference for action' directly to your subordinates certainly warrants looking into. Again, you should start by asking yourself as to why he is bypassing you. Is there some shortcoming on your part, such as your habitual resistance to his directions, indecisiveness, lethargy in acting, or your general attitude which makes him uncomfortable in finalizing action-plans with you? If these are the reasons, it is you who must reform yourself; otherwise your boss's surreptitious bypassing will soon be converted into open and defiant bypassing.

If, on the other hand, the problem lies with your boss, you will have to take up the matter with him. While doing so, you may wish to adopt the following approaches:

- highlight the damage being done to the discipline and morale among your subordinates. Be specific. Emphasize that the staff are confused as to which boss they should listen to; and
- be matter of fact. Never show personal resentment because the hurt to your pride, though very painful and important to you, is obviously of not much concern to him.

When He is Breathing Down Your Neck Maybe the boss is worried about the way things are being done, and wants to pitch in. If that is the case, you should accept his help. In case he is not sure how well the job is being done under you, give him more information:

- are your reports too infrequent? If he wants them more frequently than under the present arrangement, increase the frequency;
- do your reports contain the type of information he has been asking for? If not, include them; and
- are your reports too detailed, or lacking in details? Do the needful, in either case.

These are some of the situations, and some suggestions. There are, no doubt, many more situations calling for different nuances of remedies. You need to be alert to the *reasons why* your boss is, or has become, difficult. And you have got to take note of such a development at the early stage, before rigidities and feelings of hurt set in. What is important is that you should be alert, and should innovate remedial measures that suit the situation and the temperament of your boss.

Conclusion

In order to achieve desired goals, you as a manager must develop your efficiency for optimizing the utilization of resources placed under you. But mere efficiency is not enough. Efficiency helps you to do things right; but what you need is not only doing things right, but also doing the right things. This requires 'effectiveness' on your part.

The most fascinating resource that dares a manager to utilize effectively is the human resource. And the most challenging aspect of human resource management is the management of interpersonal relations. It is not enough that a manager be an expert in managing either his subordinates or his boss or his peers; he must be *effective* in managing all the three—simultaneously and in harmonious balance. Therefore, interpersonal relations transcend hierarchical lines; they call for constant attention at vertical as well as horizontal planes.

In order to improve interpersonal relations in organizations, it is required that each one develops an understanding of the other person in terms of his values, needs and goals, and also the type of reaction-patterns he generally maintains. There is also the need for each person to communicate honestly his thoughts, feelings, wants and beliefs, and influence the other person without being aggressive or defensive in his relationships.

The art of managing interpersonal relations hinges on a manager striking a proper balance of the age-old tussle between authority and influence. While there is no denying that authority, and its effective use, are essential in any kind of organization, undue dependence on authority alone has never worked. In fact, it almost always ends up by disrupting the whole organization. Authority is a factor of status whereas influence is a factor of stature. Stature can be earned through mature nurturing of relationships by persons who are otherwise competent. Authority usually carries sharp edges which can be smoothened by influence at the hands of a manager having maturity. A person with influence need not be too dependent on status, but he has got to make sustained inputs—not only on his subordinates, peers and boss, but principally on himself first. The inputs on himself are in the nature of self-development so that he earns positive self-regard. When he has sufficient positive self-regard, he is ready to treat others with dignity, and get the same level of dignity from them.

There are distinct differences in the approaches a manager must adopt toward his subordinates, peers and boss. Establishment of proper interpersonal relations between these calls for systematic and sustained efforts on his part. Once he acquires the right balance, his interpersonal relations can equip him with the reward of 'unfailing influence'. And this helps him climb the rungs of success to becoming a truly 'effective' manager—that is, a manager who gets the desired results without throwing his authority around!

EIGHT

Management of Tensions at Work

CHAPTER OBJECTIVES

- Show how regulating tensions is a matter of self-discipline
- Discuss why the external, so-called curative inputs alone do not work in reducing tensions

---

The Wheels of Tension

Even during the pre-historic days when life was much simpler, the cave-dwellers must have had their share of tensions. If one of them looked out of the cave in the morning and noticed that either the field was all clear for him to go out and capture his breakfast or to stay put since the tiger was around in search of his breakfast! Both of these situations generated in him manageable amounts of tension. This led to pumping of adrenaline into his blood-stream, which sharpened his hearing, eye-sight, thinking and general alertness. He was thus well-equipped and ready either for a fight to claim his breakfast or for a flight in order to escape becoming the tiger's breakfast!

Tension has been known to have the capacity to sharpen our faculties which, in turn, enables us to survive—or even surpass our hitherto unknown capabilities. This continues to be valid and relevant, *provided* we are faced with tension in *manageable quantities*.

But there is a difference! The advent and advancement of our civilization have imposed upon us a lot of social inhibitions. We can no longer straightaway translate our likes and dislikes, wishes or needs into actions in terms of fight or flight. Now, we find ourselves programmed to weigh our proposed action in terms of whether they are socially acceptable or strategically advisable. Today, we are sub-ected to tensions from two sources—one, the inevitable tensions that arise from the usual threats or opportunities in life, and the other, tensions arising out of the continuing need for suppressing or modifying our normal, natural instincts for fights or flights.

The situation at our workplace is even more acute. There are tensions galore. One has to reckon with people at work from different backgrounds with their own packages of personal ego, professional ego, power needs and power bases interacting and criss-crossing each others' paths. Then, there are a host of regulatory and inhibiting structures in the organization governing the actions and feelings of the people at work.

Today's workplace is much more complex than yesterday's. Corporate mergers, global-scale competition, growing consumer assertiveness and the irresistible impact of economic forces at the global level have introduced an inescapable need for balanced interpersonal relationships. Within an organization, relationships are built around various 'structures'. They could be related to:

♦ work;
♦ authority;
♦ status;
♦ prestige; or
♦ friendship.

Each of these structures has an impact on the interpersonal relationships which are interwoven in a workplace, actuated by interactions between varying temperaments, struggles, tussles, etc. Non-fulfillment of this interpersonal need may lead to emotional disturbance, general loss of motivation for life, and may ultimately lead to a rejection of one's self-esteem itself. All these build up a number of foci for inevitable conflicts within the organisation which, in turn, lead to tensions among the individuals working there. Thus, tensions—instead of finding an outlet through healthy fight or flight—get compulsively turned inwards, where they gnaw at your personality, tolerance and even physical well-being!

Pressure vs Tension

At this point, it would be good to recognize the distinction between pressure and tension.

Pressure   Pressure is normally not unwelcome. We all know that we function at our best when we are under pressure. The truth is that we do *need* pressure in our life in order to be 'on the go', and to ensure that our faculties are in good shape. However, each of us has our 'built-in tolerance points' up to which pressures remain productive; beyond these, they become counter-productive. But pressures of the wrong type or in wrong measures are a different matter; it is these undue or undesirable pressures that lead to tensions.

Inadequate pressure can lead to:

+ less attentiveness;
+ sleepy, slothful responses; and
+ boredom.

Too much pressure can lead to:

+ poor performance;
+ struggle for coping; and
+ tensions.

Adequate pressure can lead to:

+ alertness and attention;
+ high efficiency and effectiveness;
+ job satisfaction;
+ professional excitement; and
+ readiness and willingness for handling bigger challenges.

Pressure is the aggregate of all kinds of demands placed on us, such as:

Physical Pressure due to	*Psychological Pressure due to*
illness	paucity of time
extreme noise	difficult people
different or disagreeable food or other physical conditions	expectation or denial of career advancements
tough work or work demands	too much work
irregular or excessive physical demands for work	lack of recognition

Tension Tension is the mental–physical product of unresolved emotional conflicts. Tension is our *response* to an inappropriate level of pressure—not the pressure itself. If avenues for release of tensions are not provided or built-in, cumulative tensions become explosive and are always harmful. When pressure increases disproportionately, tension begins to manifest itself in any one or combination of the following areas of functioning:

Emotional	...	the world of our feelings
Mental	...	the world of our thoughts
Behavioural	...	the world of our actions
Physiological	...	the world of our physical responses

'Demand–supply' and 'Price' Mechanism of Tensions   Tensions are also subject to their own 'demand-and-supply' pressures! The economists say: 'Prices shall fluctuate upwards when supply does not match demand'. Similarly, when demands (of pressure) go up, more and more managers 'pay' dearly in terms of tensions, by attempting to manage in a situation when the supply *(of their tolerance)* is meagre. Short runs of continuing tension can be quite 'expensive'. But long runs can make us 'bankrupt'! The limited reserve of energy and tolerance we build up over time is the 'currency' in which tension is transacted. Under tension, we tend to draw heavily upon such reserve. Once we hit the rock-bottom of such reserve, we begin to suffer from physical and psychological seizures. There is mounting evidence that stress lowers resistance to disease. And the biggest setbacks to our immune system are caused by:

- ♦ work problems;
- ♦ unfair criticism or unfairness by the boss;
- ♦ frustrating, humiliating or irritating encounters with fellow employees; and
- ♦ feeling pressurized by looming deadlines or heavy workload.

They affect the hormonal output of the endocrine glands—generally playing havoc with the chemical balance of the entire body. When we are subjected to prolonged or excessive tensions, the chain of reactions set in motion at the physical level may be somewhat on the lines illustrated in Fig. 8.1.

The tell-tale signs of a 'stressed' person are easy to recognize. They are jumpy, edgy and peevish. They smoke or drink too much. They over-react to people around them, getting into needless arguments, and can't stay away from the toilet too long.

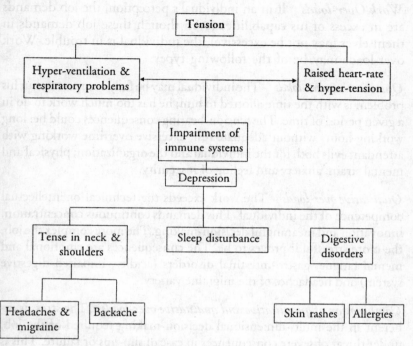

FIGURE 8.1 Chain Reaction of Tension

Which are the Occupational 'Stressors'?

Work fulfills several fundamental human needs, in addition to servicing your 'hygienic needs'. But quite a few tensions do arise from your work itself when either your needs are not being fulfilled or when you *perceive* threats that your needs are not being or will not be fulfilled.

Problems of Work-loads

It would help if you look a little closer at how stresses and strains are generated by mere maladjustments between you and your work-load quite apart from the stresses that are caused by interactions between you and your colleagues. This closer look would most likely reveal a number of causes of tensions which would open your eyes and, hopefully, lead you to self-adjustments and to easing many of your tensions. Some of these problems are:

Work Over-loads   If in an individual's perception, the job demands are in excess of his capabilities (even though these job demands in themselves may not be excessive), the individual is in trouble. Work over-loads may be of the following types:

Quantitative over-loads   The individual may be fully competent, but his problem is with the time allotted to him; he has too much work to do in a given period of time. The tension-bearing consequences could be: long working hours without adequate rest; excessive overtime working with attendant evils both for the individual and the organization; physical and mental strain, anxiety and feeling of insecurity.

Qualitative over-loads   The work exceeds the technical or intellectual competence of the individual. This demands continuous concentration, innovation and meaningful decision-making. The more complex the job, the more stressful it proves to be. The consequences are emotional and mental fatigue; gastro-intestinal disorders (acidity, impaired digestive system) and headaches of the migraine variety.

Combination of quantitative and qualitative over-loads   The stress is inherent in the multi-dimensional decision-making required of the job, under threat of severe consequences in case of slip-ups or failure. This is frequently encountered in risky, tension-filled operations like launching a new project on trial basis, 'fire-fighting' operations or tasks such as that of an air-traffic controller at busy airports, or dealings in a busy stock-exchange.

Work Under-loads   The stress in this case arises from the failure of the job to provide meaningful stimulation or adequate psychological reinforcements to the performer. Some typical situations are:

♦ dehumanizing monotony; and
♦ absence of opportunities to use acquired skills and expertise.

The common consequence of such a situation is boredom; but in some cases this even leads to hysteria, mass outbreak of illness, absenteeism, poor productivity—even sabotage in extreme cases.

Self-imposed Stresses   A little introspection can provide interesting and instructive lessons about the stresses that can maul you. These, interestingly, arise out of the 'instructions' *you impose on yourself—*

specially those of you who are conscientious performers, seeking perfection.

Many of us suffer due to our obsessions of the following kinds:

♦ whatever we do, we must do really well—*better than anybody else*;

♦ whatever we are doing, we should accomplish *really quickly* ;

♦ we must *try really hard* at whatever we are performing;

♦ we must do *the job ourselves*—even at the cost of our health or well-being; or

♦ we ought to *do things in a way that will please others*—regardless of our own satisfactions or values.

Each of these objectives is worthy of serious efforts. We cannot really quarrel with that. The problem, however, comes up when one of these over-rides what is realistic or appropriate in a given situation, or when you tend to make them matters of life and death. You must remember that these are 'instructions' we give to ourselves. We must ensure that they are made to serve us and are compatible with us; they must not enslave us!

Problems of Occupational Frustrations

Tension is also caused by frustrations from denial of what we want, or need, or feel we are not getting what we deserve. Here are some typical situations that lead to occupational frustrations.

Frustrations Whose Focus is Within Us These are the situations where:

♦ we have no say in decisions on what we want. Therefore, we are never satisfied with what is available (even though what is available is, in fact, satisfactory);

♦ what we want is not available;

♦ we act in ways which reduce our chances of getting what we want; or

♦ we have unrealistic expectations.

Frustrations That Arise Out of the 'Systems' in the Organization

Role ambiguity The performer has to keep guessing as to: *(a)* what is expected of him on the job; *(b)* what are the applicable standards of performance; *(c)* how he fits into the organization and the lines of accountability; and *(d)* how he is being assessed on his performance;

Role conflict   The job is made up of conflicting roles or responsibilities leading to conflicting demands or clashes with others. Also, when more than one senior manager demands compliance of their instructions—often conflicting ones—it leads to tension. This is more common among middle-level managers;

Poor career development   One of our powerful needs is to be assured that: *(a)* our performance is being taken note of; and *(b)* there is a system—and there are mature people—for giving shape to our career-development on the basis of merit. There is trouble when this is denied to us.

Poor communication   Even in the midst of several communication networks in an organization, *adequate* and *timely* communication are usually conspicuous by their absence—particularly communication from bottom upwards. And communication from top downwards too is often in the nature of one-way 'announcements'. The most crippling feature of communication is lack of credibility. In such a situation the grapevine takes over. And it is most frustrating for managers—and others down the line—if their main sources of information are the subordinates, the union leaders or the grapevine!

What Can We Do?

Two things are evident from the above.

One, that pressures, stresses, conflicts and resultant tensions are *inevitable facts of life* which cannot be wished away, or done away with.

Two, that *primarily it is the individual himself, through his self-discipline* who can solve these problems.

If you want to improve the situation surrounding you, you first have to change yourself; and 'changing yourself' means, in essence, 'changing your perceptions'.

Once you accept these basic facts, you can, of course, set about looking for the 'props'—techniques, built-in systems, planning-and-organizing efforts, etc. Some such 'props' have been suggested. But you must remember, there is no getting away from—nor are there any short-cuts to—self-discipline if you really wish to: *(a)* minimize the

---

Genuine Worries, and How You May Deal with Them

Sometimes you have a real reason to worry. You are in danger of missing a meeting or you have made a major mistake. Try this process to ease the situation:

Ask yourself: What's the worst that can possibly happen? Maybe your boss will yell at you, you'll miss a deadline or you'll lose a business. Often, you may end up realizing that the consequences aren't worth losing your sleep over.

Prepare yourself to accept the worst. Imagine you get sacked. Or you go bankrupt. It will be no fun to contemplate the worst, but doing so will help you confront the issue in a calmer frame of mind. By merely going over the worst that can happen, you'll also see that its possible to recover from 'the worst'.

Work calmly and methodically to improve upon the worst. Is there anything you can do to make the situation better? Make a list of steps to take—people to call, tasks you can attend to, studies and discussions you can do, help or advice you have to seek—anything that will help.

Remember: when you are prepared for the worst, either you are better able to confront it , *or, sometimes, the worst does not happen!*

---

ravages of stress and *(b)* harness your tensions into productive and opportunity-bearing forces.

For this you must first learn to control and constructively direct your tensions.

Establishing Healthy Habits

In almost every work-group, it is possible that one of the members is a tension-addict. He is in his elements when he is under tension. Under tension (and not just 'pressures'), he even works better. And in the absence of tension, he feels like a fish out of water; he slumps down to a disoriented, groping, dispirited state of being. But for most of us, tension by itself is *not* a stimulant; it has to be *made to become a stimulant.* And the chemistry required is: *develop a more tranquil state of mind.*

How can we talk of 'tranquil state of mind' in the midst of the stresses, strains and conflicts that we are doomed to live in? A very pertinent question. Look at the elemental forces in nature, and consider how it achieves equilibrium in the midst of storms and gravitational pulls and tugs. This is a convincing and inspiring pheno-menon proving the point that equilibrium, or tranquility, is actually the result of counter-balancing of seemingly diverse pulls and pres-sures, provided you take the trouble of placing these forces in a way that counter-balance each other.

To drive the point home, I quote below an excerpt from an earlier article of mine.

The Managers' Dilemma in the 80s

While the modern jet airplane goes hurtling through sub-zero temperature in rarefied atmospheric conditions at 35,000 feet, at speeds teasing the sound barriers, the passengers inside the 'pressurized-for-comfort' capsules are hardly aware of the snarling elements literally knocking at every vulnerable nut and bolt and rivet of the plane. 'Where ignorance is a bliss, it is folly to be wise!' Every uneventful journey is thus a silent but grateful tribute to this "conditioned" equilibrium of the whirlwind!

The Manager of the 80s also 'jets' through such conditioned equilibrium every day of his working life....

Tranquility of Mind 'Tranquility comes from personality growth through the assimilation of new experiences. When a person ex-periences something he cannot understand or accept... or incorporate into his established system of thinking or feeling... this becomes a traumatic damaging experience...Until the traumatic experience is reinforced and assimilated, the result is internal conflict and nervous tension.'[1]

In simple words, tranquility is the positive result of learning how to control tension. Recommended below are some well-tried and self-explanatory methods for building tranquility:

♦ allow yourself (that is, take steps to make available) sufficient time for what you are about to accomplish;

♦ recognize your limitations, and either overcome them or learn to act within them;

♦ avoid tension-causing situations;

♦ learn to say: 'no';

- tackle one job or problem at a time;
- whenever possible, pick associates who, you feel, could be stimulating;
- listen to music. Classical, devotional, ghazals, jazz, whatever suits your fancy; and make a conscious effort to let the lilting strains seep into your brain. You can actually feel the stress seeping out;
- how about yoga? It has been tried all over the world, and has proved—beyond cultural boundaries—to be literally a panacea for stress;
- take a leisurely stroll down a quiet road. Make your mind a complete blank, and just walk. (In fact, any form of exercise is likely to lower your anxiety—leading to a tranquil state of mind.)
- do your best to teach yourself to be patient.

Succumb to Worry, Die Young[2]

We have overcome many of the worst diseases of this century, but we've made no headway whatsoever against a crippling disease that lies behind many emotional and physical problems: worry. While there is no way to avoid business problems, there are ways to fight the stress they might cause.

Live in day-tight compartments: It is impossible to live in the past or the future. But, as Dale Carnegie said, 'by trying to do so, we can wreck both our bodies and our minds. So let's be content to live the only time we can possibly live; from now until bed-time.'

Focus your attention, then, on the one place you can act to achieve your ends: today. Robert Louis Stevenson has aptly put it in these words: 'Anyone can do his work, however hard, for one day. Anyone can live sweetly, lovingly, purely, till the sun goes down. And this is all that life really means.'

Many of us spend far too much time worrying about things that will never come to pass. One way to keep worries at bay is to figure out the mathematical odds that an event will actually come to pass. That helps put your concerns in perspective. For example, say you are worried about flying. The odds your plane will crash are about one in a hundred thousand. Knowing that, should you still worry?

Keep busy: It's impossible to worry if you're busy with a project, learning a new skill, helping others, or reading an absorbing book.

Choice of an Appropriate Style of Response to Tensions Since the individual himself is the central figure in coping with tensions, each of you has to adopt a style of behaviour which suits your personality make-up, actuated by the profile of your personal strengths and weaknesses.

The question that deserves examination is whether you have any choice in adopting a certain style of behaviour to improve your capacity for coping with tensions or you have to leave this as a free-floating factor, on the assumption that nothing can, or need, be done about it?

In this context, let us examine the following possible postures people around us have, or adopt:

- ◆ unassertive;
- ◆ aggressive;
- ◆ passive; or
- ◆ assertive.

The following example[3] amply illustrates these four postures:

A colleague confronts you about why the report he had asked for has not yet been completed. Some of the possible responses to this confrontation may be:

Unassertive While slowly edging away from him, you say that you are terribly sorry. You point out that he had asked for the report only yesterday, but anyway you would stay late and finish the task. You also mumble that you are inexperienced for this sort of task, that it is rather a difficult task. But you don't make an issue of it.

Aggressive With your chin thrust forward and your hands on your hips, you say that he has been already thrusting too many tasks upon you lately; that you have been too busy with other, more important tasks; that you are not at his beck and call; that he should go ahead and complete the report himself if it is that important and urgent to him.

Passive Bowing your head as the onslaught of your colleague goes on, you offer no reason or explanation, and you wait and hope that the storm will soon be over.

Assertive Looking straight into the eyes of your colleague, you say that you appreciate that the report is important for him, and it happens to be your top priority today, and that it is likely to be finished by tomorrow morning as agreed. You also say that you have been thinking of discussing the question of your own work over-load to see that some changes are made to lessen your over-burdened schedule so that you may devote your time and energies equitably to this and other tasks.

I think the following *four* observations are pertinent:

1. Under the *unassertive* style, your behaviour is aimed at appeasement. You simply wish to pacify the other person before whom you emerge as 'inferior'. Although not guilty, you are in effect taking the blame. As a result, the real problem has been side-tracked.
2. When you are being *aggressive* you will not allow the other person to dominate you. In fact, you are determined to assert your superiority if the other person tries to bully you. As a result, you do not even recognize that the other person may be having a real problem. Your main concern is to attack and silence the other person; the problem itself can wait, or go to hell.
3. As a *passive* person you just do not react, nor do you take any action; or you take as little action as possible. Hardly any moves are made to tackle the real problem. You make yourself as unobtrusive as possible.

   Under none of the above styles of behaviour, the real problem gets solved. The person(s) you interact with are either *appeased* or *intimidated* or *bypassed*, but their need for action from you remains unfulfilled. In short, *the source of tension remains alive*, and the person confronted by tension continues to remain tense—although he may think he has dealt with it.
4. The essence of *assertive* style, in contrast to the other three styles, is equality, mutuality and inter-dependence. Under this style, one treats the other as his equal, without of course accepting any nonsense. This style, however, recognizes that the persons on both sides share a problem that needs to be solved, and that it can best be solved through cooperation.

Although from this discussion, the assertive style may emerge as the most desirable, the fact remains that most of us, in varying circumstances, resort to assertive or unassertive, aggressive or passive postures or their combination. Nevertheless, in the long run and from the point of view of overcoming or minimizing your tensions adopting the assertive style as a normal posture is the most advisable.

Assuming that you select the assertive style of behaviour, you must remember that assertiveness cannot just be switched on. It can emerge and survive only when you back it up with some substance in your overall style of management. What it really calls for are the following:

♦ an examination of your current style of management;
♦ identification of the areas that need to be modified, rejected or added in the light of the pointers arising out of the foregoing discussions;
♦ doing the needful to develop your personality and capabilities to the extent that it enriches your self-esteem; and
♦ embarking upon a planned 'fine tuning' accordingly, at a pace which generates a desirable amount of pressure—not tension—for you.

Recommendations

Some Observations

Freedom from, or reduction of, tensions is very important for an effective manager. The potential of all his experience and expertise is considerably handicapped if he becomes a bundle of tensions.

Offered below are some recommendations which, if assimilated into your managerial style, may enable you to cope with tensions in a more effective way. In fact, these measures, if practised in the right spirit over a period of time, may even eliminate several tension-bearing factors from your day-to-day life at the workplace.

The key to this challenge—of 'management of tensions'—lies almost entirely with you, the individual, not so much with the organization. You cannot just stand up and declare one fine morning to your organization: 'We are under terrible tension at our place; do something!' Primarily, it requires a great deal of self-discipline and efforts along a duly identified and chosen path over a period of time IF you are really keen to secure relief from undue tensions.

> Marilyn Ferguson observed, *'No one can persuade another to change. Each of us guards a gate of change that can only be opened from inside. We cannot open the gate of another, either by argument or by emotional appeal.'*
>
> *'If you decide to open your "gate of change" to really understand and live the principles ... your growth will be evolutionary, but the net effect will be revolutionary.'*[4]

What follows are some recommendations, in order of their importance. They are primarily in the category of what *you* have to do.

What You Have To Do

One clarification at the very outset. Many junior and middle-level officers and managers harbour the misconception that it is not for them to make managerial inputs like delegation, role-clarity, job-loading, job-structuring, decision-making and ensuring discipline. Nothing could be more erroneous. Much of their tensions arise from adopting such a passive posture. Let us recognize the fundamental truth that each officer or manager is both boss and subordinate— irrespective of whether he is a junior officer or the managing director. Therefore, it will not do for you to try to wriggle out of undertaking these 'managerial inputs' on the excuse that you are only junior-level officers or managers. In fact, it is the use of these managerial inputs which can enhance your effectiveness and help you eliminate many tension-bearing situations.

The recommendations discussed below ought to be adopted as *your* tasks and responsibilities for *your* benefit and for your peers and subordinates.

Delegation   We usually find that bosses are reluctant to delegate— for a variety of reasons. As a result, amusing (but worrying) situations arise: it is the subordinate who increasingly begins to delegate tasks to you which, in reality, are his! Delegation, when properly practised, emerges not only as an instrument for 'multiplying yourself' and thus strengthening your team, but also paves the way for creating a more effective team—leading, in turn, to a more harmonious atmosphere and a significant reduction of tensions in you and within your team.

Time Management   It is well known that delegation and time management are complementary to each other. Both are important aids to curtailing tensions. It is necessary, however, to note that:

♦ what we can—and we have to—do is to manage ourselves with reference to time;
♦ the more we learn to better utilize our time, more time begins to become available; and

♦ most of us spend much of our time—almost 80 per cent—on the 'trivial many' (which yield barely 20 per cent of the results). If only we spend 20 per cent of our time on the 'vital few', we can, in due course, reap a harvest of 80 per cent of the key results!

Fairness Coupled with Firmness   Contrary to popular belief, practising fairness requires more courage and sacrifices than being firm. In order to be fair in one case, you have got to be firm with half a dozen parties or persons trying to pursue their vested interests. Opposition from vested interests must be fought with a missionary zeal—even at personal risks. It is only when you establish your reputation that you can be relied upon to be fair despite all obstacles and threats (even ridicule) that you finally earn the right or the freedom to administer firmness.

This also enables you to incorporate greater assertiveness in your behaviour and managerial style. It is the fair but firm person who ultimately succeeds in pruning, and in keeping at bay, tensions around him. He radiates calm among the people he interacts with.

Assertiveness   Your plans for consciously incorporating assertiveness in your behaviour and management style must steer clear of aggressiveness. The keys to creating enduring assertiveness within yourself are: mutuality, equality and inter-dependence, reinforced by continuing efforts to improve your over-all performance.

When you are on your way to such self-development, very few persons (including your bosses) will take the risk of riding roughshod over you and, thus, be the cause of tensions for you.

Role-clarity vis-à-vis Work Over-load and/or Work Under-load
Role clarity must provide advice or information as to: *(a)* what one is supposed to do and achieve; *(b)* under what limitations or with what facilities; and *(c)* what standards of performance are going to be applied.

You must avoid work over-load and/or under-load while assigning tasks to your subordinates—and also while being loaded by your superiors. To avoid confrontation with your superiors on this issue, perhaps the best way is to provide (to your subordinates) and to ask for (from your bosses) as much clarity about the required roles as possible. This is one area where the support and active collaboration of the top management are essential.

Communication   In reality, communication calls for an ongoing dialogue between all sections of an organization—not only on matters which the top management considers important but also on matters regarding which people at other levels want or require information, explanation or discussion on. Otherwise, the rumour-department will take over and then there is no telling what appalling distortions or mis-information would be let loose.

Above all, the soul of true communication is *credibility*; and credibility is nurtured on *integrity*. If credibility and integrity are missing, communication degenerates into a ritual and turns into an irritant. The result is tensions all around !

Sense of Humour   How about cultivating some sense of humour, if you are not endowed with it? Laugh *with* others rather than go red in the eyes and blue in the face. What is wrong with a certain degree of light-heartedness ? Even when things go wrong, what do you really gain if you and others become grim or aggressive, and then rush out to find faults with others? When you do this or allow this to happen, the mistake committed is side-tracked, and a lot of time, opportunity and good-will are robbed. It is far more important that you find out *what* goes wrong than *who* goes wrong. This can be achieved more easily if there is good-will and good humour prevailing among colleagues.

As part of the package for self-development, if you try to build up a sense of humour and the capacity to see the problems of others without unnecessary grimness, most of your problems can be solved. As a bonus you will find a significant reduction in your tensions!

Some Useful, Easy Tips[5]

1. Try this age-old remedy: Talk less, listen more!
2. Streamline your routine. Make small lists of chores that you would like to accomplish. Work up gradually to the big chores. Try and clear at least a couple of the *pending jobs* and earn some more self-esteem.
3. The right kind of breathing also dispels stress. Take a deep breath and exhale carefully, concentrating on the air leaving your lungs. Slow down your pace of breathing. Breathe from your belly, watching it expand, then contract to normal.
4. Caffeine heightens stress levels. Try cutting down on those endless cups of coffee.

5. When you feel stress creeping up on you, roll your neck a few times. Shrug your shoulders. Loosen your jaw muscles.

Conclusion

Pressures and tensions are a fact of life. You cannot banish them. You have to learn to live with them. The important question is: how do you live with them?

Certain amount and kind of pressures—even tensions—are welcome. They sharpen your capabilities and personality. They help you by equipping you to face or deal with things that propel you for greater successes in life.

But if and when you are confronted by pressures and tensions that might corrode your capabilities and personality, you have got to develop the art of channelising them along positive lines.

One major realization you must imbibe is that *you*, the individual, are the principal actor in the drama of combating tensions.

Successful management of tensions is really the end-result of integrated efforts at self-discipline and self-development over a period of time. As a result of such efforts, you are likely not only to overcome tensions but also to emerge as a more effective person who could, in all probability, contribute towards lowering the level and intensity of tensions in your workplace!

Test Yourself

Management of Tensions at Work

C. T. SCAN
(Critical Tensions Scan)

Name	Department

Scanning on Individual Basis

1. In my considered view, my five major tensions at work are:

    (i)

    (ii)

    (iii)

    (iv)

    (v)

2. The five major reasons or causes for these tensions are:

    (i)

    (ii)

    (iii)

    (iv)

    (v)

3. I feel—on introspection and while contemplating my answers to the above-stated questions—that I should take the following steps to minimize such tensions:

Screening by the Group

Members of the Group			
Names	Depts.	Names	Depts.
1.		4.	
2.		5.	
3.		6.	

1. In our considered view, the following are the five major and critical tensions which are encountered and shared by most of us at work.

    (i)

    (ii)

    (iii)

    (iv)

    (v)

2. The five major reasons or causes for these tensions are:

    (i)

    (ii)

    (iii)

    (iv)

    (v)

3. Collectively, we feel, we can do the following to minimize our tensions at work:

4. We consider that the following five steps or actions need to be taken by the senior levels of management to help us fight the causes of our tensions.

NINE

Managing Ourselves with Reference to 'Time'

CHAPTER OBJECTIVES

- Point out how time is too independent to lend itself to be 'managed' and why it is therefore important to manage ourselves with reference to time
- Provide practical suggestions for making better use of time for enhancing effectiveness

---

Introduction

The late Nobel Laureate, Richard P. Feynman had said: 'We physicists work with time every day, but don't ask me what it is. It's just too difficult to think about.' A graffiti on a wall said very aptly: 'Time is nature's way of keeping everything from happening at once.'

Physicists might say time is one of the two building blocks of the universe—the other being space. Some people believe time is the fourth dimension. A biologist sees time as the internal clock that keeps plants and animals synchronized with nature. And a businessman or an industrialist says time is money!

What is Time?

Webster's Dictionary defines time as:

- the entire period of existence of the world or of humanity;
- every moment there has ever been, or will ever be; and
- indefinite, unlimited duration in which things are considered as happening in the past, present or future.

Some scholars believe that at the dawn of human existence, our ancestors might have lived in a state of 'timeless present' with little or no sense of past or future. Only much later, they might have realized the existence and passage of time in terms of: *(a)* the movement of the planets and the seasons; and *(b)* events on the human plane. In more recent times, however, man has tried to comprehend time as the 'duration' between activities or events.

Measurement of Time

Time flows on and is irreversible. Much has been done so far to 'measure' time, rather than to understand it. Time has been broken into chronological units like decades, centuries, millennia, Christian era, *yuga* or *vikram samvat* to suit our convenience or to help our comprehension.

Ancient Indian philosophers conceived time (*Kaa'la*, in Sanskrit) as an endless cycle. Brahma is credited with a longevity of 100 divine years. Since each day of the divine year is equal to 1,000 solar years, time, according to Indian philosophers, stretches out practically to infinity. They have 'mapped out' the time spent till now on earth as *mahayuga*, made up of 4,320,000 solar years. This has been further divided into four *yugas*, i.e. ages: *Satayuga, Tretayuga, Dvaparayuga* and the current *Kaliyuga*. The lunar year is made up of 354 days and the solar year of 360 to 366 days. A week consists of seven days, and each day is made up of 60 *ghatikas* of 24 minutes each.

In the eighth century BC the Babylonians developed a year of 360 days and divided it into 12 lunar months of 30 days each. The Egyptians extended the year by five days, meant for feasting during the Nile's annual flooding. Refinements by the Romans and by Pope Gregory XIII in 1582 gave us today's Gregorian Calendar, accurate to a day in every 3,323 years!

Today, our atomic clocks measure time in 'femtoseconds'; one such second is a thousandth of a '*picosecond*'. Think of the enormity of accuracy of time-measurement available to us today: there are more femtoseconds in one second than there have been seconds in the past 31 million years![1]

Mind-boggling though all these are, they only tell us how this endless stream called time is being measured.

The Nature of Time

But what is time? Although Feynman's statement—'It's just too difficult to think about'—springs to mind, thinkers in the field of management have long realized that it is the most important and powerful resource for accomplishing anything in life. It is more precious than money, materials, even manpower.

Time is one of the greatest equalizers. The rich and the poor, the knowledgeable and the ignorant, the efficient and the inefficient—all get the same 24 hours in a day, 365 days in a year. *What is unequal is what we make of the time we have.* Some of us make the most of it, and some a mess of it.

Almost all 'too-busy' persons keep complaining that they don't have enough time. 'I wish the day had 48 hours!', they are always complaining. However, there are also people who seem to think they have more time than they know what to do with! The interesting thing is that both are complaining—from opposite poles—about the same thing, that is, the *availability* of time.

But even more interesting—and instructive—is the fact that in time management the problem does not lie with its availability or non-availability; it lies with the *poor utilization* of time. Once we learn the art of 'proper' utilization of time, we not only get over the paucity of time but more and more time becomes available to us! There is a saying that 'the truly busy man has time enough to spare!' The person who is truly busy has probably gone through the mill of accomplishing more and more in less and less time; in the process, he has had to become highly organized. In other words, he has graduated himself through the art of better utilization of time to such an extent that he now has time enough to spare—even after accomplishing a lot more than others.

A pertinent question is, 'Can we really *manage* time?' Generally, 'managing' something connotes that one is in a position to control, manipulate, adjust or secure responses to stimuli.

Unlike the other resources, time is *beyond our control and stimuli,* since we cannot do any of the following with it:

- touch;
- catch;
- accumulate;
- replace;
- see;
- feel;
- store;
- retrieve; and
- turn it on or off.

The dilemma is that, as a powerful resource, time must be utilized properly even though it is not under our control. So, how do we manage time? The grudging answer is that indeed we cannot *manage* time. What we can do—and the only thing we must do—is to manage *ourselves* with reference to time! This management of ourselves can be brought about primarily through self-discipline which, in turn, enables us to 'fine-tune' our self-organization. And then we are equipped and ready to utilize our time as best as we can!

While it is universally acknowledged that time past is irretrievable ('we cannot bring back or change our past'), it is not realized by many that we can certainly change our past by better utilization of our *present* and *future*. There are several inspiring examples of people achieving crowning success on the very issue on which they had had humiliating failures in the past. When they do so, they do 'change' their past.

The converse is also true and pertinent. While in some cases we cannot change our past, we can undoubtedly *spoil*

 ♦ an otherwise good present, by simply continuing to worry about the future or brooding over the past; or
 ♦ an otherwise good future, by not making proper use of our present.

It is worth recounting here what happened to Bahadur Shah Zafar, the last Mughul Emperor who ruled India till 1857 AD, and remained exile in Burma till his death. He was also a poet of great recognition. This is how he summed up the frustration of *his* 'time management' in a poignant couplet:

عمر دراز مانگ کے لائے تھے چار دن
دو آرزو میں کٹ گئے دو انتظار میں

'In the name of longevity, I had borrowed a time span of four days; two days were spent in wishfulness, and the other two frittered away in waiting for things to happen!'

To think that these are the expressions of self-pity of an anguished person is to miss the real point. The moral that transcends anguish and self-pity is that even an emperor, with all his power and resources, can fail miserably to create opportunities for himself if he does not organize himself with reference to time.

Steps Towards 'Getting Organized'

Auditing How We Manage Our Time

Over the years we have imperceptibly accumulated numerous habits and tendencies which work as hindrances to 'organized' functioning. Therefore, the first step for you toward getting organized is to take a close look at yourselves, before looking around to find out who or what are the obstacles to your good time management.

What you need to do is to build around the triangle comprising: *(a)* identify your time-problems; *(b)* assign and re-arrange your priorities; and *(c)* delegate as much as possible (see Fig. 9.1).

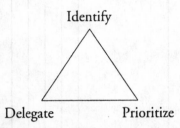

Identify

Delegate　　Prioritize

FIGURE. 9.1 The Triangle of Time Management

Identify Your Time Problems　　One simple method to do this is to open a daily time log to record how your time *gets spent* (contrary to how *you* would have liked to spend it) on a typical working day. The duration of this kind of observation could be shorter i.e., one week (not less) if your job is not too complex (for persons doing routine, uncomplicated, repetitive tasks), and longer, i.e., two or more weeks for those of you whose job has myriad complexities (for persons doing marketing, public relations, industrial relations, air-traffic control, etc.). It is important that during this period of observation, you simply let things happen as they have normally been happening. Please leave your attempts at reformation for a later stage. Although a format is given in Table 9.1 (see p. 216), it is not necessary for you to stick to it. There is a lot of room for flexibility. It is best that you design the format that suits your working pattern or personality. What is important is that you do maintain a log in which your day's activities are studied in terms of the parameters shown in Table 9.1.

TABLE 9.1: Daily Time Log

Name.............................. Period From.............To..............

Activity *Task, discussion, meeting, processing papers, visits—planned/unplanned*	With whom?	Priority category 1, 2, or 3	Started at	Ended at	No. of interruptions & duration	Quality of Result *Productive, unproductive, avoidable*

REMARKS:

Category 1: Important *and* urgent; Category 2: Important *but not* urgent
Category 3: Urgent *but not* important.

You should fill in the log preferably after each activity. The 'Quality of Result' and 'Remarks' columns, however, should be filled in at the end of the day with a detached frame of mind, in a quiet moment, after contemplating the following *seven* questions:

1. Was the time spent commensurate with the result achieved?
2. Was there any activity that went on without interruptions? How many interruptions were there, and of what total duration?
3. Which visits were planned? Were they necessary or useful? Could they have been shorter?
4. Which visits were unplanned? Did they prove to be necessary, and were they useful? Could they have been shorter?
5. Incoming telephone calls: How many ? Were they necessary? Could they have been shorter?
6. Outgoing telephone calls: Were they unplanned? How many calls were made on matters that suddenly became urgent? Could they have been shorter?
7. Meetings: How many? How many were planned, and how many were sudden?

   ♦ how many could have been shorter (by a total of how many minutes)?
   ♦ was it really necessary to call all the persons who attended?
   ♦ were the outcomes of these meetings commensurate with the time and efforts spent?

Assign Priorities   No general guidelines on how priorities should be assigned can be prescribed. However, the two overriding factors for setting priorities are: *(a)* how you would like to work; and *(b)* what you must do to achieve the desired results within the framework of your style of working. These factors determine within every one dissimilar perceptions of what is 'important' and what is 'urgent'— dissimilar, because they are so closely interlinked with your personality and your style of working. In any case, a pre-requisite for assigning priorities is that you first develop an overview of your own responsibilities, and then pattern your work-schedule according to the overall needs of the organization.

I am personally persuaded that the essence of the best thinking in the area of time management can be captured in a single phrase: organize and execute around priorities.

—Stephen R. Covey, *The 7 Habits of Highly Effective People*

Delegate

In the day-to-day work-schedule, there are *four* kinds of tasks that lend themselves to being delegated.[2]

1. *Routine tasks:* These include screening of mail, preliminary interviewing of job applicants or information-seekers, minor or routine maintenance needs. If you are too busy or disinclined to handling them yourself, you could offer them to your subordinates provided you have not already overloaded them.

2. *Tasks of lower priority:* These are not necessarily routine tasks, but are of comparatively lower priority which you would have liked to handle yourself, *if* you had the time. When more urgent matters occupy your attention, you may pass these tasks on to capable subordinates.

3. *Problem solving:* There may be tasks which still have some time-margins, and they entail problem-solving. Either you have subordinates who possess the particular knowledge or skill in that area of problem-solving or you wish to expose some potentially capable subordinates for the purpose of 'developing' them. You may wish to pass on such tasks to them even when you are not under great time-pressure because you are convinced that these tasks will provide challenges, and resultant motivation, to your subordinates.

4. *Changes in your own job emphasis:* It is usual for executive job-changes to take place—gradually as well as suddenly in some cases. Sometimes the new aspects of your jobs require more of your time and attention. In order to 'gain' the extra time, you may have to delegate the 'old' aspects of your responsibilities to capable subordinates.

Watch out for delegation from below   Usually we complain of the time-pressure imposed upon us by our boss (as perhaps our subordinates may well be doing about us imposing our time-pressure upon them!), and by the 'system' in our organization. But we are seldom aware that a lot of such time-pressure is imposed on us by our subordinates. We could be in for considerable consternation if we do a careful auditing on this point. The responsibility for such a state of affairs, however, is largely ours. Many of us have either not learnt the art of delegation, or we do not have the courage to delegate, or are prisoners of the 'do-it-ourselves' syndrome. The subordinate, who can be surprisingly shrewd, is happy to take note of his boss's hesitations and to dump upwards his own tasks in the same proportion as his perception of how much of a 'do-it-ourselves' addict his boss is!

Some guidelines for delegation

♦ select tasks that are interesting from the point of view of your subordinate's current level of skill and knowledge;
♦ delegation must provide opportunities for your subordinate's development;
♦ select the junior-most subordinate who has the skills and rank necessary to complete the assignment successfully. And the key word for this is: Entrust. Entrust the entire matter along with sufficient authority so that he can take the required decisions. This is quite different from saying, 'Just do what I ask you to do'; and
♦ do not abdicate. Provide to your delegatee the resources, authority and continuing guidance if and when he needs it. Follow up effectively: watch the progress, provide mid-course corrections and supports without breathing down his neck.

Interpreting the Daily Time Log

You must study the log at the end of the observation period of one or more weeks, as the case may be. This study should be made clinically, showing neither mercy nor ruthlessness. Carefully study the 'Quality of Result' and 'Remarks' sections in particular; this will throw a lot of light on whether your time is getting spent on doing the right things, and on doing them the right way. It will also reveal to you *the pattern* of how your time gets spent, as opposed to how you think you spend your time. Please go beyond 'studying' the time log; be sensitive and objective in your response which must result in corrective measures on your part. Deeper introspection and auto suggestion should pervade your self-improvement efforts. Here are some suggestions:

Some Introspection   Develop the habit of asking yourself—constantly, and with the intention of improving your conduct—the following *nine* questions:

1. When I come to my workplace in the morning, do I know what are my two or three primary tasks for the day?
2. Do I usually succeed in accomplishing those two or three primary tasks?
3. Do I tackle the difficult tasks when my energies are at their peak?
4. Do I usually complete my tasks by the deadline? Is it usually at the eleventh hour with a feeling of breathlessness, or is there a cushion allowing me to relax before I complete my task?
5. Do I put off difficult tasks and procrastinate?
6. Do I delegate tasks sufficiently—particularly those tasks that are well within the ambit of my subordinates' responsibilities and skills?
7. Have I been able to control interruptions? Have I been successful in curtailing their drain on my time?
8. Do I usually return phone calls when I say I will?
9. In general, do my task accomplishments amount to dealing with the vital few, or do I remain entangled with the trivial many?

This kind of self-analysis is bound to promote in you an urge for managing yourself better with reference to time. And it would be useful to check from time to time whether your time utilization is improving or not. You should extend this inquiry to its logical conclusion by identifying, and acting upon, those two or three specific steps that you feel are most relevant to you during a given period of self-development.

In the light of the realizations emerging from an in-depth study of the log, you should determine *priority categories* for the tasks that lie ahead:

♦ Category 1 could mean 'important *and* urgent' tasks;
♦ Category 2 could mean 'important *but not* urgent' tasks; and
♦ Category 3 could mean 'urgent *but not* important' tasks.

Important vs Urgent Tasks   Important or urgent tasks emanate from their interactions in the crucible of your personality.

It is more important that the tasks you handle are important rather than urgent. An important task denotes a project which has enormous potential to provide good opportunities. If you foresee it well in advance, you can attend to it in time at a relaxed pace. Conversely, an urgent task may be an otherwise manageable, opportunity-bearing one which has gone haywire because it was not foreseen well in advance, or was neglected till it became a small time-bomb, and is now ready to explode.

One criterion that you should consider important is the ratio prevailing between your urgent and important tasks. *A well-organized manager will have fewer and fewer urgent tasks bombarding his desk.* He achieves this because he had foreseen the importance of a task well in advance, and had already set in motion appropriate actions for dealing with it in a relaxed manner, so that he can give it adequate attention. He thus prevents the task from building up into a red-hot urgency. Therefore, the real test of good time utilization is that the influx of 'urgent' tasks should decline over time, and you should be dealing more and more with tasks that are important, allowing yourself sufficient time for handling them in a relaxed manner.

The Vital Few and the Trivial Many A 'high pay off' task is one that promises yields of substantial benefits such as developing untapped markets, landing a major contract, or innovative technologies leading to much higher productivity. You should, therefore, learn to distinguish between the trivial many and the vital few, and critically review the pattern of your engagements. Do you usually remain entangled with the trivial many? In any case, you should always be on the lookout for the vital few and pay timely and adequate attention to them to derive the fullest possible payoffs from them.

Therefore, while interpreting the log, you should also examine your activities in terms of their pay off. You should look upon time as a return on investment.

Adjusting to Your Personal Energy Cycle and Your Moments of Inspiration Each of us has fairly regular energy cycles—the peaks and valleys of our energies. You should observe and make notes as to which are the hours when you usually feel most energetic and productive, and when you feel weighed down with fatigue or lethargy. Once you identify these hours or blocks of hours, you can pattern your working schedule in consonance with your energy cycles. Again, the scheduling of your Category 1, 2 or 3 tasks between your high and low energy periods is very much a matter of personal choice and convenience. However, some kind of order does need to be established. You could, for instance, tackle tough, demanding tasks during your high-energy periods, and save the routine tasks for the low-energy periods.

It is advisable, however, that you devote no more than three or four hours a day to tough tasks, because it is strenuous to sustain concentration for longer periods. By the same token, it is not advisable to sidestep routine tasks, because keeping them in abeyance just because they are routine can also add imperceptibly to your anxiety.

Similar to our energy cycles, each of us has his own moments of inspiration. Some of us are more innovative—full of ideas and plans—while we are in bed about to fall asleep, while travelling to our workplace, or when we make the first contact with our office chair in the morning. Soon thereafter, though, at the appearance of the first daily chore, these moments of inspiration vanish like mist. You should keep paper and pen handy, and immediately jot down the ideas and plans as they come to your mind—no matter how crude or unworkable they may appear at that time. Refinements, workableness or priorities can be set later.

Dealing With Barriers to Time Management

So far we have discussed the methods for organizing ourselves better. But organization alone is not enough. We all know that there are numerous hindrances to the effective utilization of time. These hindrances emanate from the *systems* of the organization and others over which (and whom) we generally do not have much control.

How do you go about managing these hindrances? An attempt has been made here to discuss the possible methods for dealing with them.

System-generated Hindrances

The Desk This is the first office fixture that can create trouble. Most of us make a beeline for the desk the moment we reach office, and tend to spend much of our time in that one spot. Perhaps, the high pressures of our office makes the desk our psychological 'home' providing refuge and strength to us. But the problem with the desk is that it has a wide enough surface, and more importantly, several drawers. These are 'traps' for papers and paper-work. Because of its wide surface and drawers, papers acquire the irresistible habit of accumulating there, thus creating for you a perpetual backlog. As the papers accumulate, your guilt-laden pressure increases which, in turn, distracts you from your determination to deal with them. And the irony is that every time you do a 'spring cleaning' of your desk, you are amazed at the amount of rubbish you have allowed to accumulate! While some of it was never very important (it merely required being glanced at and passed on to others), quite some of it was indeed very important in that it had the potential for good opportunities. But your failure to attend to it in time has rendered it useless; it stares you now in your face as silent, scolding, 'time-barred' testimonies of inaction.

Is the desk to be blamed for all this? The desk, in fact, is an important milestone in your office; and it cannot be blamed if *you* do not use it properly. The desk is actually meant to be a centre for the radiation of your activities, and not as a centre for their absorption, to be kept waiting and crying out for attention.

Also, you must fight your tendency to remain desk-bound, wishing that the work should walk up to your desk. Instead, you must make it a habit to walk over to where the action is. This would give you a feel of the environment and the nuances surrounding a particular task. You would thus be sure about what kinds of actions you should take. In addition, this would also help you dispose off problems more effectively and promptly, thus substantially cutting down your paper-work and your time requirement.

Dealing With Paper-work Paper mismanagement can result in a big drain on your time, besides crippling your ability to function effectively. Neither a clean desk nor sloppiness is a key to paper management, nor is quantity the root cause of a paper glut. The real cause of a paper-work crisis is *your* problem with decision-making, that is, your inablity to decide what to do with the paper in front of you.

TRAF Technique The key to paper management is *processing*. Stephanie Winston suggests a four-stage method she calls the TRAF[3] (Toss, Refer, Act, File) Technique.

Toss Challenge the papers you are hesitant to discard by asking: 'What is the worst that could happen if I threw this out?' Nothing, in all probability. It is probably some routine weekly/monthly reports that were started years ago to fulfill some needs which have faded by now, or notices of seminars you won't attend, advertising circulars, and so on. If there are papers you are genuinely unsure about, maybe they could be kept with other papers to be filed.

Papers that are to be filed, should be segregated into papers for long-term retention, and those to be reviewed (and possibly thrown out) at monthly intervals.

Refer Decide which of the papers deserve to be referred to your colleagues or subordinates who may know more about their contents, or have greater interest in, or need to deal with. Act quickly, which means: *(a)* go through it quickly; *(b)* make comments you consider important and relevant; *(c)* request for a time-bound specific action or response if called for; and *(d)* refer to the right person(s).

While on the subject of reference, it is worth noting what some executives do. They assign one page in their notebook to each such person they have to deal with regularly. 'When I think of what I want to discuss with them, I jot it down on their page. Then, if they walk by my office or call me, I flip to their page and take care of several issues at once.' This practice has merit; you could try it out too.

Act Place all papers you have selected for personal action in one pre-designated spot on your desk. Include all those ambiguous 'I'm-not-sure-what-to-do-with-it' papers. Decisions too are actions; pinpoint top-priority tasks, and start acting from the top-priority items downwards. Avoid the temptation of 'I'll-think-about-it-tomorrow' as far as possible.

File Odd though it may sound at first, a proper filing system plays a very significant role in ensuring optimum utilization of your time.

Hidden among the papers lying about in any organization, there is a treasure-trove of valuable material, ideas, concepts, information and the potential for new opportunities. Therefore, easy access to information is the central point of filing. If you know where the required information is, you have an important resource at hand.

On the other hand, lack of easy and timely access to the right information not only consumes too much of your time, it also deprives you of the benefits of many opportunities. Besides, it results in loss of face and debilitating frustrations.

The problem about filing is not too many files or too few people who know how to file papers. *It is almost always the ambiguous or ill-defined classification system.* An effective filing system should: *(a)* group information into clear and simple categories that reflect the concern of the users; *(b)* permit retrieval of any information within three minutes or less; *(c)* facilitate orderly incorporation of new files; and *(d)* provide a simple, consistent method for clearing out obsolete files.

A common misconception is to equate the physical act of putting papers into folders with the conceptual act of classifying information into practical, usable categories. While the physical act is clearly a clerical activity, the conceptual act calls for judgement and that must be done by managers for various benefits including reinforcement of their overall efficiency and better utilization of time.

Your Role in Generating Paper-work   What about *you* as the source for generating papers and paper-work? It goes without saying that you must do unto others what you wish them to do to unto you. You should, therefore, critically examine the number and volume of papers you have routinely been generating. Ask yourself: 'Are they really necessary?' If yes, 'Are they serving current needs in their present format, presentation, data?' 'Can they be eliminated, replaced or made more concise?' 'Can their frequency be reduced?'

Table 9.2 (on page 226) shows a sample format for evaluating the need and usefulness of departmental reports. This can help in reducing or eliminating unwanted reports.

Even if you curtail just a few papers, you have not only done a lot of good for others, but provided a sizeable relief to yourself in terms of your time-utilization.

Meetings   Meetings are necessary in any organization for coordinating multi-functional activities and facilitating the much-needed network of communication. But they are a double-edged sword. They can easily lose their primary purpose and dwindle into an indulgence rather than a necessity. Each manager's time costs money; and the amount works out to be significant. (According to one study conducted in 1991, the *per-hour cost* of a middle-level manager of 15 years' standing in India came to Rs 235 for the public sector and Rs 311 for the private sector. Since remuneration in India, both in private and public sectors, has gone up at least three-and-a-half times {if not more} by 1996, these figures can safely be assumed

TABLE 9.2: Evaluating the Usefulness of Department Reports

The proliferation of internal reports has begun to cost more—in terms of time, expense and paper—than the benefit warrant. To help cut down on the number of reports produced, please evaluate each report received according to the following criteria:

Name of report	Do you receive it?	Is the report or part of it, of value?	Would a circulation copy suffice?	Too much detail?	Format clear?	Key ideas highlighted?	Frequency: cut back, increase or OK as it is?	Comments

to be Rs 825 for the public sector, and Rs 1,100 for the private sector.)

According to a study conducted a decade ago by Booz, Allen & Hamilton,[4] 299 managers in the USA with an average salary of $40,000 spent half their time in meetings. And a sizeable chunk of that time was absorbed by rambling discussions, manoeuvring around office-politics, excessive socializing, and vested-interest conflicts. Five $50,000-a-year people spending ten useless hours a week can cost an organization well over $1,000 a week.

Let us consider the casualties. The figures given above are merely the *monetary price of the time* the executives spend in meetings. What is not reflected here is the far greater amount worth of activities they could have carried out if they had spent that time merely on their assigned tasks. And what about the *opportunity cost?* If those meetings had been held for truly opportunity-bearing purposes, and they had been conducted to arrive at result-oriented plans of actions, the value of the opportunities secured could be anywhere between ten to twenty times the cost of the executive time spent!

No hard and fast rule can be drawn up for curtailing or controlling meetings. In fact, at the senior levels, meetings are desirable facts of life. It is not abnormal that almost 75 per cent of the senior managers' time gets spent in meetings at horizontal and vertical levels. But for a technical expert, even 20 per cent of his time spent on meetings ought to raise eyebrows.

What is needed is that as a responsible manager, *you* must make it a habit to individually evaluate the meetings you call in terms of their 'pay off'. Similarly, you and all your senior colleagues who usually attend meetings called by one or the other should *jointly evaluate,* periodically, whether your meetings are worth their while. Such evaluations must lead to devising equally effective alternative methods which help you cut down or eliminate time-consuming meetings. For instance, can the matter be handled by a memo, telephone call, tele-conference or informal discussion over tea or lunch? Above all, can the number of persons usually called to attend be cut down—drastically?

What follows are *four* well-tried techniques to *limit the duration* of meetings:

1. Draw up a list of the issues that must be dealt with. Obtain everyone's agreement on: *(a)* the list of items; *(b)* the period

within which these issues have to be dealt with; and *(c)* everyone's commitment that these issues must be truly dealt with, and not pushed over for yet another meeting. Highlight, by citing concrete examples, the adverse effects such as opportunity lost or worsening of the problem if immediate action is not taken.

2. Having followed 1, stick to coverage of the issues within the time limit, allowing no laxity about holding yet another meeting. Maintain the pressure gently but firmly. Keep reminding the participants about the items covered vis-à-vis the time already spent.

3. One subtle and effective way of ensuring business-like discussions is to call the meeting either before the lunch-break or before office closing time!

4. Towards the end of the meeting, wrap up the outcome—the issues covered, decisions taken, implementation planned, by when and by whom.

These are some methods by which you can make the meetings that must be held truly productive and economical in terms of time-consumption. It goes without saying that the suggestions made above must be modified to suit the prevalent relationship-environment, the style of management of the convenor of the meeting, etc. What is important is that some pre-planned method for conducting the meetings in a proper manner must be adopted if past experience with meetings has been disappointing.

Hindrances Through Interruptions

It is quite common that our best-laid plans often go haywire because of interruptions that no one can possibly budget for. These interruptions are in the shape of unexpected visitors, telephone calls that are either about trivial matters or tend to be too lengthy or both, sudden eruption of crises—often on trivial but totally unavoidable matters. All of these make demands on your time, tearing you away from high-concentration activities. Often these are demands you just cannot ignore, no matter how upset you may feel.

Interruptions are a fact of life; many of them require our immediate attention. Each organization has its own rhythm and tempo, including its volume of interruptions that are not controllable to a large extent. However, when interruptions to which you must respond begin to claim greater part of your day, almost everyday, then some deeper issues are involved and some hitherto-untried therapy is called for.

Unexpected Visitors There are always people—subordinates, peers, customers, outsiders—who barge in with their 'I-must-speak-to-you-now' persistence. It is neither possible nor wise to block all such interruptions. These people constitute a far-reaching network of contacts who may already be, or are likely to become, valuable resources. Besides, those of us who wall ourselves in too thoroughly run the risk of shielding ourselves from problems till they become crises. Therefore, it is more realistic to *limit* your control on 'barge-in' interruptions to specific parcels of your time—your 'prime-time' in particular—and be more flexible during the rest of the day.

This calls for making it known to your *subordinates* that you are not to be disturbed during specified times of the day. At the same time let it be known that you would be glad to discuss their problems during certain specified periods of the day.

Saying the same to your peers is not easy. But if they want to interrupt you when you simply cannot afford to spare the time, you have to practice the art of saying 'No'. However, it is not true that saying 'No' must entail being rude. What is required is to *explain why* you cannot extricate yourself from the task you are busy with, and then offer that you would go over to your peers' office when it suits him, or you could meet him later over a cup of tea. If his problem is genuinely urgent, you may have to set aside your own engagement. In any case, you can still bargain with him about the length of this interaction, if possible.

With outsiders who have suddenly descended upon you, an equal amount of tact, as described above, may have to be employed—with the difference that you may not send them back the first time. In case they ring you up before coming, you can still try to set up a meeting at a mutually convenient time, within a time limit.

You have to decide what your highest priorities are and have the courage—pleasantly, smilingly, non-apologetically—to say 'no' to other things. And the way you do that is by having a bigger 'yes' burning inside. The enemy of the 'best' is often the 'good'.'

—Stephen R. Covey, *The 7 Habits of Highly Effective People*

In any case, you have to establish a set routine as to which are the hours you are available for others, and see that it gets known. This may have the effect of bringing down, over time, the influx of unexpected visitors. However, the key to ensuring that you are not mistaken for a snob or a hard-to-get person is to highlight your helplessness with your own pressing tasks. Any negative feelings that your visitors may still be having has to be neutralized by your warmth and convincing evidence that you mean to help them—when you are finally face- to-face with them.

Telephone Calls   A ringing telephone is one of the most obstinate summons of contemporary life. Not to pick it up even when you are far too busy requires courage. There is no denying, though, that the telephone is one of the blessings of modern life; it has made communication fast and effective while retaining the personal touch and has spread the span of our reach far and wide. In fact, it has become inconceivable to do without a telephone in our lives.

Like meetings, this instrument too is a double-edged sword. One, it can penetrate any shields we may build around us. Two, it can reach us without any prior announcement, demolishing, at times, our most creative moments. It renders us almost helpless in the sense we can hardly ignore it. Three, if either party does not watch out, the conversation on this instrument can threaten to become far too lengthy and time-consuming. And then, there is the universal problem of people making unnecessary calls simply because it is so easy to do so.

The telephone is meant to serve us. Therefore, ensure that you don't end up the other way around—with you serving the telephone. Here are *three* suggestions:

1. If you happen to get a long-winded caller on the other end, you can politely but firmly tell him that you have another chore on hold, and could he either tell you the gist of what he has to say quickly or could he, or you, call back at a time suggested by you?
2. When *you* wish to make calls, consider the following suggestions:

    ♦ When you are *about to make the call*:
      • jot down on a piece of paper all the essential points which you wish to cover during this conversation, and keep it in front of you during the call;
      • refer to a notebook where you have been writing down other points for taking them up at a later date with the person you

are about to call; and

- anticipate: *(a)* the information or past correspondence *you* might need; and *(b)* the information or references *he* may need during this call and keep all such papers handy on your desk before making the call.

Now you are ready to make the call.

- ♦ When you *make the call* :
  - during the conversation, keep ticking the points as you deal with them; ensure that your list has been covered. Before ringing off, consider whether this is the right moment to take up the additional points which you have brought forward from your notebook. If appropriate, deal with those points as well—thus giving yourself a bonus; and
  - in case the matter regarding which you are about to make the call requires talking to more than one person, consider carefully the sequence in which you will call the people concerned. Call that person first who has the requisite information but not the last word; and call that person last who has the last word but who needs to know what the others concerned think or feel about the issue.

By following these suggestions, you won't have to call the concerned persons back and forth, and you will save a lot of time besides doing your job in an efficient way.

3. When you *return calls* maintain a meticulous record of the calls you did not attend, and the promises you made to call back. Failure to do so might result in missing out on some potentially useful information. Besides, that does lead to misunderstandings.

- ♦ as far as possible, consolidate all return calls, and make them during one block of time;
- ♦ again, anticipate the inquiries and references that might crop up, and keep all such information or references handy (as suggested above in the context of your going to make a call);
- ♦ make up your mind as to what you need to achieve from making these calls, and aim at the desired results; and
- ♦ practice what you want others to follow: be as brief and to the point as possible.

You as an Interrupter ! Though a very obvious and legitimate question, it is amazing how often we miss putting it to ourselves.

It is precisely for this reason that I raise it so pointedly here. As part of your efforts to get organized for the best possible utilization of your time, you must constantly audit your own habits in terms of the various issues that have been discussed in the foregoing pages. And the same criteria and corrective measures should consciously be applied to yourself. This will not only raise your credibility with those from whom you expect cooperation, but will also contribute greatly to the cumulative efforts of others in the organization to usher in more effective time-management.

Search for Perfection? Yet another element which works out as an obstruction—not interruption as such—to time-utilization is the desire to be perfect. Perfectionism is a compulsive striving for an *ideal* of excellence or organization far beyond any actual utilitarian purpose. It is like insisting on a Rolls Royce for transporting furniture. Striving for perfection up to the point of actual requirement is understandable; it ceases to be desirable when it is pursued for its own sake—far beyond the requirement. The relevance of these observations is that it takes a great deal of time and effort to seek perfection which, in turn, leads to delays. Besides, it takes its toll in frayed nerves on the part of your collaborators and frustration on your part. Examples abound of the so-called 'perfect job' that never gets done—or done in time!

You must ask yourself the following *five* questions whenever you are trying to do a task with finesse, and wish to end it with a flourish:

1. Are you putting in (or considering putting in) disproportionate efforts into the task? Do the means suit the ends?
2. Does the pay-off on the task warrant the efforts? Where is the point of diminishing returns?
3. Is there a simpler, less exacting way to accomplish the results required?
4. Will the attention invested in this task be at the cost of neglecting your other tasks?
5. Does the proposed perfectionism pose the threat of missing your deadline?

Conclusion

Time is the most powerful, elemental, basic, natural factor. It is also a very significant resource for all human efforts and enterprises. While other resources can be controlled and manipulated, time is beyond anyone's reach. And yet it just cannot be ignored or done without. As eloquently brought out in H. G. Wells's *Time Machine*, changes of unbelievable magnitude in the universe, as also in human lives, take place merely by the operation of time—all other factors of space, systems, people, institutions remaining the same. This powerful resource is also scarce and totally unretrievable. Once it slips through our fingers, it is gone for ever. So, how do you manage such an uncontrollable resource, especially since manage it you must? All you can do—and must do—is to *manage yourself* with reference to time.

This realization—that it is you who have to be managed—immediately brings the ball into your court. The first step is to draw upon your reserves of self-discipline. The objective of self-discipline is to so fashion your reflexes, habits and attitudes that you achieve the best possible utilization of the available time. Non-availability of time has never been the real problem; it has always been one of *mis-utilization of time.* The interesting thing about the relationship between utilization and availability of time is that the better you utilize your time, the more time becomes available to you! Once this realisation is grasped by you in the right spirit, the areas where you need to concentrate your efforts will easily reveal themselves—ranging from filing, paper-work, meetings, telephones, dealing with system-generated interruptions to human interrupters, including yourself! And once you learn the art of utilizing your time to its optimum level, the dividends that accrue to you and to your organization as a whole can be amazing.

TEN

Leadership: Some Pragmatic Approaches

CHAPTER OBJECTIVES

- Explain the significance of competence and character for enduring leadership
- Offer practical steps to improve competence and character

Introduction

Managers come in all shades and complexions. Some are specialists, and some are generalists. Some are perfectionists. Some are autocrats, and some are democrats and some believe in laissez-faire. Some are hoarders of power and authority, while some are great believers in delegation. Some seek popularity and a lot of visibility, and some are the 'back-room boys', content with silently doing their assigned tasks. *But those who are effective managers are invariably the leaders*!

In the context of 'delayering' and 'flattening' of organizations being pursued these days, the question that has been gaining currency is: 'Should a manager attempt to be a leader? Wouldn't it be enough if he does well in his traditional and much-needed "managerial functions" of planning, organizing, directing, staffing and controlling?'

Well-known author and educator, Bergen Evans expressed this cynical view: 'For the most part, our leaders are merely *following out in front*; they do but marshal us in the way that *we* are going!' Another writer, Henry Miller has yet another view: 'The real leader has no need to lead—he is content to point the way.'

So, do we really need leadership? What precisely is leadership? Who are or can be leaders? And what practical steps can one take to *become* a leader?

Notwithstanding the many challenges to the very institution of leadership, what stand out time and again are some *basic, real-life* requirements for effective management. That is, there must prevail at the workplace ongoing and balanced interactions between three important elements, namely: *(a)* the manager himself; *(b)* the group he has to manage; and *(c)* the circumstances surrounding these two. These interactions should be so channelized that they lead to achieving predetermined objectives by the best possible utilization of available resources. The real crunch, though, comes when managers try to rely solely on efficiency. They then find out that with all the required non-human resources—money, materials, plants, machinery and technology—having been procured, installed and primed up, *it is the crucial human resource that breathes life into the other resources and gets them going.* This undoubtedly requires the managers to secure *continuing, motivated contributions from the human resource.* While motivation can be promoted, *to some extent,* by structuring the non-human resources and the work itself, it thrives primarily on *effective management of the human resource* through leadership. And when a manger eventually attains effectiveness in these areas, it means that he has graduated—slowly but steadily—*from the status of a manager to the stature of a leader!*

Thus, you can see that the business world has good reasons to believe that *leadership is a requirement of the job of an effective manager*—be he in business, in government, in the army, or any other institution that influence our lives.

Evolution of the Concept of Leadership

The question, 'What is it that makes a person an effective leader?' has been engaging the attention and study of thinkers for a very long time. Plato, the Greek philosopher in the fifth century BC, and Chanakya, the Indian philosopher, economist and strategist in the fourth century BC, made a detailed study of leadership. Chanakya went beyond mere studying; he even put into practice his theories on leadership. And he succeeded in shaping a young man of humble parentage but immense potential into a wise and powerful emperor!

However, this subject has continued to remain both interesting and baffling. During the past 85 years alone, more than 3,000 books and articles on leadership are believed to have been published, and dozens of leadership theories proposed.[1] Yet, we still know relatively little about the factors that determine the success or failure of a leader. Like motivation, no universally accepted theory of leadership has been developed. As James Burns, a dedicated student of leadership, says, it is 'one of the most observed and least understood phenomena on earth'.

Debate continues on whether a leader is 'made' or 'born' with special qualities—such as a 'commanding personality', 'a magnificent hypnotic speaking ability' and a 'booming voice', or even 'imposing good looks'. Yet another idea that has persisted is that a leader must have some charisma—a quality that inspires undying loyalty and devotion among his followers in spite of his not possessing any worldly powers. Defying the exclusivity of these 'theories', we see several 'live' examples—in politics, in athletics and in business—of real leaders not necessarily possessing towering stature, throbbing voice or hypnotic eyes. Some of the quietest and most unobtrusive managers are known to have made their mark as the most effective leaders.

Given below are *five* common denominators of leadership derived from the various conclusions about leadership:

1. It actually represents a category of behaviour that encourages and helps the followers to do their best.
2. It is a dynamic process in which an individual behaves in a manner that *influences* others to follow him willingly to help produce desired results.
3. Leadership is the 'the art of influencing individual or group activities—and securing willing cooperation—for achieving the desired objectives of an organization'.
4. Leadership is something more than—and beyond—power or authority of the leader; it implies some degree of voluntary compliance by the followers.
5. From managerial perspective, leadership represents the ability of the leader to influence his subordinates to willingly commit themselves to perform specific tasks associated with goal accomplishments; and, in that process, derive satisfactions and pride in their 'contribution'.

Some Major Theories on Leadership

What follows are the results of the important researches and experiments on leadership that have proved to be landmarks in the field of management studies.

The 'Trait' Phase As already mentioned, the debate on the subject of leadership had started as early as the fifth and fourth century BC by Plato and Chanakya. While Plato believed that leadership was hereditary, Chanakya proved by his experiment that leadership could be inculcated.

By the end of nineteenth century, it began to be conceded that while leadership was essentially hereditary, its 'traits' could be learned. This marked the beginning of the 'trait phase' of leadership research which attempted to identify those specific traits that made a person an effective leader. Eventually, the following 'list' of traits was identified:

+ personal courage;
+ enthusiasm;
+ self-esteem;
+ self-confidence;
+ sense of responsibility;
+ sense of humour; and
+ communication effectiveness.

No one can really quarrel with the relevance of these traits. However, it is not at all easy for any one person to acquire all these traits. Besides, it is questionable whether it is really necessary that a leader must possess all these traits simultaneously!

The 'Behavioural' Phase From the 1940s, researchers shifted their attention to the study of leader-behaviour, marking the beginning of the behavioural phase. The emphasis shifted to how leaders behave rather than what traits they possess—*what they do, and how, rather than on what they are.*

Ralph M. Stogdill and his team began their studies[2] in 1947, and came up with the findings that effective leader-behaviour is multi-dimensional, that effective leaders exhibit different behaviours in different situations.

They talked of 'consideration structure' which emphasized the psychological closeness between the leader and his followers. They found that 'supervisors with the best records of performance. . . focused their primary attention on the human aspects of their subordinates' problems, and on endeavoring to build effective work groups with high performance goals.'[3]

Another school talked of the 'initiating structure' which emphasized that leader-behaviour was oriented toward attainment of goals. Under this the leader laid down as to who shall do what, how much, by when, and on what standards of performance; and he structured his subordinates' behaviour by directing their activities toward getting the work done.

It was ultimately concluded that while both are necessary for an effective leader, it is more important for him to know how to strike a balance between the two that is appropriate for the particular situation.

In retrospect, these studies are acknowledged to have served as springboards for leadership researches that followed, particularly those that centred on another very important factor—the situational differences that influence leader effectiveness.

The 'Situational' Phase   By the late 1960s, research began to shift decidedly toward a 'situational perspective'. Contemporary theories about leadership are almost entirely 'situational in nature. In contrast to the earlier theories which focused on leader behaviour, *these new theories attempt to explain effective leadership in the context of the larger situation in which it occurs.*

Fred E. Fiedler propounded the 'contingency theory of leadership'[4] which held that effective leadership was contingent upon the *match* between *(a)* a person's leadership style; and *(b)* the 'favourableness' of the leadership situation.

Three factors determined the degree to which a situation can influence a work group:

1. *Leader–member relations:* The better the relations between the leader and his group members, greater is the cooperation and compliance by the members.
2. *Task structure:* The greater the degree to which a group's assignment is programmed and spelled out in a step-by-step fashion (reminiscent of Taylor's scientific management), the higher are the chances of the leader enjoying more influence over his subordinates.
3. *Position power:* The more power and backing from his superiors a leader possesses for rewarding and punishing, hiring or promoting his subordinates, the more power he wields over his subordinates.

What these observations amount to, in simple terms, is that the situation holds the key to a leader's effectiveness. The 'situation' itself is the product of the equation that is established between the:

♦ concerned person's personality;
♦ resultant pattern of relationships he has with his followers; and
♦ position that results with regard to the structure of tasks.

Styles of Leadership

Leadership style is a much-talked about topic. It refers to a leader's manner of acting in a work situation. Some talk about the autocratic style, others about the democratic style. Yet others talk about the 'people-oriented' and 'task-oriented' approaches of leaders. Behind all this talk, there is an implied inquiry whether there is a *specific style* that is *best* for the manager. Stated very simply, leadership style refers to a leader's manner of acting in a situation; and it depends largely upon his personality. Therefore, prescribing the best style of leadership for general adoption is unthinkable.

It can be stated that:

♦ effective leaders do not fall into a fixed style permanently;
♦ leaders don't have to worry about 'style'. They let others worry about it. Leaders themselves are better off taking note of the situations and circumstances surrounding the task and the current mental state of their subordinates, and then casting themselves into that mould of leadership style that has the best chance of achieving the desired results; however,
♦ they have to abide by a pre-condition: their readiness to adopt varying styles must not degenerate into unprincipled, incomprehensible or unpredictable actions on their part. They must remain steadfast to certain core principles in their behaviour toward subordinates and to the problems or opportunities they tackle at that point of time.

Autocratic vs Democratic   It is commonly believed that the autocratic leader tries to influence his followers by telling them *what* to do, and *how* to do it; and the democratic leader believes in *sharing* his leadership responsibilities with his followers by *involving them* in the planning and execution of tasks. The autocratic leader assumes that his power is derived from the position he occupies and the support he enjoys from his superiors; and he proceeds on the notion that the subordinates are innately indolent and they prefer to be led (in keeping with Theory X of McGregor[5]). The democratic leader assumes that his power is granted by his group; and he proceeds on the notion that the subordinates are basically '*not* passive or resistant to organizational needs', and they can, with motivation, be made self-directed and creative at work (in keeping with Theory Y of McGregor).

Laissez-faire Psychologist Kurt R. Lewin[6] identified laissez-faire as a *third form* of *leadership*. Under this style of behaviour the members of the group come to believe that they can do however and whatever they want to. No policies or procedures are established; everyone is left alone with no attempts to influence anyone else. In this situation, the formal leadership role stands abdicated and, therefore, whatever leadership is being exhibited is *informal* and *emergent.*

Figure 10.1 depicts the three styles of leadership in terms of their lines of communication and influence on the subordinates.

There exists, of course, a wide variety of styles of leadership ranging *between* these *three* styles. Robert Tannenbaum and Warren Schmidt[7] have depicted a broad range of styles as a continuum moving from autocratic or boss-centred leader-behaviour to democratic or subordinate-centred leader behaviour at the other end. There are researches and prescriptions galore: Robert House's *Path-Goal Theory,* Robert R. Blake and Jane S. Mouton's *Managerial Grid,* Victor Vroom and Philip Yetton's *Normative Theory,* etc. It is understandable that the main concern of all these researches and studies has been to discover a single *ideal* type of leader-behaviour, if possible. But such an objective has proved to be unattainable—even unwise.

So, where do we go from here? To be fair, all these painstaking studies, researches and their findings make great, eye-opening reading. They have contributed, in parts, valuable insights into the phenomenon of leadership. But what is their practical value? Most of them are good descriptions tending to end up as prescriptions, with little or no practical guidance or built-in clues as to how a person wishing to shape himself into a leader can translate them into *his* plan of actions.

Therefore, I propose not to elaborate upon them any further. Instead, let us turn to some down-to-earth observations in the hope that they may prove helpful for an aspiring or existing leader.

DEMOCRATIC STYLE

- Leader is in touch with all concerned

- Encourages all-round communication

- Provides sense of direction

- Gives and seeks feedback from all

- Conducive to team spirit

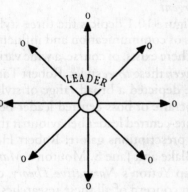

AUTOCRATIC STYLE

- All directions from the leader

- No feedback given or sought

- No communication among the followers

- No concern for team spirit

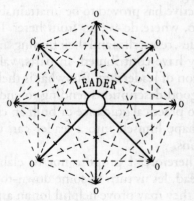

LAISSEZ-FAIRE SYTLE

- No directions from anyone to anyone

- Everyone free to do what they wish—but for what purpose?

- Everyone in touch with everyone except with the leader!

- Any team spirit

FIGURE 10.1 Styles of Leadership

Pragmatic Approaches to Leadership

I now propose to lay before you my suggestions, under two broad headings:

+ approaches to leadership; and
+ steps towards leadership

Approaches to Leadership

These approaches are a prelude to the steps to be taken by you for effective leadership. They comprise primarily the approaches you should integrate in your thinking and behaviour for paving the way to emerge as leaders. It also means re-orienting, where necessary, *your attitudes* and *angles of vision* on matters related to leadership.

To emerge as a leader, you must:

+ be yourself;
+ have self-esteem;
+ consider leadership as a transaction;
+ be 'open' and seek 'feedback';
+ be consistent;
+ be flexible;
+ be up-to-date on information;
+ be decisive;
+ be accessible; and
+ develop your charisma.

Let us discuss what these qualities mean in concrete and 'implementable' terms.

A Leader Must Be 'Himself' Determine after adequate introspection as to 'who' you are. What are your characteristics that are ripe, or can be refined or reinforced, for being used as *your* qualities for leadership? Maybe you feel good about your persistence, finely-honed logical mind, good imagination or creativity, or the values you possess. Work with what you have. Identify your leadership strengths and use them, and further refine or strengthen them.

In this context, a leader must first be himself. There is no *one* way to lead. Good leaders come in more than one personality type; they may be loud or quiet, aggressive or easy to get on with. As an aspiring leader, do not make the mistake of trying to mould yourself after a so-called 'role model'. You must be yourself.

Have Self-esteem As an aspiring leader, you must have a positive self-image. You must *deserve* respect from yourself. This does not come merely by wishing it. You must so build yourself up on *competence* and *character* that you are able to look into your own eyes in the mirror without flinching. Unless you possess genuine reasons—deep down—to respect yourself, others cannot be expected to respect you. Similarly, you must believe in what you do or propose to do, which means your sense of values must be intact in respect of the projects you have undertaken. Only then will you be able to show real enthusiasm. This, in turn, will rub off on your followers as well. They will unhesitatingly look upon you as their leader and be infected with a go-getting team spirit.

What's Right With Me?

Many of us would hesitate to ask this for fear of sounding conceited. But such hesitation or guilt about being conceited would be misplaced. We get better at whatever we subject to keener study or thinking. This is true both about our strengths and weaknesses. If we focus only on our mistakes, we can be sure we shall become more adept at making them; the converse is equally true about our strengths. If Edison had allowed himself to be swamped by his 5,000 mistakes while he was working on the electric light bulb, the world would have had to wait for God knows how long before getting electric bulbs.

Learn from your achievements—not your mistakes. Study your successes because your future successes are dependent on your current achievements, not merely on avoiding of the mistakes you have already made. Identify where, and in what, your strengths lie, and build on them. You will no longer feel limited by your current job and skills, but will be able to meet obstinate challenges and promising opportunities with a measure of confidence hitherto unknown to you!

Consider Leadership as a 'Transaction' The relationship between a leader and his followers is built up—slowly and steadily—over a period of time; and all the time an exchange or transaction goes on whereby the leader both *gives* and *gets* something. *You give some things*—challenging assignments, guidance, training, delegation in order to develop the followers, support, recognition, fair treatment. *And you get some things*—cooperation, dedicated team-work, loyalty, enthusiastic work and strength resulting from these factors.

Make concerted efforts to remain in touch with your subordinates—particularly with the problems they may be facing. This would enable you to provide support, encouragement and advice to your subordinates. Such convincing evidence of your interest will propel them, in a natural way, to be *more inclined to respond to your leadership*. This will encourage and help them to do their best for you and your projects.

The things you do—to yourselves and to your followers—are more important than the traits you are born with. *You may not be able to help what you are, but you do have a lot of control over what you do.*

Communicate—be Open and Seek Feedback   One important catalyst in communication is 'openness'. The more you open up, the more your subordinates will open up to you.

You should take a close look at the quality of your communication. Has it been confined to merely 'announcements' or directives from you downward? Are you 'included' by your subordinates in what they think, feel or plan in response to *your* communications to them? Do they respond to you positively, or are they indifferent or even hostile to you or to your messages?

Business involvement is an essential facet of the kind of communication that builds up your leadership. Effective communication is not complicated. The best communication at the workplace is that which concerns the work, and is conducted as a direct exchange between you and your subordinates. Make it a point to get your people together for some relaxed conversation about the current performance of the organization, the hopes for the future, etc.

Another important ingredient of good communication is that you must be a good listener. Give the subordinate a chance to talk about his job. Listen to his problems; ask questions. By doing so you will accomplish several things: the subordinate will welcome the chance to express his feelings, needs and desires; he will in all probability reveal facts and feelings you need to know if you are to remain in touch with the affairs of the organization that are relevant to you.

Yet another—even more important—ingredient of good communication is the credibility you build up among your subordinates.

Your people must believe you, and believe in you.

People acknowledge their superior as credible when they perceive him as being:

- ♦ trustworthy;
- ♦ knowledgeable about what he talks about;
- ♦ dynamic;
- ♦ sincere; and
- ♦ a person who has sense of direction.

There are no short cuts to credibility. At the same time, a leader in particular cannot afford to do without it.

You can earn this credibility only by consistently demonstrating that you are true to your words and deeds, that you can be relied upon, and that you have the courage of your convictions.

Be Consistent A leader is someone his followers want to be sure they can depend on; and the essence of dependability is consistency. However, consistency does not lie in always doing everything the way it has been done before, down to the last detail. What we are talking about is *consistency in the essentials.*

> *People can't live with change if there's not a changeless core inside them. The key to the ability to change is a changeless sense of who you are, what you are about and what you value.*
> —Stephen R. Covey, *The 7 Habits of Highly Effective People*

This simply means that the general principles you subscribe to and take your stand on should be known to everybody—and everybody should be able to reasonably predict how you will act in situations attracting those principles. One of the essentials of leadership is that you be even-handed and consistent in administering policy. Once you begin to make exceptions that are incomprehensible, your credibility for consistency is in jeopardy.

Be Flexible Adapt yourself to new situations with sensible changes. As in life, things are always changing in the business world too. But not many of us get used to changes; and this leads to alarming problems—like missed buses, explosive crises, etc.

Remember that when changes are imminent, your subordinates look to you for clarifying vital issues and their implications, for guidance or for clear evidence that you (and they) are in control, and you know which way to turn. In fact, your subordinates measure your leadership abilities, to a considerable extent, in terms of their perception as to how confidently—and successfully—you respond to change.

Be Up-to-date With Information   You must possess up-to-date knowledge and skill—*and you must know how to use them with expertise.* Nothing impresses your subordinates more—and secures their acceptance of your leadership—than convincing evidence that you are abreast with all there is to know about: *(a)* technical know-how related to the jobs you and your people are engaged upon; and *(b)* what is going on at all levels of the operations you are responsible for.

Additionally, you must continue renewing yourself. As a corollary to the mind-boggling advancements in technical knowledge fields, you have to acquire knowledge or skills in areas that may be *new to you.* For example, in almost any area of operation, it has become essential for you to become computer-literate, more consumer-sensitive or acquire more refined skills for management of the human resource at your level.

As the eminent industrialist, Clarence Randall, once remarked, a leader must:

+ know;
+ know that he knows; and
+ make it known that he knows.

Be Decisive   You must be willing and able to take clear-cut decisions *and* actions—without procrastination. Remember that while decision-making must be a participative process, the 'taking' of decision must be done by you, the leader. The buck must stop with you!

Some managers go overboard in their attempt at turning decision-making into a group activity. They call meetings, consult endlessly with subordinates and are constantly asking: 'What would you do?'—even when they know what they want to do. This is not appreciated by the subordinates. While they welcome being consulted, they do expect their leader to take decisions. They grow uneasy and lose confidence with a leader who can't seem to make up his mind, or who is unwilling to take responsibility.

The right thing to do is that *you* must decide. Your subordinates will follow you if you are decisive—even when they may not agree with all of your decisions.

Be Accessible Be around when needed and listen with under-standing. It is not enough for you to be out in the front. You must also be in step with your people—visible and available when, and where, they need you. This goes a long way in infusing confidence and rapport between you and your subordinates. Besides, by being where the action is, you too get a deeper insight into—and a feel of—what is really going on.

'Charisma' Matters—and it Can be Developed All said and done, there is such a thing as 'charisma' in a leader. It is that special quality in some persons that makes others *want* to follow their lead. This component of a leader transcends the procedural or rational aspects of leadership; it is something intangible and yet very real and very effective.

And charisma can also be developed. Keen observation has shown that charisma is usually made up of the following ingredients:

♦ dedication;
♦ sincerity;
♦ involvement;
♦ earnestness regarding goal and work;
♦ relational approach toward followers; and
♦ result-orientation.

This combination of ingredients, when possessed by a leader, has often proved to be infectious for the followers; in due course, they are convinced that the charismatic leader is a good influence on them, or he is in a position to do good to, or for, them.

The interesting thing about these ingredients is that they are certainly *acquirable*, if only a manager sets out to do so.

Steps Towards Leadership

The attitudinal re-orientation discussed above constitutes the 'approaches' towards leadership. They pave the way for you to take concrete 'steps' towards attaining and retaining the stature of a leader. They comprise the following:

♦ job restructuring;
♦ moulding a winning team;

- delegation;
- competence;
- character; and
- ability to deal if and when leadership is challenged.

The demarcation I have made between 'approaches' and 'steps' is primarily for your easy understanding, but in reality, there is bound to be a lot of overlapping.

Let us now turn to the pragmatic steps towards achieving leadership.

Job Structuring and Job Enrichment   How tasks are presented to your subordinates has the power to make the tasks sufficiently challenging and interesting (or not) to them. In fact this 'how' has often proved to be a very potent motivator in itself. This calls for a self-renewing desire and ability on *your* part as the leader to innovate. This innovation is necessary for injecting newer dimensions into the jobs. Without these innovations, your followers have to keep working repeatedly and thus suffer the agony of monotony and a feeling of under-utilization. This is where *job structuring and job enrichment* come in.

There are *two* other facets of this issue:

1. Tell your people what to do. This is, of course, part of your job. But *how you tell them what to do* can help you become a better leader. Begin by telling them *why* the job is to be done. You may add what happens next so that they realize how their function ties in with other functions. If possible, *show as you tell*—either by example, illustration or by showing samples. Let them talk—about when, where and how they would do the job.
2. The above process is not complete unless you tell them what job standards shall apply—in terms of quality, cost, time-limits and quantities. But be careful; don't give them impossible jobs or standards. Unrealistic goals invariably become demotivating; they freeze even capable workers into inaction or end up with messy actions.

Structure the job on these lines for each subordinate. You may well be on the path of practical leadership.

Mould a Winning Team   You must possess or acquire the art of moulding a winning team. This takes effort and determination, and a few coaching skills. You can do this in *five* ways:

1. Create a shared sense of purpose. Clarify the vision, and let your team-mates see the logical goals by themselves. You should thus be able to focus the energy of the team to enable it to accomplish extraordinary things.
2. Make the goals 'team-goals'—not your personal goals. Unless the whole team wins, no one wins. A good leader always uses the first-person plural, 'we' and 'our', and emphasizes how everyone's work has importance, and fits in with the overall scheme of things. Invite participation; let decisions bubble up from the team. Don't dictate solutions.
3. Make each member responsible for the team-product. You should make each team-member feel that his contribution plays an important role. Show your team-members what effect *their* actions will have on the total organizational objectives.
4. Share the glory, accept the blame. As a leader, it is your duty (privilege?) to spread the benefits around when things are going well. You should pat your people on the back, get a write-up in the company newsletter or take such measures that spread the good word around. But when things go wrong, you must not point accusing fingers at your team. You should accept the blame publicly, then speak privately with the team about how things could be improved.
5. Be involved. Gone are the days when it was easy for the boss

---

Leader vs Boss

A leader, and an aspiring leader, would do well to remember the distinction between a 'boss' and a 'leader', and choose his role carefully. We reproduce below the wise statement of Gordon Selfridges, the founder of the famous and prestigious London departmental store:

'The boss depends upon authority; the leader on goodwill.

The boss inspires fear; the leader inspires enthusiasm.

The boss says "I"; the leader says "We".

The boss fixes the blame for the breakdown; the leader fixes the breakdown.

The boss says "Go"; the leader says "Let's go".'

to stay aloof. Now the boss concept itself has yielded place to the 'leader' concept. You, as the leader, have to remain involved all the time so that you can have an exact idea of what is going on, and what help and directions you should offer.

Practice Delegation   You must try to understand the significance and benefits of proper delegation. It is primarily a tool for fully developing the potential of your subordinates and, ultimately, for generating motivation among them. Therefore, you must select such tasks for delegation that would be interesting and would stretch their capabilities. You must invest time and efforts in your subordinates so that you may reap the full benefits of their contributions at a later stage.

It is important that you budget for mistakes that your subordinates might make. This is a price you have to pay for enabling them to learn, while you try to 'develop' them through delegation. But you must also stand up for them if they get into trouble.

Competence and Character   I now take up these two ingredients which I believe to be the *real keys* to leadership. They are like the pillars on which the effectiveness of leadership rests. And these can be built up—step by step—along pragmatic lines. Even if you are somewhat deficient in the other ingredients of leadership discussed so far but are sound on these two, you have fairly good chances of emerging as leaders among your people.

The suggestions and ideas discussed here can easily be put into practice since they are well within the competence of most people who wish to develop leadership qualities.

Competence   Let me begin with an imaginary—but universally pertinent—description of what invariably happens when someone is placed as a supervisor of a *new* team. The first couple of days are, of course, spent by the supervisor settling down in the new setting. On the surface, both sides extend a generous offer of goodwill and cooperation; but beneath the surface, there is intense watchfulness for discovering noteworthy characteristics—especially the 'chinks in the armour'. And then, maybe on the second or third day, the supervisor is approached by an innocent-and-helpless-looking subordinate (usually the 'elder brother' among the subordinates) seeking guidance for solving a problem related to work. The subordinate goes to some length emphasizing that he has tried all he knows, but has failed to find a solution (of the problem which may or may not be real); and then he asks the supervisor for guidance. If the supervisor: *(a)* does not come up with the correct solution, *(b)* is unable to see through the bluff in case the so-called problem is a practical joke; or *(c)* takes too long, in the subordinate's opinion, to come up with the correct solution, he runs the risk of being 'written off' immediately by his most important clientele, i.e., his subordinates. In fact, the rest of the subordinates are eagerly waiting at that moment to get the 'verdict' on their new boss. It would be 'good news' to them if their representative declares that the boss does not know enough. Immediately thereafter, the grapevine gets into gear to find out what strings this boss might have pulled to reach that position! In any case, regardless of what opinions the top management may have about this supervisor and what other good qualities he may indeed possess, more than half his claim to lead his team has suffered a major setback.

The moral of this story is that the single most important requirement of a leader is convincing evidence that he is competent.

You can give concrete proof of your competence in the following *seven* ways:

1. You, the leader, must possess adequate knowledge and skill relating to the gamut of tasks that are carried out under your jurisdiction.
2. The brilliance you may have displayed 'once upon a time' either of knowledge or skill is not good enough; you have to keep yourself abreast with the latest advancements in these areas. You must update yourself continuously.
3. You must be decisive, and your decision-making style should, as far as possible, be participative.
4. You must be accessible. But mere accessibility will not do; your people must be convinced that you are a good listener.
5 You must dare to be different when warranted—not just for the sake of appearing different, but for sound reasons. This can happen only when adequate knowledge and skill lend to you the courage of your conviction.
6. You must take full responsibility for the resources placed at your command—both physical and human. Particularly, with regard to the human resource, you must constantly do your best to develop them through delegation and offer of challenging tasks.
7. You must own up the mistakes, if any, your people may commit; and, where justified, you must stand up for them.

On a superficial view, these requirements may appear to you as a tall order. But it deserves to be reiterated that these are essential for developing your competence. And it deserves to be emphasized that there are no short-cuts to competence. And what is the problem, anyway? These are all down-to-earth actions that you can practice very well.

Character 'What next?', assuming that a person has acquired adequate competence. You must know from your experience of various kinds of people that there are many people who are held in awe for their competence but are *not* regarded as leaders. In fact, they are feared or hated! Character in a leader occupies the same importance as competence. A person with great competence but no character is as ineffective as a leader of people as one who has abundance of good character but no competence.

> *If I try to use human influence strategies and tactics of how to get other people to do what I want, to work better, to be more motivated, to like me and each other—while my character is fundamentally flawed, marked by duplicity and insincerity— then, in the long run, I cannot be successful. My duplicity will breed distrust, and everything I do—even using so-called good human relations techniques—will be perceived as manipulative.*

—Stephen R. Covey, *The 7 Habits of Highly Successful People*

What exactly do we mean by 'character'? And can we really mould our character—soon enough to be of use *now*?

We concede that a person's character is built up, inch by inch, over a long period of time as a result of the cumulative impact of his experiences with diverse situations and people. Usually, such a 'distilled' character is so deeply ingrained that it is too difficult, if not impossible, to change.

What I have picked up for your consideration here are the mental qualities—such as behaviour, temperament and attitude. We know that a person's *moral* nature, values or qualities cannot be changed— not even after years of efforts. But what can certainly be altered is his *attitude* and *behaviour*—provided, of course, he is willing to make the effort for self-development.

Actually, what really counts in relation to your followers is: *(a)* how you reveal yourselves to your people as a *fellow human being;* and *(b)* how you behave during your day-to-day, work-related, interactions with them. It is my belief based on experience—and I hope to be able to demonstrate this here—that a person's 'character' in relation to his mental activities, attitude and behaviour can certainly be changed, over a reasonably brief period of time, if he undertakes to make the change with sincere efforts.

One pertinent question is: Why call this 'character'? Why not simply call it 'behaviour' or 'attitude'? The choice I have made is deliberate. It is based on the belief that once the recommended changes in behaviour and attitude are adopted and practised, and the person concerned realizes the enormous benefits he has been deriving from them, it is quite possible that he will automatically internalize them. And when he does so, it might even change his 'character' in the long run!

With this in mind, I offer here a few suggestions which require that a leader—and any one aspiring to become a leader—makes only *some* adjustments in his pattern of behaviour and style of management. In fact, the 'adjustment' itself is confined only to: *(a)* subtle shifts in *emphasis* in his normal behaviour or attitude; and *(b)* introduction of some newer elements in his *style* of management.

Emphasize What—not who—Goes Wrong (or Right)! Whenever something goes wrong, the natural tendency is to find out *who* made the mistake—with an implied exasperation at the person. Let us ponder over the implication. If the boss's reputation is that he goes after the subordinate who makes a mistake, and that he makes it hot for him, any of the following *three* set of situations may prevail—singly or collectively:

1. His subordinates would not like to take any risks in what they are required to do. No initiatives, no decisions if risks are involved. Just carry on the routine, or work in a routine manner.
2. In spite of great caution, if something does go wrong, all subordinates would become united in making sure that the boss does not get to know of the mistake. He may suffer the embarrassment of learning about the mistake in his own section/department from outsiders!
3. If the mistake is too big to be concealed, the concerned subordinate would try his best to pass the blame on to someone else.

The net effect is that the leader does not have a 'team'; he only has a cluster of subordinates, with no bond between them and the boss, or among themselves.

If, on the other hand, the boss has a reputation that he is more keen to find out what goes wrong rather than go after the person who made the mistake, his people will operate in a tension-free atmosphere. They would collaborate with him to track down the cause(s) of the mistake, and do something to eliminate such mistakes. They would strengthen team-spirit, and the boss would have a team he can rely upon for taking initiatives!

When things go right, it is equally frustrating to single out a 'who'. Anything that comes out right is the result of the pooled efforts of more than one person. It is another matter that one of the members might have spearheaded the success. When only one person is singled out for the praise or indulgence, the others who usually contribute to the efforts silently but significantly are likely to feel left out. No matter what camaraderie prevails in that group, it is bound to wear off over time if this practice continues.

I am not saying that the 'who' should not be identified when things go wrong or right. In fact, the person should be identified because he may need help or even disciplining when things keep going wrong; or he may need commendation or accelerated developmental inputs when things keep going right. What I am recommending is that *the emphasis* should be more on finding out *what* goes wrong or right.

Emphasize the 'why' of a Task   Managers, in their keenness to be explicit, spell out the 'what', the 'how', the 'when', the 'how many', and the 'standards of performance' while assigning tasks to their subordinates. Unfortunately, in most cases, they miss out on providing the 'why' of a task. The pity is that they make this omission unwittingly. By failing to do so, they create a gap between their and their subordinates', objectives. By not letting them be part of the excitement of the challenge surrounding the task, they make the subordinates feel that they are outsiders who are merely expected to do what they are told to. Thus, the subordinates are robbed of the opportunity to get involved, to feel the excitement of challenge, and to get motivated.

Again, in this case too, all that the managers have to do is to incorporate in their normal interactions the element of sharing with their people the 'why' of a task—of course, to the extent the other organizational considerations permit them to do so.

Welcome Strong Subordinates Strong subordinates are those who have a mind of their own, who demonstrate knowledge or skill superior to others, and who have the courage to speak up even contrary to what the boss has been saying or doing. When the boss spots such subordinates, he usually becomes apprehensive. He even feels insecure, and tries to steamroll such subordinates by using his authority. He goes on to systematically demoralize such subordinates; he either ignores their suggestions, or silences them with sharp reprimands or transfers them to other departments when they become a pain in the neck.

This attitude must be forsaken by the boss because it is he who loses more than the subordinate. He denies to himself and to his team the benefits of better quality of contributions. Even greater is the loss to the team. Instead of re-invigorating the team by welcoming such subordinates, the boss actually demoralizes the others and impoverishes the team. If he feels insecure, he should understand that he himself is to blame. In fact, he should welcome such subordinates because they give him the much-needed signal that the time has come for him to sharpen and upgrade his own knowledge or skill.

Go for the Right Questions (the Right Answers will Take Care of Themselves) Especially those managers who have built up impressive track records of successes become vulnerable to one obstinate ailment: rushing out with answers. Quite possibly this mental state is brought about by their well-earned self-confidence (which imperceptibly grows into a kind of arrogance bred by over-confidence). The result is that even before a problem or an issue has been fully unfolded to them, they think they know exactly what it is about, and tend to consider any further diagnostic deliberation a waste of time. They eagerly come out with *their* decision as to what is wrong and *their* prescription of the 'right solution' by drawing from the storehouse of their past experience. What they usually miss is that they may have come out with the 'right answer' for the 'wrong question'! This results in a double damage: *(a)* the problem gets worse; and *(b)* the subordinate who consulted the 'expert' feels frustrated because he was neither heard fully nor given the opportunity to 'participate' in working out the solution.

Therefore, *all* managers—especially the experienced and successful ones—must watch out against this tendency; they must always invest adequate time and attention to make sure that they have fully understood what the right question is. Once they know the right question, finding the right answer is usually not a problem. And the 'rightness' of the right answer lies in working it out with the subordinate consulting the manager.

Practice Fairness Coupled with Firmness The popular notion about fairness is being soft, accommodating, nice to people. And firmness, on the other hand, is regarded as being tough, strict, difficult, saying 'no' most of the times. But the fact is that it requires more courage and guts to be fair than firm. Actually, fairness and firmness are simply two sides of a coin. Every time we wish to be fair to one person, we have to be firm with half a dozen others who may prey upon us with their vested interests. Besides, the difficulty about being fair is that we have to abandon all other worldly-wise, self-interest-centred considerations and compromises, and go in for what is right purely on merit. Whenever, one is in the process of debating whether to be fair or not, a lot of tempting arguments from within—and advice from others—raise their heads, suggesting that fairness is an antiquated concept, that we should be smart, worldly-wise, and do something which promotes *our* interest—never mind fairness.

But you as a leader are under close watch all the time—not only in terms of your deeds and words, but especially in terms of *your intentions*. It is imperative that your decisions or actions are transparent in regard to your adherence to fairness and being even-handed. Over time, people must come to believe that you are *predictable*, that whenever you have to choose between fairness and unfairness, you can be relied upon to be fair—even though it may entail a lot of personal sacrifice and risk of unpopularity among those with whom you shall have to be firm.

Some of you may choose to be smart and not go in for the rigours of being fair. In that case, you cannot 'eat the cake and have it too'; you will remain only a boss—you cannot become a leader! Because, 'fairness-coupled-with-firmness' is inseparable from the profile of a leader.

Be People-oriented, but with Goal-achievement as the Objective The real test of all that a leader has, and does, is whether he can create goal-congruence among his people and ensure goal-achievement by them. In that context, all the shifts in emphasis and changes in attitude and behaviour and management style that have been suggested above are meant to ultimately usher in a team-spirit that would motivate your people to do their best to achieve the desired results for the organization.

Therefore, do remember that the above-suggested 'reforms' introduced by you are not merely exercises in self-improvement nor mere attempts at enriching the environment around you. These have a specific purpose; they must inculcate among all team-members a will to achieve the desired results. All your actions, and inputs, must be geared to that objective.

Given below are *eight* observations distilled from the foregoing discussion:

1. A good leader may or may not be a good manager of resources, but a good manager has got to be a good leader. It is, in fact, a *requirement of his job* that he ultimately emerges as a leader of his men.
2. The skills required for a balanced management of the human and non-human resources can certainly be picked up (provided, of course, the person has basic intelligence, aptitude and willingness). Hereditary qualities, if any, are welcome, but their absence is certainly not a limiting factor for the acquisition of these skills.
3. Leadership is not tied down to any one style, such as authoritarian, democratic or laissez-faire. There is a saying in Hindi: 'शहर सिखावे कोतवाली' which means: 'It is the profile of the city and its people that teaches the Sheriff how to do his job!' An effective leader does well not to feel tied down to any one approach; he is perfectly justified in moving from one approach to another in order to meet the situations facing him.
4. Leadership is not tied down to hierarchy, either. It is not dependent on *status* alone; it is a matter of *stature* as well which can be acquired over a period of time by how the leader acts in challenging or normal situations, and how he behaves with his people. In a nut-shell, it comes from the maturity you have acquired over the years.

> *Maturity is the balance between courage and consideration. If a person can express his feelings and convictions with courage, balanced with consideration for the feelings and convictions of another person, he is mature, particularly if the issue is very important to both parties.*
>
> —Stephen R. Covey, *The 7 Habits of Highly Successful People*

5. Since situation plays a very important role in the exercise of leadership, any one in a given situation who, by his actions and behaviour, influences the actions, behaviour and *feelings* of others, plays the role of a leader in that particular situation.

   Therefore, leadership is not restricted or reserved only for the superiors. In a typical workplace, one comes across any number of examples where the so-called subordinate either saves a ticklish situation or comes up with ideas brighter than the boss's. In such situations, he has acted as a leader, and such leadership initiatives deserve to be encouraged and recognized.

6. Following from the above, those who are not bosses must not resign themselves to the idea that they are not, or cannot be, leaders. Each one has the responsibility—and should be given the opportunity—to exercise leadership whenever demanded by situations; and he should rise to the occasion—not only for the good of the organization he works for, but also for his own self-development.

7. Among wise managers there is a growing realization that the position called 'manager' may not exist in the foreseeable future. What will be needed are 'leaders' possessing vision for the future and the ability to coach and guide their people to achieve full potential. Simply being an efficient manager wouldn't be enough. More than ever, businesses, schools, even charitable institutions, civic groups, need *leaders* who can help people achieve their potential. Once their potential is achieved, 'efficient managing' can be relied upon to take care of itself. Leaders in future, therefore, will have more to do with 'developing people' than 'managing' things themselves.

8. Loyalty does not come from simply wishing it, or by trying to be liked by your people. In fact, your primary concern should not be to make yourself liked by your people, if you want that they should really like you. Instead, you should develop a sincere and genuine interest in your people, and your being liked by them will follow naturally.

   Today, if you were to believe some people, loyalty is dead. They emphasize that today the relationship between the boss and his/her subordinates is strictly a matter of 'What have you done for me lately?'; nothing matters except the rupees in the pocket. Perhaps this view reflects the frustration of those managers who haven't bothered to develop the warm, direct, person-to-person relationship with their associates that leads to loyalty. True, employees aren't as loyal as they used to be; they require a lot more convincing evidence that their bosses have a genuine interest in their well-being. But this is certainly something that you can work on.

What if Your Leadership is Challenged?[8]

Even the most seasoned bosses run into a situation where their leadership is challenged. The important thing for you is to recognize such a development in its *early stage*, and take effective steps to eliminate the causes before the resistance or opposition develops beyond control.

Here are *five* typical symptoms:

1. Excessive or frequent need for disciplining the subordinates for bypassing, negligence, even insubordination.
2. Grievances galore of all kinds, and trivial matters being blown out of proportion.
3. Reluctance to cooperate, increasing need for arguing or cajoling them to get even simple tasks done.
4. Slump in overall performance record.
5. The boss's leadership being ignored, in the sense that his people no longer ask questions or look up to him, and try to make their own decisions.

These are serious symptoms, and they mean that you have been neglecting the 'scene' for too long. More than doing something *to* the subordinates, these call for you to have a serious look at yourself and do something to yourself!

Any one of these symptoms calls for two-pronged action:

♦ you must keep a cool head. You should deal with *individual cases* and not take a single case to be representative of all; and
♦ you must resist the temptation to 'make an example'. If you do so, it may turn out to be the spark that lights the explosion. Instead, you should look for the *underlying causes of the trouble*, and deal with them.

As part of your introspection, as well as your plan of action, you should seek answers to the following *six* questions:

1. Have you been failing to make decisions promptly enough?
2. Have you been collecting all the facts before making your decisions?
3. Have you been 'selling' your ideas and decisions by explaining the 'why'—or have you been relying too much on your authority?
4. Have you been allowing personal feelings—friendships, animosities, etc.—to influence the running of your affairs?
5. Have you been allowing your staff to have some say on solutions of group problems?
6. Have you been taking positive steps to underline the group nature of the work—such as group-goals and group achievements?

Honest and ruthless answers to these questions will themselves suggest to you what remedial measures you must undertake—immediately, and in the long run. They will also tell you where your deficiencies lay, and what you must watch out against in future.

Conclusion

Although 'leadership' has been much discussed, researched and written about, it remains extremely elusive—as far as its adoption by most people is concerned. However, much ground has been covered, and a number of misconceptions have been removed due to these researches and the ongoing discussions they have generated. For instance, leadership is not a bundle of in-born traits; there is nothing hereditary about it, and much of it can be learnt. Even though 'charisma' is an important element in leadership, there is nothing mystical or supernatural about it. The ingredients that build up 'charisma' can be identified, and broken down to components which can be learnt, practised and integrated in your behaviour and style of functioning. Leadership is not necessarily based on authority or hierarchy; anyone who, in a given situation, is required to—or comes forward to—handle the problem or challenge, becomes a leader—at least during that situation. The more participative and result-oriented a person, the greater are his chances of emerging as a leader. The cornerstone on which leadership rests is the art of 'managing' human resource effectively, in which 'development' of the people has now acquired great importance.

There has been an age-old tussle between authority and influence. Authority is what a 'boss' relies upon for getting things done. Influence, on the other hand, is the power to produce results through reason, personal examples, and the followers' desire to fall in line with their superior or guide. This is what a 'leader' relies upon for getting things done. Managing by authority implies direct control and manoeuvres for obtaining desired results—with or without the willing cooperation of others. Managing by influence, on the other hand, hinges on the willing cooperation of others. Such cooperation emanates from the followers becoming convinced about the rationale of the desired results *and* the leader's sincerity about the development and betterment of his followers—simultaneously while he is getting things done by them. The followers grow in their belief that their leader can 'deliver the goods' and that they are going to benefit in several ways by following his lead. Authority depends on status; influence depends upon stature.

As a leader, you must steer clear of the slippery grounds of authority which create bosses; you must rely, as far as possible, on influence which will finally shape you into a true leader.

The various branches of management of human resource (such as decision-making, delegation, communication, etc.) are like the 'rivulets' which, if managed effectively, can come together to form a mighty 'river' of motivation. It is the leader who can give direction to these rivulets. Under effective leadership, the 'river' of motivation can gather a natural momentum of its own, which, on the one hand, can ensure impressive position and gains for the organization, and, on the other, lead greater number of employees towards self-actualization.

The two pillars on which leadership rests are competence and character. The specific connotations of these terms have been spelled out. They can certainly be acted upon and given shape to on the practical plane. Unless these are integrated by the boss into his management style and personality, he cannot become a leader. In fact, a leader may not be handicapped even if he is ignorant about all other researches and techniques of leadership. If only he builds himself up on his competence and character, he can emerge as an enriched leader.

In the ultimate analysis, a leader is like a 'guru'—a philosopher, friend and guide. He teaches, he becomes a work-partner, he guides without seeming to do so or without having to throw his weight around.

ELEVEN

Your Sublimation as an Effective Manager

Introduction

Imagine that you as a manager have acquired all sorts of skills and attitudinal accomplishments that you consider important for proper functioning. Also assume that you do utilize these qualities in your day-to-day working to the best of your capability. Still, in the ultimate analysis, the one paramount criterion on which your efforts shall have to be evaluated by yourself and by others around you, is: how effective have you been?

This criterion of effectiveness is invariably concerned with whether your efforts have produced the required *results* with reference to the problems or opportunities around which you have invested all your efforts. Further, are your efforts likely to produce *desirable results* and not just the required results? The test of such 'desirability' is: how enduring and free from adverse side-effects your efforts prove to be now, and in the long run. Also, do your efforts and style of working today invigorate you and your team so that you can be depended upon to *repeat* such performance whenever required? Or have you 'spent' yourself and your team during this project to the extent that every-thing has started falling apart, and your team is gasping for breath?

These are the questions that should propel a manager to apply the acid test to all his efforts and expertise. The name of that acid test is:

effectiveness!

It is necessary here to emphasize the fundamental difference between efficiency and effectiveness—two words that generally tend to be understood and used almost synonymously.

Implications of 'Efficiency' and 'Effectiveness'

Consider this: A manager may be very efficient, but that does not necessarily make him effective as well.

Efficiency is generally concerned with 'how well' and 'how much' a task has been performed. Some of the factors contributing to the efficiency of a person are his intelligence, knowledge, skill and imagination. A highly intelligent person can be clever, but that does not make him wise as well. A highly efficient manager can be competent, but that alone cannot guarantee his being effective as well.

Effectiveness relates to *the contribution* a manager may have made while performing his tasks—in terms of 'what results', 'how much' and 'what quality'. The factors that determine a managers effectiveness are:

- the extent to which he achieves results—not just performs tasks;
- the extent to which he goes beyond what is normally required of him; and
- the extent to which this quality in him is *(a)* self-sustaining; *(b)* on-going; and *(c)* motivational for others.

Effective people are not problem-minded; they're opportunity-minded. They feed opportunities and starve problems.

But is there a chance that efficiency is not the answer? Is getting more things done in less time going to make a difference—or will it just increase the pace at which I react to the people and circumstances that seem to control my life?

Could there be something I need to see in a deeper, more fundamental way—some paradigm within myself that affects the way I see my time, my life, and my own nature?

—Stephen R. Covey, *The 7 Habits of Highly Effective People*

This comes from dedicated, systematic working by persons mellowed with maturity. Intelligence, knowledge, skill and imagination—the components of efficiency—are, no doubt, important supportive factors and are welcome; but they alone are not enough. Many brilliant people turn out to be failures as result-achievers, whereas even plodders (like the tortoise in that famous allegory) emerge as very effective result-achievers.

The features of efficiency and effectiveness can be summarized as shown in Table 11.1.

TABLE 11.1: What is Efficiency and Effectiveness

Efficiency is	*Effectiveness is*
◆ Concerned with 'how well' and 'how much' of a performed task.	◆ Concerned with desired results: • delivers the goods; • happens on time; • is cost-effective; and • leaves no side-effects.
◆ Relies on: intelligence, knowledge, skills and imagination	◆ Relies on: wisdom
◆ Almost uni-dimensional: • the specific 'target' is the target; and • neither the manager nor his superiors expect anything more.	◆ Multi-dimensional: • the 'contribution' is the target; • going beyond the confines of the current assignment; and • a 'motivational process' which is self-sustaining and ongoing.
◆ Doing things right	◆ Doing the right things

How do you go about acquiring effectiveness? Is there a set of exercises, prescribed steps, or exclusive qualities that we can adopt, and thus hope to make ourselves effective as managers? Disappointing though it may seem, the answer is: 'No'. Effectiveness does not even have an entity of its own; it is the sum total of a number of attributes, qualities and attitudes that go into 'distilling' effectiveness in you.

Take the case of a chemical compound. It too has no entity of its own; it is created when a number of specific ingredients are put together in such a manner that the desired chemical reaction is set into motion. Some atoms of a specific kind and potency are brought together to produce the required molecules, and some molecules of desired number and potency are brought together to, finally, create the desired compound. Take away the atoms , and the molecules will not be formed, and thus the compound itself will not come into being; or you may get a monstrous compound instead!

So much for the ingredients making a compound! Then there is the important question of providing, and maintaining, the ambiance; for example, the right combination of temperature, atmospheric pressure and other catalytic factors. In other words, the right environment. It is true that for creating the same compound under varying combinations of temperature, pressure and catalytic factors, the formulation of the ingredients themselves may require suitable variations.

This is equally true of managerial effectiveness. In order to upgrade yourself from an efficient to an effective manager, you will not only need to imbibe certain 'ingredients' determining your style of management, but also create and maintain a conducive 'environment'.

I shall now attempt to suggest both the 'ingredients' and the 'environment' which ought to propel you towards managerial effectiveness. Let me emphasize here that these 'ingredients' are essentially the managerial qualities and know-how that have already been discussed in the preceding chapters; and the 'atmosphere' comprises the *attitudinal alignments* that have been recommended earlier. While summarizing those qualities and attitudinal factors here, I hope to convince you that your managerial effectiveness can be acquired only when *you* make use of those qualities and attitudinal factors in unison and in an integrated manner.

Steps Toward Managerial Effectiveness

Be a 'Professional' Manager

Simply stated, this means you must get rid of ad-hocism—whether it resides within you or is being imposed upon you by others. You must decide and act on reason, anchored on those core principles which you have reasoned out, tried out and adopted on your own. You must not be arbitrary and 'seasonal' in your practice as a manager. For this, you have to take the following *six* steps:

1. Liberate yourself from subjectivity, impulsiveness, guess-work, unpredictability and irresponsibility.
2. Identify your targets in the context of your organization's chosen goals, and challenge yourself and your colleagues to achieve the

required as well as desirable results.

3. Achieve your targets by all means. But watch out against this target-achievement becoming an obsession in itself, goading you to do so by hook or by crook. Your target achievement must be tempered by your insistence on the 'style of your management'. And your 'style' must be based on: *(a)* time-tested managerial principles; *(b)* motivational inputs; and *(c)* continuous monitoring that your will and capability as well as that of your team-mates gets reinforced—not worn out—as you proceed from one target achievement to another.

4. Develop your people, through delegation and empowerment, to reach their highest potential while you involve them in achieving the agreed targets.

5. Treasure your ethical and moral principles, and stand up for them transparently.

6. Be open to criticism, and have the courage to amend your ways once you discover—or it is pointed out convincingly—that your decisions or actions are wrong.

Be a Motivator

Rely more on motivation among your people for obtaining their willing, and ongoing collaboration with you in achieving targets and producing results. Do remember that continuing motivation stems not so much from monetary rewards and other material benefits; its perennial fountainhead is *your* participative work involvement with your people on tasks that offer professional challenges to them.

Implications of 'Morale' and 'Motivation'   'Motivation' flows from a state of mind, from an inner urge within people—whetted by suitable challenges—to give their best and to rise to their full potential. This can come primarily from your *quality leadership* and not just from morale-building inputs.

> *You can buy peoples hands, but you can't buy their hearts. Their hearts are where their enthusiasm, their loyalty is. You can buy their backs, but you can't buy their brains. That's where their creativity is, their ingenuity, their resourcefulness.*
> —Stephen R. Covey, *The 7 Habits of Highly Effective People*

Morale is derived from the satisfaction of the 'hygienic needs' such as:

♦ good wages;
♦ good amenities at the workplace and at home;
♦ good working conditions; and
♦ good treatment from superiors, peers and subordinates.

These may ensure that your people are 'not dissatisfied'. But this cannot be stretched to mean that they are 'satisfied'. All that happens with good morale is that your people feel fine; this does not necessarily lead them to a state of on-going motivation!

Job-restructuring and Setting Challenging Goals   In addition to morale-building, continue innovating on job-restructuring with a view to 'building-in' motivation in the jobs themselves. Set goals in such a way that they tone up the content of the jobs your subordinates are required to do. Towards this objective: *(a)* set specific and challenging goals; *(b)* seek your subordinates' participation in setting such goals; and *(c)* be available to them without, of course, breathing down their necks.

Your Leadership   Let your subordinates benefit from your leadership. Do the following specifically:

♦ find out what they think;
♦ keep telling them what's going on;
♦ make life easier for them, which simply means: ensure better quality of working life so that they work in a better way and produce more;
♦ give them goals which they collaborate with you to set;
♦ challenge them to achieve; and
♦ appreciate what they achieve.

Practise Delegation   Actual delegation must be preceded by the following assessments and effective actions that are called for:

♦ what tasks can be delegated and to whom?
♦ who are worthy and ready now in terms of their skills, skill-needs, knowledge, maturity and dependability?
♦ what kind of training, briefing, empowerment, support and help a delegatee needs from his superior? and

♦ what can the superior do to present the tasks to his subordinates in such a manner that they appeal to them as sufficiently and manageably. . .
  • challenging;
  • stimulating; and
  • s-t-r-e-t-c-h-i-n-g?

As a prerequisite to practising delegation, you have to first develop in yourself the following *two* attitudinal approaches:

1. Your style of decision-making comes first.
   ♦ you must be decisive. You should have the courage to be conclusive and free from hesitations; and you should come forth with decisions at the right time. You may be in haste to take a decision, but that must not mean you take hasty decisions;
   ♦ you must genuinely believe in participative decision-making. This means that at the decision-making stage, you may seek as much consultation as necessary with your colleagues and subordinates for analyzing the issue and generating the alternatives for your decision; and
   ♦ when it comes to deciding, *you* take the decision. But once you take the decision, you must share the reasons behind your decision with your collaborators. Only after this, should you exhort them to lend their hands and hearts for faithfully implementing your decision.
2. Your delegation must lead to: *(a)* desired results; and *(b)* progressive development of your people. You must resist the temptation of practising delegation for the sake of delegation.

Be a Communicator

Always remember the vital importance of communication for your effectiveness as a manager. Communication is not a vehicle for handing down information and instructions only; it must be used for conveying and receiving information, ideas, feelings, attitudes, suggestions and commands—with the intention of evoking discriminating responses resulting in desired actions.

You must also remember the following *three* fundamental tenets of communication:

1. He communicates the most who listens more than he speaks.
2. No matter how good you are at using the 'techniques' of com-

munication, you cannot succeed unless you have built up a respectable fund of credibility in the eyes of your communicatees.
3. No communication is complete or worth your while unless you build up an ongoing and reliable chain of 'feedbacks'. Such feedbacks cannot function if you depend on your band of 'reporters'. It can function and thrive only if there is transparency on your part. The more you open up—and are convincingly perceived by your people as being open—the more they shall open up to you.

Take Care of Interpersonal Relations

Interpersonal relations hold an important key to a manager's effectiveness. You have to be alive to the sensitivities of people around you at vertical and horizontal planes. And you have to fine-tune your attitudes and behaviour based on integrity, mutual respect and innate goodwill. You must also ensure that such attitudes and behaviour—and your intentions behind them—are as *transparent* as possible.

Here are *four* suggestions:

1. You must rely more on 'influence' than on authority. This calls for building up your style of decision-making and actions on the basis of reason, participative functioning as far as possible, and personal touch which slowly and imperceptibly builds up your 'charisma'.
2. You must remain yourself. This implies: *(a)* that you don't try to pretend to be someone else; and *(b)* keep working upon yourself till you can legitimately respect yourself for your proven accomplishments and other qualities.
3. While dealing with the people around you, always remember that there are people who are: *(a)* difficult; and *(b)* with difficulties. You must accordingly determine your attitudes and behaviour *and* your plan of action for smoothening your working relationships with them. As an effective manager, you go beyond simply smoothening your relationship; you help them resolve their own problems.
4. Never treat a complaint lightly. Attend to it with due seriousness, respect and promptness. By all means be strict—even harsh where there is no alternative—but also remember to *empathize* with the other person.

Manage Yourself with Reference to Time

Remember, the real problem with time is not with its poor availability but with *our* poor utilization of it. The more you refine your time-utilization techniques, the richer you become with time. A *truly busy* man (which actually means a highly organized person) has time enough to spare!

Here are *three* recommendations:

1. What is the predominant combination of your tasks? Are most of them 'urgent' or 'important'?
2. If the majority of them are 'urgent,' you have—and *you* are—a problem! You have reason to be concerned with your style of functioning. It means that you have not been far-sighted enough, or alert enough, to take timely and corrective measures with problems or issues. Had you attended to them at the very beginning, they would have been easy enough to tackle. Today, they are just 'ticking away' on your desk as small or big time-bombs—throwing you off balance and making you handle them in panic and haste.
3. You should so pattern your work-schedule that you progressively have more of the important jobs on your hand than the urgent ones. This would mean that you are far-sighted and getting better organized, and are able to tackle your tasks with a more relaxed and composed frame of mind. Thus, you have time enough to spare.

Manage Your Tensions

When you master the art of managing interpersonal relations and your time, most of the causes of your tensions are removed, or at least minimized. Nevertheless, there is a lot more you can achieve in this area if you concentrate on self-discipline, with particular reference to the following *four* factors:

1. Distinguish between *pressure* and *tension*. Manageable amount of pressure is normally welcome. It sharpens your faculties and keeps you on your toes in a healthy way. Tension, on the other hand, is our *response to pressure*, not the pressure itself; but when your response becomes disoriented and beyond your emotional-mental capacities, it corrodes you.
2. Beware of under-loads as much as over-loads of work. Both of them cause tensions. Audit your style of working. Are you generating

self-imposed stresses in the form of undue insistence on: *(a)* perfection; *(b)* doing much of the chores yourself; or *(c)* trying to please everybody?

3. Persist with your efforts to secure tranquility of mind. Try to believe that this can be achieved. Towards that end *(a)* allow yourself sufficient time for the task in hand; *(b)* recognize your limitations, and either overcome them or act within them; *(c)* cultivate a sense of humour and try to break down too much reserve or sternness if that has taken hold of you; *(d)* learn to say 'no' without being rude or arrogant or abrupt; and *(e)* listen to music, take up yoga if possible, go for leisurely strolls keeping your mind blank.

4. Cultivate assertiveness, but steer clear of aggressiveness, obstinacy and dogmatism. As a prerequisite for acquiring assertiveness that is effective, do a lot of introspection and package your capabilities and style of working and interacting with others in such a way that, ultimately, everyone including yourself concedes that your assertiveness is truly well-deserved and well-intentioned.

Be a Leader—With Trust in Yourself and Without False Modesty

An effective manager cannot but be a leader. Leadership is a requirement, not a matter of option, for an effective manager. Remember the following *four* requirements:

1. Your leadership qualities do not have to be god-given. They can certainly be developed and acquired through self-development. In fact, much of the recommended attitudinal changes and capability refinements can go a long way in bestowing upon you the right to leadership *IF* you cultivate and internalize them in your style of management.

2. What is most important is that you make the fullest possible use of these attributes for the development of your people and for creating a winning team around you. What is the use of having excellent qualities if they do not touch, and enkindle, the lives of those who depend upon you to show them the way for their self-development and proper utilization of talents? It is in this sense that leadership must be viewed as a transaction.

3. Always rely more on being the leader of your men than on being their boss. Recognize the power of 'positive influence'; it is far

superior and enduring than throwing your weight around.
4. Above all, recognize that 'competence' *and* 'character' are your most important assets as a leader. Everything else pales into insignificance if you are not—or not perceived as—a man of competence and character. There are certain pragmatic and specific measures you can take to modify your attitudes and behaviour in order to be so perceived.

The Sublimation

While you may be at different stages of self-development along the various steps discussed above, there are some basic factors of managerial effectiveness that you must never lose sight of. I shall dwell upon just two of them here.

Distinguish Between 'Fake' and 'Real' Effectiveness

Fake effectiveness comes in two shades: 'personal' and 'apparent'.

Personal Effectiveness Usually self-seeking and ambitious managers emerge as very effective in realizing or satisfying their *personal* objectives. They have their own hidden agenda which they are busy implementing silently. That such a practice leads to poor decisions and disrupts the organization's objectives are not of much concern to them.

Or, they turn the workplace into a hobby centre, pursuing what catches their fancy rather than what the organization really needs.

Or, they go meticulously about their empire-building within the organization, surrounding themselves with yes-men, with facilities and status-symbols that they want for their personal aggrandizement.

Apparent Effectiveness Punctuality, good attendance, not fully utilizing leave-quota, prompt disposal of queries, quick decisions, good public relations: these are practised and cited by some managers as *their* claim for effectiveness.

Claims of this kind can only provide an aura of effectiveness. With or about such managers, the following *four* questions start raising their heads, sooner than later:

1. Quick decisions are fine, but what is the quality of these decisions?
2. Good attendance, punctuality, not fully utilizing the leave-quota are not unwelcome, but what is the quality and quantity of work done during the manager's presence at work?
3. Promptness is welcome, but is promptness in itself a blessing? What is the quality and usefulness of the decisions taken or the tasks accomplished promptly?
4. Good public relations are, of course, desirable, but are they enough or are they really required in all situations, and should they be pursued for their own sake?

Real Effectiveness   Merely discharging duties is not as important as obtaining results. Each task performed must emerge as a contribution—transcending the formal demands contained in the job-description. Here are *seven* pertinent criteria of real effectiveness:

1. What *more* do you, as a manger, contribute beyond the strictly formal demands of your job? Merely citing the *amount* of work tackled from your in-tray or highlighting the promptness with which that was accomplished is no measure of the 'contribution' you make to your assignments.
2. Achieving a one-time or uni-dimensional objective is not enough. Your achievements by the very nature of your functions must be multi-dimensional and on-going.
3. You may have well done what you have handled. But what you may have left undone, or done inadequately, may have tremendous repercussions. Therefore, talk not only of what you have done, but contemplate on what you have not yet done.
4. It is good that you solve problems, but it is more important for you to produce creative and preventive alternatives so that such problems do not recur.
5. It is good that you economize or conserve resources that are scarce or costly, but it is more productive for you to use up the resources in such a way that value-added output is ensured.
6. It is good for you to be important, but it is more important for you to be good.
7. Finally, the crux of real effectiveness is: *Doing the right things is effectiveness*; doing things right is efficiency.

What are the Organization's and Manager's Responsibilities for Managerial Effectiveness?

Both the organization and its managers have to share the responsibility for creating situations that are conducive to enhancing managerial effectiveness. There are a number of impediments that are system-generated; they can be removed through the will and efforts of the organization in particular. Similarly, there are a number of improvements that are essentially matters of self-improvements, capable of being achieved only through *your* determined efforts.

The primary purpose of the following discussion is to highlight the issues that an organization and its managers should be aware of, and should address themselves to. They should plan and implement actions to improve matters. The choice of the manner and sequence of such actions must, obviously, be influenced by the situations peculiar to the organization and its managers.

Understanding the Manager Today   Time and experience compel us to recognize that managers do constitute a special class in themselves deserving greater attention and understanding from the organization. Some of the special factors justifying special attention for managers are:

♦ highly analytical and capable of judging the gap between precepts and practices of their superiors, and are thus prone to suffer from disillusionment;

♦ closer to the seat and process of decision-making at the top level, and are therefore in a position to see through the real intent of the decisions taken by the higher-ups;

♦ when they are taken for granted, they suffer internally and go on internalizing and 'filing in' their grievances, until an outburst becomes inevitable; and

♦ intelligent, professional people who, given the choice, would not like to be demanding or vociferous.

Manager's Participation in Management   Taking note of a manager's sensitivities as enumerated above, it becomes all the more pertinent for an organization to ponder over the question whether its system permits its managers to have true participation in management. One of the grave omissions in respect of managers has been taking their participation for granted. True, managers are invited to participate in furnishing information, diagnosing problems, even suggesting alternatives. Thereafter, the decision is taken by the superior; and that is fair enough because he indeed is the one who is expected to take decisions. Where the unintended failure creeps in is that usually the superior merely tells his collaborating managers what decision he has taken. He rarely explains to them the reasons or rationale behind his decisions. He fails to do this in most cases because it simply does not occur to him to do so. Nevertheless, would mere announcement amount to real and adequate 'participation' by the concerned managers in decision-making?

Consider this. To the employees down the line, managers are like the photograph negatives from which the prints of the management's wishes and plans are made and handed down. As we know, a print will be only as clear or blurred as the negative it is printed from. If efforts are not made to clearly explain *to* the managers the management's reasons and intents behind decisions or plans of actions, how can they succeed in explaining matters to subordinates, or in implementing decisions with conviction and in a proper manner?

Role-clarity Even at very senior levels, absence of, or chaos with regard to, role-definition has been known to generate utter demoralization, gnawing insecurity and deterioration in performance on the part of even those who have otherwise been veteran winners. A manager's effectiveness demands that he must:

♦ understand the overall contribution his unit is required to make to the organization. In other words, he must know what *his superior* is responsible for;
♦ understand his own role in his unit, that is, he should know what *he* is responsible for—in terms of knowing and achieving;
♦ establish specific objectives with a well-defined time-frame—for himself and his team-members;
♦ own up his responsibility for his and his team's actions; and
♦ obtain feedback on his team's progress towards his unit's objectives.

In a nutshell, he should not be content with just performing, but should see his performance in the total perspective. Role-clarity must be taken up as a task that takes precedence over any other planning task.

Result-oriented Performance   Close on the heels of the foregoing comes the need for a well-established system in which managers are enabled to know what they are expected to achieve and contribute toward the objectives of their unit or department—in the overall context of the organization's objectives. They should not only know this but they should be enabled to accept this. It is the responsibility of the organization (especially the seniors) to support the proper functioning of such a system by making regular use of brainstorming sessions. Such sessions should be so conducted that the managers' contributions are determined by a consultation between the concerned managers and their bosses. The overall departmental objectives should be broken down to achievable individual tasks or assignments, and agreements should be reached with individual managers for achieving such targets. This should be closely reinforced by regular reviews of the progress, and by offer of help and guidance from superiors or other more suitable sources. Such reviews also reveal whether the goal originally set was realistic, and whether lessons can be learnt from past experience for setting up and achieving similar targets in future.

Target-achievement vs Performance   Appraisal of performance must not be clouded with concern for target-achievement alone. It must equally concern itself with looking into, and evaluating, the style of management and the quality of efforts employed by the manager or others down the line.

When achieving set targets becomes an obsession with a manager, he could tax, over-stretch and throw out of gear all the resources placed at his command—men, money, materials or the requisite discipline and culture. He may, thus, leave behind him a panting and gasping unit. Targets achieved in such a manner may turn out to be not only too costly in the long run but even counter-productive. Therefore, the organization must judge a manager's performance not only in terms of the target achieved by him but also on the basis of his 'style of management' and 'quality of his efforts'. In short, his performance as a manager of resources must be the true test.

Manager's Responsibilities

Building up an environment cannot be a one-way traffic. The question: 'What can the organization do for us?' automatically begs the counter-question: 'What can we do for the organization?'

Enumerated below are some of the areas which the managers are fully responsible for developing on their own:

♦ motivation;
♦ delegation;
♦ communication;
♦ time management; and
♦ leadership.

To sum up, it is actually the *net effect* of several developmental processes—both at the organizational and individual manager's levels—that brings about managerial effectiveness. Table 11.2 may help to emphasize this fact.

TABLE 11.2: The Essential Contributors

The Organization	Individual Manager
♦ Participative decision-making and implementation	♦ Participative decision-making and activities
♦ Mangers' and workers' participation in management	♦ Delegation in practice
♦ Free and all-round communication with a lot of transparency	♦ Communication based on credibility
♦ Role-clarity	♦ Role-crystallisation
♦ Result-oriented performance system—with equal emphasis on 'achievement' and 'style of management'	♦ Leadership resting on competence and character
♦ Extensive use of 'quality circles' or similar forum	♦ Better time-management

Conclusion

Managerial effectiveness is the ultimate test of all the self-development a manager may have done. It comprises a single but most important judgemental question: 'True, you have acquired impressive qualities and capabilities? So what? What contribution can you make?'

In the all-important efforts to enhance managerial effectiveness, an organization must continue to generate internally the power to maintain its edge over others if it is to survive the onslaughts of competition, technological changes and other challenges. It is essential for this purpose that each section of an organization functions efficiently. But any obsession with efficiency alone can prove to be counter-productive —even dangerous—for the organization. It is essential that the 'various streams of efficiencies' are harmonized and harnessed together so that they turn into a mighty river of effectiveness within the organization. Towards that end, it is essential to have a clear grasp of the fundamental distinctions between the real meanings of, and popular notions about, oft-repeated terminologies such as 'efficiency' and 'effectiveness', 'morale' and 'motivation', 'target-achievement' and 'performance'. It is also necessary to reflect upon the proper understanding of such distinctions in our day-to-day functioning, and in the values held dear by the organization. The seniors in an organization must always remember that an 'effective' organization is responsible not only for itself and its employees; its effectiveness also lies in how well it balances its attentions to the needs of both the inside and outside world, in order to protect and promote the interests of a far wider circle of stakeholders.

Both the organization and its managers have to share the responsibility for creating situations that are conducive for enhancing managerial effectiveness. There are a number of impediments that are system-generated; and only the will and efforts of the organization can remove them. It has to begin by understanding its managers more empathetically, and ensure that the managers do participate in management as a priority over others' participation in management. The manager must be provided as much role-clarity as possible; and result-oriented performance system should be installed and operated earnestly with full involvement of the seniors.

However, building up and maintaining an environment for effectiveness is not a one-way traffic. The question: 'What can the organization do for us?' automatically raises the counter-question: 'What can we do for the organisation?' There are a number of improvements which, essentially, are self-improvements—capable of being achieved only through determined efforts by you, the *managers*. Some of the areas which you are fully responsible for are: *(a)* practising communication, delegation and time-management; *(b)* securing from the resources placed at your command—particularly through the efforts of your human resource—the best possible 'value-added' outputs, and toward these objectives *(c)* inculcating in yourself the effective reflexes of true leadership built on the twin pillars of competence and character.

Managerial effectiveness is concerned with doing the right things— and not merely doing things right. This can gradually be attained by well-conceived and synchronized efforts on the part of both you and your organization. Once you have attained this state, it can liberate you and your organization from the problems or handicaps that arise from a lack of motivation, sense of belonging, delegation or leadership.

On the 'action' plane, consider the following *seven* propositions. But go beyond 'considering'; try and integrate them into your lifestyle. You will soon realize that they go a long way to make you compellingly 'effective':

1. Most of the qualities or attributes recommended here are usually already within you. Whenever you bring yourself up to: *(a)* listening to others; *(b)* drawing lessons *of your own* from what you listen; and *(c)* acting upon such lessons, you are bound to be well on the way to enhancing your all-round effectiveness.
2. Soon after you open up to others—and you are *perceived* by them as open—everybody will respond and open up to you too.
3. Have confidence in yourself, and others will do so too.
4. Don't tell or proclaim; *show* what you can do.
5. Treat people as you would like to be treated by others.
6. Always offer more than expected.
7. You won't always have what people ask for; but offer something else approximating or surpassing what they want from the vast repertoire of your experience and competence.

And you will find that there is no looking back—both for you and your organization!

References

CHAPTER ONE

1. Thapar, Romila, *A History of India,* Penguin Books Limited, 1975, pp. 78–135.
2. Thakore, Dilip, 'Unforgettable Business Leaders', *Gentleman,* August, September and October 1996.

CHAPTER TWO

1. *The Hindu Survey of Indian Industry,* 1995.
2. Business World, 6–9 March 1996, p. 51.
3. 'The Quality Revolution in Indian Industries', *Business Today,* 7–21 January 1995.
4. *Business Today,* 7–21 January 1995, p. 19.
5. *Business Today,* 7–21 December 1995, pp. 81–94.
6. Kannan, N.G., 'Harnessing People Power', *The Times of India,* 20 March 1996.
7. Vishwanathan, Anand, 'Caring For Customers', *Business Today,* 7–21 October 1994.

CHAPTER THREE

1. Frederich W. Taylor's testimony, 'Hearings Before the Special Committee of the House of Representatives', 62nd Congress, 4 October 1911, Government Printing Office, 1912, p. 1388.
2. Maslow, A.H., 'A Theory of Human Motivation', *Psychological Review,* 50, 1943, pp. 370–96.
3. Herzberg, Frederick, Bernard Mausner, Barbara B. Snyderman, *The Motivation to Work,* Wiley, New York, 1959.

CHAPTER FOUR

1. Krein, Theodore J., 'How to Improve Delegation Habits', *Management Review,* 71, May 1982, p. 59.

CHAPTER FIVE

1. Adapted from Walter Ducket's *Check Your Decision-Making Skills,* Supervision, 1987, p. 41.

CHAPTER SIX

1. Bedeian, Arthur G., *Management,* The Dryden Press, Illinois, 1986, pp. 530–32.
2. Howe, Robert H., 'Eclipse of the Sun', *Army* 13, 1963, p. 31.
3. Fries, Charles E., *Linguistics and Reading,* Holt, Rinehart and Winston, New York, 1963, p. 57.
4. Sussman, Lyle, and Sam Deep, *The Communication Experience in Human Relations,* South-Western Publishing Co., Cincinnati, 1989, p. 6.
5. Mehrabian, Albert, *Silent Messages,* Belmont, CA, Wadsworth, 1971, p. 44.
6. Fallom, William K., *Effective Communication on the Job,* AMACOM, New York, 1981, p. 4.
7. Kossen, Stan, *The Human Side of Organizations,* Harper & Row, New York, 1983, p. 73.
8. Pollock, Ted, 'Listener's Quiz', *Supervision* 33, 1971, p. 22.

CHAPTER SEVEN

1. Arnold, Stanley, and Ray Josephs, 'Getting Along with Superiors' in *For Executives Only,* Englewood Cliff, N.J., Prentice Hall, Inc., 1985.
2. *The Times of India,* 1 April 1996.
3. Uris, Auren, 'Effective Communication' in *The Executive Deskbook,* Van Nostrand Reinhold Company, New York, 1976, pp. 20–23.

CHAPTER EIGHT

1. Dr. Funk, David, *Release from Nervous Tension,* Ballantine Books, New York, 1981.
2. Levine, Stuart R. and Michael A. Crom, *The Leader in You,* Dale Carnegie and Associates Inc., 1994.
3. Arroba, Tanya and Kim James, *Pressure of Work,* South-Western Publishing Co., Cincinnati, 1984.
4. Kumar, Sheila, 'Try Some Stress-Busters', *The Times of India,* 21 March, 1996.
5. Covey, Stephen R., *The 7 Habits of Highly Effective People,* Fireside Book, Simon & Schuster, New York, 1994.

CHAPTER NINE

1. Boslough, John, 'The Riddle of Time', condensed from *National Geographic* by *Readers' Digest,* June 1991.
2. Uris, Auren, *The Executive Deskbook,* Van Nostrand Reinhold Company, 1976, pp. 93–94.
3. Winston, Stephanie, *The Organized Executive,* Warner Books Inc., New York, 1983, pp. 35–81.
4. Ibid., p. 148.

CHAPTER TEN

1. Burns, James M., *Leadership*, Harper & Row, New York, 1978, p. 2.
2. Shartle, Carrol R., 'The Early Years of the Ohio State University Leadership Studies', *Journal of Management*, Fall 1979, pp. 127–34.
3. Likert, Rensis, *New Patterns of Management*, McGraw-Hill Book Company, New York, 1961, p. 7.
4. Fiedler, Fred E., *A Theory of Leadership Effectiveness*, McGraw-Hill Book Company, 1967, New York.
5. McGregor, Douglas M., *The Human Side of Enterprise*, McGraw-Hill Book Company, 1960, New York.
6. Lewin, Kurt R., 'Leader Behaviour and Member Reaction in Three Social Climates', in *Group Dynamics: Research and Theory*, 1960.
7. Tannenbaum Robert, and Warren H. Schmidt, 'How to Choose a Leadership Pattern', *Harvard Business Review*, March–April, 1957, pp. 95–101.
8. Uris, Auren, *The Executive Deskbook*, Van Nostrand Reinhold Company, New York, 1976, pp. 141–43.

Index